When Schools Work

When Schools Work

Pluralist Politics and Institutional Reform in Los Angeles

BRUCE FULLER

Johns Hopkins University Press

Baltimore

Johns Hopkins University Press
2715 North Charles Street
Baltimore, Maryland 21218-4363
www.press.jhu.edu

Library of Congress Cataloging-in-Publication Data

Names: Fuller, Bruce, author.
Title: When schools work : pluralist politics and institutional reform
in Los Angeles / Bruce Fuller.
Description: Baltimore : Johns Hopkins University Press, 2022. |
Includes bibliographical references and index.
Identifiers: LCCN 2021018592 | ISBN 9781421442778 (hardcover) |
ISBN 9781421442785 (ebook)
Subjects: LCSH: Public schools—California—Los Angeles. | Education and
state—California—Los Angeles. | Academic achievement—California—
Los Angeles. | Educational change—California—Los Angeles.
Classification: LCC LA245.L6 F85 2022 | DDC 370.9794/94—dc23
LC record available at https://lccn.loc.gov/2021018592

A catalog record for this book is available from the British Library.

*Special discounts are available for bulk purchases of this book. For more information,
please contact Special Sales at specialsales@jh.edu.*

CONTENTS

Notes on the Vernacular   *vii*

Prologue. Pluralist Politics Move Institutions   1

1 Civilizing Los Angeles   16
WITH MELISSA ANCHETA AND SARAH MANCHANDA

2 Palace Revolt   53

3 Outside Agitators   93
WITH MALENA ARCIDIACONO, CAITLIN KEARNS, AND JOONHO LEE

4 Organizing Pluralist Politics   126
WITH SARAH MANCHANDA

5 Pluralist Politics and Institutional Reform   147

Acknowledgments   *177*
Notes   *181*
References   *197*
Index   *211*

Let me clarify a few terms that appear throughout the book. I follow custom by abbreviating *Los Angeles* with the ubiquitous idiom, *L.A.* This sparse acronym began appearing in the 1870s but was not used much until the 1920s, after film and entertainment industries grew in prominence nationwide. The use of *L.A.* became the norm in the 1950s, as war veterans, midwesterners, and Blacks (again) flocked to a burgeoning labor market.[1] Abbreviating the Los Angeles Unified School District poses a related quandary. The *Los Angeles Times* to this day alternates between L.A. Unified and LAUSD. I opt for the former to avoid yet another acronym, along with signaling the irony of purported unity amid an institution that seems rather diffuse. The first known written use of *Angeleno*, designating a resident of Los Angeles, California, occurred in 1857, says *Merriam-Webster's* dictionary, although its earlier use is likely among Spanish-speaking Californios. The residents of more than a hundred towns in Latin America, each named Los Angeles, are typically dubbed Angelenos.[2]

Latino is preferred to *Latinx*, except when quoting someone. That's because only university professors and elite groups use *Latinx*, not the diverse array of Hispanic-heritage peoples on the ground. Just one in four Latinos surveyed in 2020 had heard the term *Latinx*, and just 3 percent use the term in everyday conversation.[3]

I deploy the word *tribe* when referring to ethnic or social-class groups, including the white Protestant tribe. This label is defined in the Oxford English Dictionary as "a social division in a traditional society consisting of families and communities linked by social, economic, religious, or blood ties, with a common culture and dialect."[4] Joel Kotkin begins his prescient book, *Tribes*, this way: "Born amidst optimism for the triumph of a rational and universal world order, the twentieth century is ending with an increased interest in the power of race, ethnicity, and religion."[5] Or, to paraphrase Robert Frost: home is the place where, when you have to go there, they must take you in.

When Schools Work

Pluralist Politics Move Institutions

Schools fail our kids miserably, critics claim. Don't our tax dollars, intended for classrooms, get diverted to education bureaucrats and fat teacher pensions? Then, civic leaders dodge efforts to shake up this entrenched institution, failing to purge lousy teachers and lift student learning? The skeptics respond by inflicting market competition on public organizations, portable vouchers for parents, or private-like charter schools. Meanwhile, politicians on the Left, hemmed in by union stalwarts, seem to protect anemic schools, preserving grossly unequal opportunities afforded our children.

This book challenges these naysayers on two scores, telling how a variety of activists built a feisty democratic politics, then breathed new life into a moribund institution once given up for dead: public schools in Los Angeles. A fresh generation of civic players—forming a vibrant network of civil rights litigators, Black and Latino leaders, pro-equity nonprofits, reform-minded teachers, and wealthy donors—would unite against a shared enemy by the 1990s. The foe held in common was the arcane regime that centrally regimented life in nearly one thousand schools dispersed across Southern California.

The *new pluralists*, as I dub them, sprouted from a kaleidoscope of racial histories and cultural identities. These youthful agitators devised a politics founded on mutual respect for one another along with shared enthusiasm for inventive policy. Most fundamentally, they distanced themselves from the old polarity marking urban politics, one that pits corporate moguls against protective labor leaders, including powerful teachers' unions. Meanwhile, distant managers of the education bureaucracy, housed inside their twenty-eight-story fortress downtown, showed little concern for regressively funded schools, the steady loss of caring teachers and middle-class families, the bleeding of dropouts from dreary high schools. So, this virgin civic terrain became a proving ground for the new pluralists, as they forcefully prodded the hidebound institution of schooling in the subsequent quarter century.

Acting from various corners of the civic stage, the insurgents were animated by a set of principles, and they were united in their struggle to challenge, even subvert, the central bureaucracy. The new pluralists advocated for better teachers, for rigorous and nurturing social relations inside schools. They went to court to win progressive funding for schools in the poorest stretches of Los Angeles. They created engaging schools that mirrored the city's widening diversity, expanding racially integrated magnet schools, creating small high schools to serve immigrant neighborhoods, and, most controversially, establishing scores of charter schools run beyond the reach of education officials downtown.

The new pluralists battled a politically protected regime that had long delivered spotty results for kids and families—schools that enforced a uniform cultural agenda and segregated children along familiar lines of race and social class. This book chronicles the rise of this counterinsurgency, a diverse array of activists who envisioned a thicker, more inclusive civil society, one that sparks evocative strategies for altering key institutions in human societies. These pluralists, speaking back to the critics, teach us about how deeply democratic politics can be fostered in the American metropolis, then how inventive policies spur institutional change.

Early in this volume, you will meet the youthful activists who premiered in the civic arena well over a generation ago—challenging established interests, organizing rallies before the L.A. school board, and taking to the streets when necessary, as they saw it. These proliferating ethnic activists and nonprofits began to nurture student leaders inside high schools, along with taking their case to bipartisan mayors, reform-minded funders, and journalists. They borrowed more from Western humanism and the Latino spirit of *familismo* than from market-oriented neoliberalism. Yet, the new pluralists were less interested in ideological categories and more intent on creating culturally respectful and effective schools.

A moderate wing emerged among this spectrum of rabble-rousers, soon enlisting progressive lawyers, descendants of the civil rights era, to successfully move new dollars to schools serving poor families. They pushed to clarify what children should be learning, then nudged teachers to respect all students, deracializing expectations about who can aspire to enter college. These *loyal insiders*—

the moderate pluralists—retained faith in the basic institution, the Los Angeles Unified School District. But they drew on notions of neighborhood control and liberalized options to create scores of small "pilot schools," which emphasized social justice, theater arts, and high-tech curricular themes. Finding allies inside the bureaucracy, the loyal insiders expanded magnet schools and founded dual-language campuses, where L.A.'s colorful groups could hear their native tongue and see their own heritage in nearby schools.

A more militant wing of pluralists simultaneously emerged in the 1990s, the faction I call *civic challengers*. These outside agitators, often fueled by wealthy Democratic donors, aimed to bring down the central institution of L.A. Unified. Giving up on the bureaucracy's capacity to innovate or respond to the cultural rainbow that is Los Angeles, the radical pluralists since 1992 erected nearly three hundred charter schools, more than any region in the nation, from storefronts in weathered strip malls to expansive campuses in pricey West L.A. The charter sector now draws one-fifth of all students within the district's bounds. These taxpayer-funded yet privately run campuses punched a sizable hole in the system's budget, prompting tradition-bound education authorities to rethink their vast archipelago of schools.

This L.A. story took a surprising twist early in the twenty-first century: children's learning curves began to rise. The behemoth institution of L.A. Unified, written off as hapless and ineffectual, came alive with a pulse, a beating heart. Reading and math scores for Latino and white students proceeded to climb (more than one grade level) over the subsequent two decades, as gauged by a careful federal assessment of learning in L.A., finally leveling off in 2019. Other barometers of pupil progress climbed as well—enrollment in college-prep courses rose, student discipline incidents fell, and graduation rates steadily increased.

This book delves into the pivotal technical question of what policy innovations actually worked to lift student learning in Los Angeles. In addition, I back up the story to examine how this fresh generation of activists devised a more inclusive and democratizing politics that motivated inventive reforms, at times resulting in lasting institutional change. These contemporary pluralists never aspired to merely rearrange deck chairs on this organizational *Titanic*. Instead, they stirred widely diverse families and students to advance their shared interest in quality schools, then worked the inside and outside game to remake this public organization—one that hosts a feeling of belonging, places animated by warmly demanding educators and motivated students.

I aim to inform a wide range of civic reformers, searching for organizing tools and policy options that truly move public institutions. In this book, I argue that lasting institutional change stems from a new civic politics, one that spurs evocative reforms and disciplined attention to implementation. The evidence detailed in the middle chapters informs educators, civic groups, policy makers, and allied scholars on the surface question of what works. More deeply, I question typical assumptions about how metropolitan politics works (or doesn't work), especially when aimed at upending recalcitrant institutions. I articulate a novel theory of how civic activism—rooted in cultural, ideological, and pedagogical communities—can cohere and reshape key organizations. For the new pluralists challenge how we define the role and inner workings of "public" institutions in cosmopolitan societies, along with the shifting collective action of the state.

This volume builds from my study of politics and institutional change in Los Angeles over the past quarter century. This intriguing metro area reveals the drivers and lasting organizational effects of cosmopolitan pluralism. We also observe similar dynamics of diffuse democracy in other arenas—say, environmental and feminist movements, or the coalescing politics around ethnic identity. Los Angeles offers an illustrative canvas for coloring in the prior global and local forces that motivate the rise of pluralist politics. These antecedents include the global migration of labor into cities and suburbs, bringing a flourish of cultural variety; the pursuit of authentic identities in which one securely belongs; and the widening rejection of melting-pot assimilation, as well as the implications for how diverse parents raise their children.

The contemporary pluralist terrain does pose threats to faith in once-sacred institutions, from regimented bureaucracies to the Western canon. The world has not simply grown flat economically; it's becoming an egalitarian web of ethnic and linguistic settlements, nonprofits, and village loyalists. This makes for a more dispersed urban politics, yet with the organizing potential to coalesce around institutional change. Indeed, what's remarkable about this L.A. story is how respect for centrifugal forces is weighed against the pursuit of common cause—in our case, the quest to recast public schools.

A Politics to Remake Institutions

I returned to my hometown of Los Angeles like any curious scholar, eager to dig into a consequential question: Why had student learning, out of the blue, steadily drifted upward during the opening decades of the new century? How did kids from diverse working-class families across a sprawling metropolis somehow beat the odds? After pursuing a variety of clues and characters, I realized the underlying story was not simply about crafting inventive reform under a weathered education regime. The deeper plotline was driven by a new politics, one that resembled—yet moved beyond—earlier notions of democratic pluralism. These underlying dynamics led to new questions: Why did this chromatic array of activists surface in the late twentieth century? How did these novel pluralists go about reshaping the entrenched institution of public schooling?

What organizational mechanisms worked to buoy student achievement or narrow inequality?

The new pluralists you meet are rarely satisfied with policy talk or sporadic news headlines. Instead, they dig into organizational trenches, seeking ways of making schools more respectful and supportive inside, and distributing resources fairly among campuses. You will meet Maria Brenes, an L.A. native who attended Harvard University before returning to East Los Angeles. She designed small high schools across immigrant neighborhoods, then pushed to expand access to college-prep courses. There's Karen Bass—an emergency-room nurse turned local organizer in (then) predominantly Black South L.A. Her young nonprofit, the Community Coalition, would help win fresh funding for central-city schools. She, along with Aurea Montes-Rodriguez, took on defensive labor leaders to revamp teaching staffs at flailing high schools while nurturing a fresh generation of student activists who rallied before the school board, helped get out the vote, and sparked instant rallies greased by social media.

They allied with others, such as Yolie Flores, an insurgent school board member, keen on options for parents, who led a palace revolt inside L.A. Unified to hand off more than one hundred schools to seemingly liberated principals and equity-minded teachers, even uniting with charter school advocates to subvert business as usual. Many new pluralists, rooted in the progressive Left, did not rule out market competition, especially in poor Latino or Black communities where parents grew desperate to find safe schools and caring teachers. Nor did these emerging agitators shy away from exercising levers of central authority to redistribute school funding or to mandate wider access to college-prep courses. The new pluralists drew from a variety strategies and playbooks, like a young coach frustrated by conventional wisdom.

Their L.A. story flows from the perennial challenge of how activists in civil society attempt to remake slumping institutions—organizations that fail to deliver quality results or public firms that no longer host vibrant places in which to work. Huge bureaucracies come to mind—say, the downtown post office or the Department of Motor Vehicles. Many private firms suffer similar calcification, like banking conglomerates or health care companies that click into autopilot when a client or patient dares to ask for help. The new pluralists of Los Angeles invite us to examine the potent interplay between a democratizing politics and institutional reform.

A variety of reformers and theorists of organizations have put forward logics for how to bring feckless institutions back to life. These include simplifying production routines or tightening the reins of management. Neoliberal advocates embrace this mechanical model, eager to specify pieces of knowledge that all students must acquire, tidbits that can be tested effortlessly. President Barack Obama's earlier strategy to raise test scores by holding teachers' feet to the fire offers one example, tying human merit to how quickly children digest facts. It's an admirable goal when many teachers—too often in Black, brown, or poor white communities—fail to impart basic literacy or elementary mathematical concepts. Obama's strategy borrowed from Al Gore's earlier campaign to "reinvent government," defining production goals centrally, then nudging institutions to innovate locally. This kind of "systemic reform" borrows from Max Weber's analysis of bureaucratic controls a century ago, narrowing what students are to learn (the product), then regulating the behavior of teachers who must get with the (centrally set) program. Their agenda was applauded by civil rights activists and pivotal independent voters, long frustrated over the insularity and seemingly pallid character of public schools.

Other advocates of institutional reform draw faithfully from economic theory. These market enthusiasts scoff at attempts to wring stronger performance out of what they see as spent public institutions. Better to simply blow them up. It's competition among schools—ideally animated by decentralized firms liberated from any central authority—that will fuel gains in organizational quality at a lower cost, all the while nimbly responding to differing curricular preferences held by parents. Market advocates believe the public monopoly of schooling, manipulated by self-interested officials and union chiefs, must be torn asunder.

Market remedies visited New Orleans in the wake of Hurricane Katrina in 2005. After the hurricane swept out a largely corrupt political order, a wave of charter schools swept in. New teachers arrived in the decimated city. These presumably agile schools took root, detached from any centralized power, and student performance steadily climbed (at least in subjects tested by the state), as political scientist Terry Moe has detailed.[1] Better to let a thousand organizational flowers blossom, competing for clients and families, so the pro-market argument goes. Only then, as the market adherents claim, will conventional educators be forced to innovate—to find quality teachers, purge mediocrity, and become efficacious as institutions.

A complementary line of thought emphasizes how the resilience of education bureaucrats or labor unions is rooted not simply in raw political power but in habitual expectations of what schools must normatively look like.[2] Standardized tests, traditional school subjects, didactic teaching—these are the trusted and deeply institutionalized signs of how schooling is supposed to work, as sociologist John W. Meyer argues. When Weberian descendants or market reformers attempt change, it's the classroom routines and rituals that sustain uninspired schools. The state, in tandem, exercises a "third face of power," as Stephen Lukes calls it, protecting the interests of constituent members whether public organizations deliver hard results for clients or not.[3] In turn, educators and union members pay "rent" to abiding politicians, a transaction that ensures the steady flow of public funding for jobs, pensions, and the like.

That said, my research team uncovered a new political theory of institutional change in Los Angeles, one that moves well past these polarizing stalemates. These divisive dialectics yield no way forward, setting bureaucratic regulation and cultural regimentation against faith in markets. The young activists emerging a generation ago in Los Angeles fell into neither camp. They drew on a variety of reform logics: loyal insiders jamming for change from within and civic challengers banging on the stalwart institution from the outside. This new pluralism—occupying civic territory distinct from neoliberal notions of efficiency or protectionist instincts of labor chiefs—spurred creative policy options and a diversifying mix of new school forms.

The immediate roots of cosmopolitan pluralism in California tie back to the 1960s, when the once golden state suffered dark days of inner-city riots, failed efforts to desegregate schools, and a vicious backlash against taxes and people of color. America's politics, of course, still suffer from this tortured aftermath. Yet, by the 1980s, young activists began surfacing in Los Angeles, rooted in communities defined by language and race. A segmented politics was brewing in the wake of demographic variety and economic upheaval across metropolitan centers. The nation had come to reflect "all colors of the rainbow," as Jesse Jackson infamously proclaimed at the 1988 Democratic National Convention in Atlanta, punctuating this moment of cultural and political challenge. Ethnic minorities no longer aspired to simmer in that mythical melting pot, to subordinate to a uniform, often plain-vanilla ethos.[4] Alternative values and ideological differences—from what language to speak or religion to follow (if any) to confronting gendered and racialized roles—now surfaced with lasting force. The old notion of assimilating into some bland stew was giving way to respect for, even curiosity about, cosmopolitan variety.

Such deep contention and cultural division play out in how we raise and school our children, along with the institutions entrusted with this essential human task. Should educators nurture inquisitive and creative youths, or fit them into an unfair pyramid of occupations? Who's racial or class heritage should be trumpeted in the curriculum? How much should children learn about creationism, slavery, or sex? Philosopher Walter Feinberg defines the pluralist turn as when members of "many different cultures should be allowed to pursue their own meanings and traditions in their homes, churches . . . and in their communities."[5] But how to devise a politics that advances shared pathways toward opportunity while crafting institutions that reflect cultural variety? This dilemma besets the central state, along with how we define common cause amid fracturing tribes and identities. Public schools became ground zero for preserving or subverting particular cultural forms and language, as civic activists rushed to various fronts of the culture wars. The global pandemic that arrived in 2020 only sharpened the disparities in learning and opportunity that beset

America's children raised on segregated islands populated by separate social classes.

The fusion of particularism and politics recently arose in New York City, where the mayor came under fire when failing to enforce state education statutes, after orthodox leaders of Jewish yeshivas skipped any teaching in English. This occurred after the mayor had loosened health regulations for circumcisions, then flouted orders to vaccinate Hasidic kids against measles—all the while gaining this community's political support.[6] (The mayor would later fine Hasidic families who held wedding parties as Covid-19 ravaged the city.)

Indeed, cultural pluralism has long intersected political power in cities. The rise of Irish or Italian regimes in the nineteenth century comes to mind. But these were ethnically arranged efforts to control jobs, status, and uniform public institutions. Instead, it's the spread of *cosmopolitan pluralism*—denoted by respect for differing tribes, lifestyles, and civic roles—that powers the new pluralists. They are bent on *altering* and *diversifying* public organizations. They do not seek standardized or dominating forms of institutions. Whether this novel rendition of pluralism serves to erode the central state or discount a shared common good is a sticky question to which I return.

What's key in understanding the new metropolitan pluralism is how this third political terrain, entered and explored over the past quarter century, offers a policy laboratory of sorts, allowing plural kinds of organizations to flourish. This institutional renaissance in Los Angeles was sparked by the legitimization of multiple ethnic leaders, diverse nonprofits, and reform-minded educators. In turn, the child-rearing ideals and social norms pursued by plural activists became embodied in *organizational diversity*. Witness the resulting spread of magnet and charter schools, small high schools, and dual-language programs. Pluralist politics, in short, legitimates differing cultural frames that sustain local forms of language, membership, and ways of raising the next generation. And sometimes this coheres into alternative forms of social organization.

Organization of the Book

I tell this story in three acts. Chapter 1 describes key historical forces that set the stage for political realignment in contemporary Los Angeles. The new pluralists that arose in the education sector essentially challenged the established regime set in place by Yankee Protestants in the latter third of the nineteenth century. This once dusty town soon resembled an imagined society, eventually a metropolis defined by demographic variety, economic disparity, and cinematic fantasy. Yet, back in 1870, this Spanish-speaking settlement was a rugged agricultural outpost of five thousand residents, enveloped in pastoral haciendas, citrus orchards, and vineyards.

In all of fifteen minutes, one could walk from the weathered Franciscan plaza, strolling past dilapidated shops and ragged cantinas before turning down a dingy alley of adobe hovels that housed farmhands and outcasts of every creed and color. Civilizing this mélange of misfits and heathens soon after the Civil War was the immediate challenge that confronted arriving ministers and investors. These fledgling capitalists, spent gold miners, and ragtag laborers conspired to subvert the authority of comfortable Californios, mostly ranchers who were born in this northern territory but were also of Mexican lineage. Eager advocates of common schooling from the Midwest and New England soon followed. These migrating educators and Protestant stalwarts—forming the first Progressive coalition—aimed to weave these rough-edged Angelenos into a single moral and cultural fabric.

To build a vibrant city on this arid plain surrounded by mountains and scrub brush required a modernizing infrastructure, starting with water, electricity, and rail lines north to San Francisco or east to Kansas City. So, those seeking private gain stirred civic authorities to tax this scruffy citizenry to invest in grand public works, stretching roads and electric streetcars across the region and channeling water south to Los Angeles from mountain snowfalls more than two hundred miles away.

These early developers required cheap labor for their massive public works. Soon, a diverse array of workers and craftsmen were arriving from all corners of the globe: Chinese and Japanese immigrants, former enslaved Blacks from the American South, Canadians and Eastern Europeans, recurring waves of Mexican families displaced by failed farms or socialist revolution. This bevy of workers laid out the town's gravel roads, drove spikes into rails, and extended irrigation ditches that set Los Angeles abloom by the late nineteenth century. This same "uncivilized" variety of foreign families also stirred Protestant leaders to expand common schools, to "Americanize" these strangers into a Yankee melting pot. These institutional pillars—enforced by the moral aspirations and raw power of white Protestants—would spark resistance and reform by contemporary pluralists a century later.

Chapter 2 moves forward to contemporary Los Angeles as racial and economic stress literally ignites the city. The Watts Riot in 1968 set fire to a mostly Black stretch of South L.A. Emerging Black and Latino leaders turned to better schools as one key path toward racial justice. They rallied with Jewish liberals, attempting to desegregate campuses. The civil rights movement took hold nationally, and federal courts initially aided the cause under the integrating logic of *Brown v. Board of Education*. Yet, this proved to be a short-lived and divisive crusade, one that sparked a devastating backlash among white suburbanites and anti-tax conservatives.

The poverty and injustice vividly revealed on the nightly news would inflame the sensitivities of ordinary Americans. In Los Angeles, the resolve of the new pluralists would be forged during this political firestorm. It only grew hotter and more damaging following voter approval of California's Proposition 13 in 1978—starving public institutions of taxpayer support and fueling anti-immigrant sentiment. Nativist tensions came to the surface, a suburban revolt against the city. These descendants of Yankee Angelenos openly expressed racist fears and moral trepidation toward Black and Chicano activists—the new civic players who solidified their own ethnic identity and now pursued political influence.

This widening coalition of neighborhood organizers, civil rights lawyers, progressive funders, and reform-minded teachers began to reframe how public schools must be improved across this far-flung metropolis. That is, how to recast schools in which learning aims were clear, quality teachers were emboldened, and campuses were equitably financed. After all, public education was supposed to be the key institution to fairly distribute children's opportunities. California had made progress in equalizing funding among school districts, yet racial gaps in the achievement of students, along with their ultimate futures, remained wide. Black Power and Chicano movements pressed for civic respect and cohesion inside their communities, not simply for rights attached to lone individuals. Yes, liberal Western traditions demanded tolerance of, and protection for, all individuals. But these emerging pluralists asked the collective question: How to rebuild thick-skinned institutions that had long reproduced inequalities in Los Angeles?

The old *economic Left* was pulling apart from a more diverse and younger *cultural Left*. Economic justice was a factor, yes, but schools exemplified institutions that must advance cultural integrity, a feeling of affiliation and efficacy among one's people. By the early 1990s, these plural agitators and nonprofits were moving beyond the spent polarity, where old capital locked horns with often intransigent labor leaders. The new activists, instead, envisioned institutions that spoke to a variety of cultural experiences, languages, and social mores. These plural groups carved out fresh civic ground on which they could pursue a rainbow of identities and economic fairness. They aimed to nurture a feeling of affiliation and efficacy within one's particular community while uniting around a common cause: building diverse and potent public schools.

To get this story right, this book delves into the first-person as well. It's the local activists, like Bass and Brenes, or the ACLU attorneys and insurgent teachers, who have animated pluralist politics in Los Angeles. "Are we not living in a world of power, resistance to power, and conflicting social movements," sociologist Alain Touraine writes, "rather than a universe of rules, institutions and socialization processes?"[7] It's these compelling individuals, the advocates on the street and those leaning into policy circles, who motivate this story. These ma-

turing activists, climbing aboard the civic stage for the first time, held little
affinity for corporate elites or aging unionists, labor organizations who begrudg-
ingly accepted Black members and excluded Latinos until the late twentieth
century. Instead, the new pluralists marked off a third political ground from
which they mounted a flurry of policy initiatives.

Chapter 3 examines how the civic challengers would split the pluralists' civic
terrain, breaking from the loyal insiders to become outside agitators. Both wings
of the pluralist movement shared certain principles: eroding the bureaucracy's
central authority, spurring organizational innovation, and building warm and
demanding schools that mirrored L.A.'s cultural pastiche. All aimed to raise the
learning curves and engagement of kids. Yet, in 1992, after becoming the nation's second state to publicly fund charter schools, the market-friendly civic
challengers no longer assumed that L.A. Unified would ever sustain reform from
within. The entrenched power of "educrats" and teachers' unions would ensure
that schools remained as they were. The arrival of bullish charter school
investors—notably Bill Gates, Netflix founder Reed Hastings, and the late developer Eli Broad—cheered the civic challengers and further undercut L.A.'s
old politics of education.

The well-heeled donors arriving on the civic stage in Los Angeles were less
interested in nurturing a democratic discourse over how to fix public schools.
Instead, they preferred to buy political influence. Eli Broad, Reed Hastings, and
Michael R. Bloomberg, New York's former mayor, recently contributed $7 mil-
lion to a pair of pro-charter candidates running for the L.A. school board.
Southern California had become a proving ground for a larger national contest.
Still, many charter advocates echoed core tenets of the new pluralists: site-level
control of schools, campuses that speak to particular cultural communities (and
languages), flexible labor rules to enhance the teacher's role and relationships,
and distributing dollars to schools in poor neighborhoods. The old Progressive
alliance, which had united labor and education bureaucrats for decades, expressed little enthusiasm for this novel agenda, which soon cost this old guard
dearly in popular legitimacy and political clout.

This chapter details the controversial victories won by differing civic challengers. We discover how liberalizing the way parents select schools, along
with the charter revolution, did empirically contribute to the sustained rise of
student learning in L.A. But this competing network of campuses further separated strong from weaker students, even in this city dominated (demographi-
cally) by working-class families of color. We arrive at the paradox of pluralism.
The new pluralists advanced a bevy of institutional reforms, then watched
achievement rise over the subsequent generation. But neither the loyal insiders
nor the outside challengers formulated a policy strategy that narrowed racial and
class-based gaps in pupil performance.

Chapter 4 explores the inner workings of community organizing, the bedrock strategy of new pluralism on the pro-equity Left. I spent nearly a year with Sarah Manchanda inside the Community Coalition (known as Coco in local parlance). Founded by Karen Bass to combat the crack epidemic nearly four decades ago, this South L.A. group also turned to school reform and youth organizing, aiming to build a participatory politics from the ground up. Coco serves an integrated blend of Black and Latino families, set amid unwalkable boulevards, aging apartments, and dingy strip malls—still just twenty minutes south on the Harbor Freeway from gleaming skyscrapers downtown.

Inside Coco, the personal becomes political, a safe haven where inner-city teens learn about the roots of poverty and racial segregation in L.A., mentored by twentysomething organizers to become savvy and engaged activists. When a certain reform hangs in the balance, Coco joins with allied groups to rally thousands of students and parents—calling for equitable financing of their schools, enriching teacher quality, or shrinking police presence on campus. Trauma and uncertainty at home inevitably erode the confidence of these adolescents, as Coco staff nurture teens' own inner growth while analyzing how to attack institutionalized disparities and cultural disrespect. This chapter illuminates the intriguing nexus of personal and political in fostering an authentic democratic discourse.

Chapter 5 delineates lessons learned in Los Angeles over the past quarter century, takeaways and empirical findings that may generalize to the work of activists and policy makers beyond Southern California. I highlight the reforms that gained popular legitimacy, matured, and successfully altered the hard-shelled institution of public schools. In this final chapter, I ask whether the radical civic challengers, after diversifying the city's population of schools, proved more successful than their moderate comrades, the loyal insiders. Of greater consequence, I clarify what both pluralist camps teach us about the politics and organizational models that have lifted public education in Los Angeles. I conclude that cosmopolitan pluralism stirs a fresh politics of education, one that can shake and improve once recalcitrant institutions.

Fellow scholars offer broad shoulders on which this study stands. Jeff Henig, a political scientist at Columbia University, has detailed the widening panoply of actors who formulate a variety of education policies, then labor in their implementation to achieve institutional change. Sure, presidents and governors, along with local school boards, pronounce on policy. But their logics and codified actions typically percolate up from the hearts and minds of local civic activists. "They are altering the battleground on which competing visions of American education will be fought, both day to day and over the long term," Henig writes.[8] He has been an inspiring interlocuter on the topic and a critical reviewer of my work over the years.

Susan E. Clarke and colleagues earlier detailed in *Multiethnic Moments* how race and demographic shifts may at once democratize and fragment the local politics of education. Their rich case studies describe the rise of equity-minded activists in the education sector, including those who challenge the preservation emphasis of many union leaders.[9] Clarke accents a theoretical quandary pursued in the L.A. story as well: Do plural ethnic leaders, civil rights activists, neoliberal marketeers, and pedagogical reformers inevitably press disparate policies, or can they unite around a common cause? I advance this conversation by showing how many in the pluralist network do not accent social justice in their notions of reform—be they charter school advocates, teacher or pedagogical innovators, or neoliberals—while they do share core principles with their equity-focused brethren. I also endeavor to understand the historical forces that gave rise to these various pluralists and how they pursue inventive policy options.

New Pluralism—Its Promise and Perils

The characters who motivate this tale are colorful and provocative. Their verve and untiring struggle for better schools remain quite palpable. But you may ask, Is this story of pluralist politics and institutional change all that new? Certainly, the ideals and prickly features of pluralism have long preoccupied civic leaders and scholars alike. Earlier conceptions of pluralism, like those advanced by political scientist Robert Dahl, came under attack for siding with Thomas Jefferson's romanticized view of states' rights. Jefferson preferred a weak central state to preserve a racially arranged economy. Dahl's textbook notion of compromise—as plural stakeholders deliberate around the table to reach a compromise—assumes a dominant cultural frame and seamless (capitalist) political economy. This harmonious view of getting to the common good, a favorite of civics teachers, feels naive in contemporary times, given the rise of well-financed interest groups. It tastes like "faux pluralism," in Nicholas Lemann's words, "a pluralism without strife."[10]

This functionalist rendition of pluralism contrasts sharply with, say, Václav Havel's emphasis on how a civil society, thickened locally by nonprofits and volunteer groups, must balance the rationalizing tendencies of central states. The Czech playwright and anti-Soviet dissident viewed intermediate collectives—churches, labor guilds, and civic clubs—as vital nodes of social solidarity, keeping in check otherwise unbridled markets and authoritarian bureaucrats.[11] It is this cantankerous version of pluralism that rings true in Los Angeles, one tied to identity politics and respect for human difference, a cosmopolitan dynamic animated by a widening array of civic players. Each group builds from its particular dialect or customs while bridging over to allied tribes when a common cause arrives in plain view. These new pluralists may work toward a compromise with established interests, or they may opt to devise local institutions that mirror their own cultural fabric, mores, or everyday lifestyles. These plural dialects do not necessarily arrive at a single cultural frame or standard institution.

Dahl did invite debate over the proliferation of differing nodes of social authority or modest organizations pursuing alternative ideals, "a plurality of relatively autonomous organizations within the domain of the state." These social collectives include, like Havel's, the ties that bind: civic groups, political parties, and religious sects. Yet, Dahl viewed these nodes of authority as exercising a conserving influence, providing "intimacy, affection . . . trust and faith," where "socialization into community norms for the preservation and transmission of culture" occurs for children and families.[12] Back in L.A. by the 1990s, diverse ethnic leaders, language groups, and pedagogical reformers began to build differing kinds of schools, human-scale institutions that mirrored the cultural and political variety of this vast metropolis. In turn, it became heretical to urge a return to nineteenth-century common schools. Instead, particular identities and educational philosophies become embodied in equally diverse schools.

The blossoming of cosmopolitan pluralism—marked by proliferating nodes of social authority—flows from the confluence of currents that joined forces in the latter third of the twentieth century. These included the spread of postindustrial forms of production that rejected top-down regimentation; the global migration of labor, followed by the fight or flight impulse displayed by dominant (white) groups; the pursuit of, and tolerant respect for, ethnic and linguistic identity (forsaking the melting-pot narrative); a revolt against uniform moral strictures and central regulation of personal behavior; and polytheistic social ideals and authorities, from plural ways of raising children to alternative lifestyles among the grown-ups. In my earlier book, *Organizing Locally*, I examined how these unrelenting forces have pushed big institutions and private firms to decentralize control out to local players, a pluralist form of social organization that discounts universals.[13] The present volume now delves into how these same forces operate to distribute social authority and influence across multiple nodes in civil society. In turn, these decentered agents engage in collective action (policy) that may drive lasting institutional change.

That said, a baffling dilemma arises as contemporary pluralists subvert central authority, in our case the hog-tied L.A. school bureaucracy. If a coherent center is brought down, does that not open space for markets to rush in? Is not a centered state necessary to fairly distribute wealth and opportunity? After all, the pluralist city displays "the coexistence of several sources of legitimate authority within a territory . . . among which the authority of the state is but one among many such sources," as theorist Victor Muñiz-Fraticelli argues.[14] Still, we discover how thick networks of pluralists do form steady coalitions to pursue a common cause.

The multiplicity of authoritative nodes is rooted in various wrinkles of human difference—race, class, gender, language, spirituality—ideally blended with a dash of cosmopolitan tolerance for one another. This runs counter to how some political scientists, like Clarence Stone, argue that it's the *unity* of civic groups that leads to policy success, tied to a racially integrating Atlanta in his case.[15] Civic capacity, for Stone, is associated with consensus among disparate groups active in the civic arena. But it's impossible to meander through L.A.'s retail haven of Koreatown, ancient Jewish delis across from CBS Studios, bodybuilders on Venice Beach, or music clubs in Latino Boyle Heights, then attempt a single story of how Los Angeles coheres. So, we must ask whether such cultural vitality serves to erode civic cohesion or instead energizes a vibrant politics of pluralism, as differing groups gain a spot on the civic stage?

We also see in Los Angeles how, as cosmopolitan pluralism wins legitimacy, activists spawn a variety of human organizations—from farmers markets to self-help networks, yoga studios to inventive schools. It's these proliferating locations of social membership, built by civic players with particular tribal or philosophical roots, that challenge the once dominant authority, earlier lodged in a centralized apparatus or uniform ideology. The cultural turn, arriving in the wake of the 1960s, signaled the end of "monistic thinking," as William E. Connolly put it.[16] Once contemporary activists infuse institutions with plural ideals or devise new organizational forms, these dispersed points of social nexus enjoy growing credibility, gaining particular customers or clients. Then, as the state deems, say, bike lanes, affordable housing, or charter schools to be legitimate social forms—worthy of public support—each sector grows its own constituency. It's a diffuse political economy of pluralism that's come to characterize the civic square, no longer one dominated by the interests of capital or staid labor.

Yes, cosmopolitan pluralism may undercut the capacity of civic leaders to move in a unified direction in certain cases. Warring factions have come to resemble porcupines, "plagued with the pricks of each other's quills," as theorist Michael Oakeshott stresses.[17] Still, I discovered in Los Angeles how pluralist contention—animated by a widening and more inclusive array of activists—moves citizens to prod tired institutional regimes. One promise of contemporary pluralism is to democratize power and create institutions that embrace human variety while securing common pathways to shared opportunity. I invite you to ask how this book informs these sometimes competing ideals. You may discover a promising civic dynamic that fosters inventive policy and rekindles nimble and effective institutions, finally delivering on their virtuous promises.

CHAPTER I

Civilizing Los Angeles

WITH MELISSA ANCHETA AND SARAH MANCHANDA

The West which so lightly and cruelly separates and scatters
people can bring them together again. The binding force of
civilization and human association is as strong   as the West's
bigness and impersonality.

—Letter from Susan Burling Ward, 1882,
Angle of Repose

A novel politics of education did not magically appear in contemporary Los Angeles. This realignment emerged rather glacially, amassing force by the 1990s to upset the city's century-old political regime. To fully appreciate this break in who marshaled influence in civil society, we must grasp the aging institutional pillars and economic disparities new pluralists aimed to confront. This historical detour helps to explain why these youthful activists surfaced and why school reform became so central to their agenda.

Harking back to the latter third of the nineteenth century, this chapter highlights the ideological and material cornerstones that defined how this tiny arid town had to be civilized—a religious conversion of sorts pressed by early Yankee investors, Protestant leaders, and assimilation-minded Progressives. This historical tale opens with men made rich from the Gold Rush and carrying familiar California names—Crocker, Hearst, Huntington, and Stanford—now taking their capital south from San Francisco to the new frontier of Los Angeles. The US Army and profiteering lawyers had already seized land and political power from Spanish-speaking Californios (who had earlier subjugated native peoples).

These nascent capitalists needed first to build a small-scale civil society, then gain political support for massive public works, bringing water, trade, and electricity to Southern California. After all, the driving notion of Manifest Destiny, America's justification for conquering the West, required that Yankee conquerors must somehow tame its "bigness and impersonality," as novelist Wallace Stegner emphasized. How to civilize L.A.'s ragtag mix of five thousand residents in the 1870s would be a challenge for arriving investors and Protestant ministers from the Midwest and New England. These pious settlers had never encountered such a bedraggled blend of unruly, often violent gold miners, Mexican farmhands, Chinese rail workers, and formerly enslaved Blacks, which they arrived to find in this dusty town.

Undaunted Yankee leaders mobilized their great civilization project on three fronts: building massive public infrastructure, legitimating capitalist investment and cultural hegemony under the umbrella of Protestant morality, and socializing new generations of Angelenos within regimented, centrally run public schools. Contemporary pluralists, nearly a century later, would define their political identity by challenging these earliest institutional and economic foundations.

The pillars set in place by nineteenth-century business leaders and Protestant reformers would prove durable well into the twentieth century. But they were shattered in the early 1990s, during the era framed by the Watts and Rodney King riots, along with the ugliness of racial segregation and the deep inequities exposed across Los Angeles by this urban violence. Well-paying manufacturing jobs, once elevating a broad middle class, moved overseas. Public schools that had long nurtured white students of Midwestern roots now hosted mostly brown kids of working-class origins. And the century-old polarization—pitting anti-tax business leaders against union chiefs—offered little light for escaping the dark hole into which L.A. had fallen.

Into this political vacuum, the novel and plural network of civic leaders entered the political scene, intent on reshaping the institution of public schooling—this unexpected coalition of Black and Latino leaders, revitalized civil rights advocates, inventive educators, and corporate moderates. But let's first examine the early institutional pillars—erected by Yankee profiteers and Progressives in the late nineteenth century—that the contemporary activists would later seek to topple. For this L.A. story begins a century earlier.

Civilizing Angelenos

The Yankee profiteers and Protestant preachers began arriving in Los Angeles not long after the nation's civil war. These confident *Americanos*—as dubbed by incumbent ranchers, traders, and edgy outlaws, most speaking Spanish, in this Franciscan mission town—sought spiritual resolve by securing a comfortable life here on earth. It was couched within pious commitment to family, hard work, and the Yankee tribe, punctuated by a desire for racial purity. Traveling from New England or the Midwest, these optimistic Yankees arrived with heavy

Protestant baggage, for the millennial project was at once moral and economic. These descendants of Martin Luther—educated Anabaptists, Congregationalists, Methodists, and Unitarians—preached that idle hands made for devil's play. Instead, material progress would result from religious piety and nose-to-the-grindstone grit, what became the driving ideology for transforming this semiarid basin into a garden of prosperity. It was to become a spacious suburban paradise, dodging the degradation of industrial cities back East. Hollywood, for example, founded in 1903 as a dry and Christian community, would become "a lazy little village in its shining pink stucco dress, dreaming peacefully at the foot of gentle green hills," as Cecil B. DeMille described.[1]

This first institutional pillar offered a unifying moral framework, at least for white Protestants, along with a tacit notion of modern progress that demanded material growth. Yet, building a vibrant economy atop this dry, sun-drenched plain required ambitious public works and cheap labor, the second cornerstone on which modern Los Angeles was built. Early investors and growers would entice a spectrum of poorly paid laborers to this spartan land of promise. They included diverse seekers and survivors from many parts, migrating from China, Mexico, and Europe, along with white laborers down on their luck and recently freed slaves from the American South. This polyglot of a working class stretched rail lines for thousands of miles, coming south from Sacramento and San Francisco, east to Denver and Kansas City. They blasted tunnels through Southern California's parched mountains to carry fresh water to expansive citrus orchards. Such unheard-of infrastructure projects required collusion between private investors and municipal officials, all of whom profited from taxpayer financing of shared public infrastructure, legitimated by the Protestant conception of progress.

The recurring waves of arriving immigrants, so necessary in fostering modern Los Angeles, redoubled the urgency of civilizing all these strange, morally shady foreigners. This fledgling town was "full of oddities and whimsicalities," Harvey Rice wrote in 1869. "Half the population is Mexican, and the other half American, English, Irish, German, and the Lord knows what." Even among the literate classes, the diversity had become breathtaking. "You read Spanish, French, German and English newspapers," wrote Benjamin Taylor in a letter from Los Angeles. "It is as many-tongued as [a] Mediterranean sea-port."[2]

So, what forms of public action and institutions could effectively socialize and incorporate the offspring of this colorful settlement into a modern Protestant way of life? Building a network of common schools—just as Protestant leaders had done in the Midwest and New England—soon became a core element of public infrastructure. Modern schooling was to pull all tribes into a shared moral frame and produce the skills demanded by L.A.'s modernizing economy. Yet, this third cornerstone of Los Angeles society soon prompted debate over which ethnic whites and foreign "others" should be incorporated into civil society.

Which ethnic tribes, beyond the Yankee class of merchants, educators, well-off ranchers, and business leaders, would become *civilized*? The new *Americano* leaders spoke of these others in racialized tones. James Woods, a Presbyterian minister, attributed weekly murders to the immoral character of "the low drunken Mexican or Indian class." A letter from one Frank Lecouvreur in 1871 described residents of Chinese descent as "Mongolians" and heathens. Another visitor, Harriet Harper, described Main Street in 1888 as adorned with "lazy bars across the clustering adobes, [where] the Mexican with his broad sombrero . . . lived [his] dreamy, purposeless life."[3] Protestant leaders and early Progressives were equally skeptical of the European immigrants, Jews, and poor "pikes" from the South. But they wagered that by spreading uniform and ethically infused common schools, most groups would become properly civilized. They pressed to expand public education and created adult literacy and hygiene programs—well into the twentieth century—to "Americanize" the waves of immigrants that just kept coming to Los Angeles, arriving by wagon, train, and, eventually, sleek automobiles.

Built atop this three-ply bedrock, a vibrant metropolis would flourish, an invented Arcadia stoked by California sun and fertile soil, that would escape from East Coast stuffiness, along with the unfettered resolve of early investors and dirt-poor settlers. Few could have predicted in the 1870s that Los Angeles would become one of the largest, most culturally alive cities in the world. At first, it appeared "bone dry, lacking a natural harbor, and isolated from the rest of the country by expansive deserts and rugged mountain ranges," one historian writes. "A backwater without the water."[4] But this fledgling town would be spirited by Protestant verve, potent doses of capital, and grand public works. All greased by upbeat boosters claiming medicinal miracles from the damp sea breeze, hyped by gutsy swindlers and land speculators.

Southern California held great material promise in the eyes of merchants, builders, and rail barons. Many arrived in L.A. from San Francisco or Sacramento with mounds of capital to invest, wealth earlier gained by selling supplies to gold miners or banking their hard-fought riches. Midwest growers, drawn by cheap farm- and pasturelands, would join these eager capitalists by expanding livestock herds, vineyards, and citrus groves. But the unfettered pursuit of private gain by rail barons and land traders—set against the backdrop of widening inequality and municipal corruption—sparked political tension and calls for civic-minded government in the late nineteenth century. Profits for the few kept rising, essentially by socializing the cost of public works—endless rail lines, aqueducts bringing water, and sprawling housing developments. Efforts by white Protestant educators to sand down the serrated edges of racial resistance

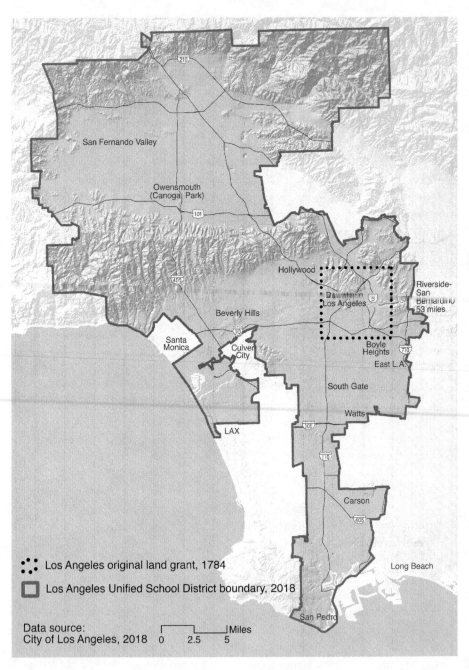

San Fernando Valley

Owensmouth
(Canoga Park)

Hollywood

Downtown
Los Angeles

Riverside-
San
Bernardino
53 miles

Beverly Hills

Santa
Monica

Culver
City

Boyle
Heights

East L.A.

South Gate

Watts

LAX

Carson

Long Beach

San Pedro

⋮ Los Angeles original land grant, 1784

☐ Los Angeles Unified School District boundary, 2018

Data source:
City of Los Angeles, 2018

0   2.5   5 Miles

Original Los Angeles boundary (1784) with L.A. Unified School District. City of Los
Angeles, 2018

and class conflict added fuel to L.A.'s eventual political fire. That said, the institutional cornerstones—a Protestant moral frame, collateral faith in public works, and the common school's pivotal role in civilizing all those foreign others—sustained a dominant political regime well into the 1950s. This edifice formed the ideological bulwark, the old normal, against which contemporary pluralists would eventually revolt.

Protestant Verve and Public Works

The first Yankees arriving in Los Angeles found no city of angels. Woods, the Presbyterian minister, recorded the grim details of ten murders during his first weeks in this motley settlement, arriving from Massachusetts in 1854. His diary told of a pueblo "not of angels but of demons," as historian Kevin Starr paraphrased. "All around my house near the head of main street, are hundreds of Spaniards in all sorts of revelry and noise—men on horseback—women on foot—children crying," Woods wrote, "as would remind me of bedlam."[5] A young vaquero (cowboy) found rough justice, yanked from the town jail and lynched by a mob led by the mayor. It seemed a lawless outpost that mixed "the cow-town ambiance of saloons, gunslingers, and vigilantes with the ambiance of a farming center of vineyards and orange groves," as Judith Raftery described.[6] A scattering of hotels, sundry stores, and saloons dotted sandy Main Street. Strolling down several village blocks, one would pass a riot of fruit sellers, breweries, two churches, and warehouses filled with grain from surrounding wheat fields while "packs of mongrel dogs roamed the town like mangy sentries," Marc Weingarten writes.

This bedraggled town hosted only a few thousand residents, many crammed into adobe hovels adjacent to the original town plaza, a social tinderbox of spent miners, formerly enslaved Blacks, Chinese and Mexican farmhands, derelicts, and gun-slinging desperados. They gained national notoriety in 1871 when a deadly riot broke out, setting white and Mexican laborers against their Chinese counterparts. It flared up in "Nigger Alley," ignited by disputed claims over an enslaved female held by a Chinese clan. By nightfall, some thirty-nine Chinese men hung from gateposts of nearby corrals. H. H. Bancroft, chronicler of early California, called Calle de los Negros "a hotbed of depravity," home to "Asiatic, African, and European, Latin and Indian [who] lived in unholy association, and for vocation followed thieving and murder."[7]

So, arriving Americanos went about building a more civil society, animated by Protestant notions of progress and collateral faith in public works. The fledgling Yankee government started small in 1871, when city fathers purchased a fire engine paid for with fines levied on those held for public drunkenness.[8] It was "probably then the toughest town in the West," read one column in 1872. On Saturday nights, the central "dance house" was a "general rendezvous of . . . low, dissolute, and degraded specimens of humanity, both male and female."[9] Protestant leaders pressed to regulate drunkenness and dances, rallying early civic groups like the Church Federation and Civic Righteousness League.

Well-educated ladies—coalescing around a newly Progressive identity—worried over the "row of saloons and bordellos off the plaza," from which emanated "the sounds of banjo music, curses, and gunfire."[10] The town council, ignoring opposition from labor guilds, voted to forbid alcohol at public celebrations, and soon, with the advent of silent films, they outlawed "movies of an immoral nature."[11] The state legislature aimed to stamp out traditional Mexican rites and pastimes, imposing fines on "barbarous or noisy amusements," festivities that applied to bullfights, horse racing, and cockfights.[12]

Civilizing these strangers required unrelenting civic action to advance a proper Protestant morality, set within a proscribed racial order. The 1870 census recorded that nearly one-third of all Los Angeles residents were nonwhite or foreign born.[13] Viewed through Yankee eyes, this raised the danger of interracial cavorting, a thinning out of Protestant blood and virtue. "Miscegenation was a sin against Protestant individualism," California writer Richard Rodríguez argues. The new arrivals to L.A., these pious disciples of John Calvin and Martin Luther from the Midwest, drew apart from native peoples. But "in Mexico the European and the Indian consorted."

Protestant self-reliance soon tied middle-class status to securing a humble cottage some miles from this long-gritty downtown. Henry Hancock, as early as 1857, carved out thirty-five one-acre lots from old pueblo lands that extended two miles south along Main Street.[14] The city's expansive footprint soon stretched ten miles east to west, making Los Angeles the largest urban area in America, geographically speaking. It wasn't simply "the laying out of suburban neighborhoods with picturesque winding streets and landscaping to suggest [ancient] Arcadia," argues urbanist Wade Graham. "What was new . . . was the illusion that it wasn't a city [but] the city dressed as the country, made up of detached houses . . . each a castle standing alone in pastoral splendor."[15] One report by the US Census Bureau in 1881 noted that three decades after Los Angeles "was captured by American forces . . . Americans now predominate, and to their energy and perseverance the prosperity of the place is due."

Quenching a Thirst

Above all, the town's Yankee leaders were eager to find water, one essential step in building a modern economy that would be founded on vast citrus orchards and grazing livestock. Earlier colonial leaders, chartered by Mexico City since the sixteenth century, had employed zanjeros to clean sewage and dead bodies from shallow channels (zanjas) that ran off the Los Angeles River. But stronger earnings for growers, vintners, and merchants depended on capturing water in

1874. North Main Street in Los Angeles, looking south toward the courthouse, largest building on left. Tracks were for horse-drawn trolley cars. Photo courtesy of Los Angeles Public Library, Security Pacific National Bank Collection

surrounding mountains, constructing reservoirs, and channeling water into the otherwise bone-dry L.A. basin. And this required ambitious public works, unprecedented efforts made credible in the eyes of Yankee voters and Spanish-speaking Californios. Established investors put their own capital on the table, men like Mark Hopkins, Collis Huntington, and Leland Stanford. But they required a financial match from taxpayers, the diverse and often uncivilized local electorate, as theses profit-seekers saw it.

The tension between private gain and shared infrastructure, including common schools, would of course persist into contemporary times. This contestation, most relevant to our story, resulted in a lasting political polarity that set nascent capitalists against early Progressives, a two-sided dialectic baked into the institutional origins of modern Los Angeles. The Progressives—led by the wives of well-off merchants and bankers—would create a variety of civic institutions to invite disparate foreigners and domestic strangers into the Yankee mainstream, a cause taking shape in the late nineteenth century. First and foremost, early Progressives pressed to expand schools and socialize disparate groups into the Protestant fold.

These Progressives largely abided by the cultural tenets of the Protestant ethic, which legitimated commercial expansion and the headlong spread of white suburbs, where a more virtuous (and white) morality could thrive. Yet, the commercial class and budding Progressives debated whether to buoy poor families, even invite some into civil society, and how much taxpayers should spend on institutions bent on incorporating these disparate outsiders. Progressives in Los Angeles also struggled to purge corrupt municipal officials, eventually aiding wider reforms in California, then accented by Theodore Roosevelt's presidency in the first decade of the twentieth century.[16]

Still, the dominating project of L.A. investors and city fathers was to rally public support for economic growth soon after California's statehood. This agenda inevitably led back to the immediate civic problem: capturing water and channeling it downtown. Enter Canadian Prudent Beaudry St. Anne des Plaines. Long on title and cupidity, but short on personal virtue, Beaudry saw in water a ripe investment opportunity. He had done well in San Francisco, moving his merchandise shop to Los Angeles in 1853. Beaudry came with a cache of silver that had been smelted up north, a not-so-portable yet entirely fungible form of capital. For a thirsty town hoping to expand agriculture, trade, and sun-drenched tourism, Beaudry realized that big money could be found in water.[17] First producing ice from lake water fifty miles north, he transported huge blocks on mules down to the city.

Beaudry soon personified the political tension between taxpayer-financed infrastructure and the unabashed pursuit of profit. In the late 1860s, he partnered with John S. Griffin, a local school superintendent, to form the Citizens Water Company. They proposed a fifty-year exclusive monopoly to manage the town's water supply. Beaudry's firm promised a variety of public benefits: free water for city offices, fire hydrants at downtown intersections, and $50,000 in gold paid to the town. The municipal council passed the lucrative deal on a 3-2 vote in 1868, backing this taxpayer-capitalized private venture: "Cities and towns can never manage enterprises of that nature as economically as individuals can . . . and is made a political hobby," one council member said at the time.[18]

But the deal was vetoed by mayor José Cristóbal Aguilar, once a zanjero, an old-school pluralist with strong ties to the ranchero class of Spanish-speaking Californios. He preferred to protect the common good rather than subsidize private gain with taxpayer dollars. Aguilar emphasized how the deal's terms were "so indefinite . . . that in the course of time great questions may arise with other vested interests, [such as] cultivators of the soil." A compromise emerged: a thirty-year lease with the town, which retained the power to set water rates. Even under less favorable terms, Beaudry would profit handsomely, building several small reservoirs in coveted highlands, like Echo Park and Lincoln Heights, early upscale neighborhoods. Still, reining in Beaudry's profit-seeking would prove difficult for Aguilar, after Prudent Beaudry was elected mayor of Los Angeles.

The spread of rail lines across Southern California—fed by tracks that snaked down from San Francisco, eventually routed to the vast Midwest—also entangled ambitious investors and municipal officials in the latter third of the nineteenth century. Profitable railroads, especially the Southern Pacific and Santa Fe rail lines, delivered waves of cheap labor and migrating farmers to Los Angeles, not to mention unheard-of wealth to the firms' owners, including the infamous "robber barons," Huntington and Stanford. Many blame the automobile for the dismal aesthetics and nagging alienation that contemporary L.A. often connotes. But the region's infamous sprawl began long before the Model T or Ford Mustang. It goes back to electrified rails, put down in the 1880s, stretching to outlying suburbs before World War I. Electric rails weaved through once-thriving orchards and cattle lands, paved over with tiny stucco homes for the aspiring middle class, transporting the first commuters to jobs downtown.

This fusion between profits and public works again surfaced in 1872, when Yankee civic leaders urged voter support for a deal that would richly benefit Leland Stanford. The town's Common Council hoped to float public bonds to finance Southern Pacific's rail line down from Northern California. A second route was to run east to Colorado over the San Gorgonio Pass, two hours east of Los Angeles. Stanford had cemented his partnership with Huntington and Mark Hopkins Jr. while serving as governor. "Stanford knew that the key to building his railroad was to accrue power in the public sphere," as Weingarten argues. The Southern Pacific's lobbyist up in Sacramento, the state capital, freely handed out stock shares to legislators. California's chief justice infamously flashed his rail pass for free rides, no matter how far his destination.[19]

But the question of publicly financed bonds to support Stanford's own company became hotly contested. Dueling campaigners climbed atop soap boxes in the old mission plaza to make their case, still the center for civic debates. Pamphlets expressed opposition from the impoverished "taxpayer," asking whether they would be exploited for free with slight public benefit ("*Pro Bono Publico*," read one sign). Opponents "bewailed the waste of the people's money and bemoaned the increase of taxes," wrote one journalist. "Impassioned orators, from the stump, with the money of the rival corporations jingling in their pockets, pleaded with the obdurate voters."[20] Editorial boards and business owners opposed the deal, arguing that Southern Pacific's owners already grew wealthy at taxpayers' expense. But voters sided with Stanford, voting 1,896–650 in favor of subsidizing the rail giant. Four years later, in 1876, his engineers—aided by hundreds of Chinese and Mexican laborers—completed a seven-thousand-foot tunnel through the mountains an hour north of downtown, opening a direct route to San Francisco.

The Santa Fe train was not far behind, spurring stiff price competition. A ticket from Kansas City to L.A. fell to one dollar one way, bringing fresh waves of new arrivals. Developers accelerated the subdivision of orchards and grazing lands across Los Angeles. Investors speculated over property titles, like trading hog futures, never intending to farm or live on the land. Between 1885 and 1887, more than $200 million in property was purchased. Sixty "townsites" were put up for sale in 1887 alone, soon hosting subdivisions adjacent to rail stations, which now spread across Southern California.

Land developers steadily conspired with city officials to plot the next train station, extending farther out from downtown. Competing rail companies petitioned the Common Council to grant exclusive franchises for profitable routes: south to the industrializing Watts District, west to Santa Monica beaches, a station placed in the town with a pitch-perfect name, Bliss.[21] "It would never do for an electric line to wait until demand for it came," one rail enthusiast argued. "It must anticipate the growth of communities and be there when the home builders arrive."[22] Huntington Land and Improvement Company subdivided vast tracts of grazing lands and orchards. Even its competitor, Suburban Homes Company, invited a new rail line to Van Nuys in 1912, "instantaneously bring[ing] a town into existence."[23] Henry Huntington (Collis's nephew) would eventually lose money on his electric-rail empire but reap huge profits by selling land and erecting thousands of middle-class homes.[24]

A final episode illustrates the collusion between profiteers and city officials—both sides motivated to build massive public works—a tale immortalized in the Roman Polanski film *Chinatown*. The L.A. water chief, William Mulholland, advanced a harebrained scheme in the early 1900s to bring much-needed water 233 miles south from the Sierra Nevada mountains. Mulholland approached developers to win public support for his far-fetched project. Local voters agreed to finance two public bonds that funded one of the longest concrete channels ever attempted (second only to the Panama Canal at the time). A roaring river of water arrived in November 1913 before a cheering crowd just twenty-six miles northwest of downtown.

Harrison Gray Otis, publisher of the *Los Angeles Times*, had editorialized in favor of the Owens Valley aqueduct, secretly investing in the Suburban Homes Company, along with his business partner, Henry Huntington. They invited Isaac Newton Van Nuys, a born-again Baptist born of Jewish descent, to help them buy land north in the San Fernando Valley—precisely where the gushing aqueduct would eventually deliver unlimited water. This profiting cabal watched their land values skyrocket, as this once-arid land soon hosted untold acres of citrus orchards and housing tracts. Attending celebrants noted this amazing feat of engineering, along with the resolve of white Angelenos. "The character of the people," one educator wrote, was exhibited by this one of two "monuments to

1886. Los Angeles High School at Temple and Broadway Streets, opened in 1873. Photo courtesy of Los Angeles County Library, Security Pacific National Bank Collection

the force and faith of the citizens of Los Angeles" (the second a massive harbor arising in San Pedro, a half hour from downtown).[25]

By World War I, investors and municipal officials had already completed a breathless array of public projects—bringing water, electricity, and rail lines to Los Angeles from afar. Suburbs had sprouted across Southern California, commuters tied to jobs via electrified rail lines. The faction of profit-seekers and city leaders certainly fostered remarkable commercial growth, along with early suburban sprawl—all fueled by a robust citrus industry, steady home construction, and L.A.'s now national reputation for sandy beaches and year-round leisure. A small and culturally homogenous circle of civic leaders had established these political conditions for capitalist expansion. They had successfully conspired to "encourage developers and authorities to convert a countryside of farms, ranches and wasteland into a conurbation of electric railways, motor highways, public utilities, and suburban subdivisions," as historian Robert Fogelson writes.[26] Or, the "subsidized monopolization" of the Golden State, as native Joan Didion more skeptically puts it.

Civilizing a Bounded Society: Protestants and Progressives

Early do-gooders—mostly well-off ladies who lunched—recognized that economic growth required cheap labor, and this resulted in deepening disparities, at least under Protestant precepts of progress in the final two decades of the nineteenth century. So, these early civic activists, coalescing under the Progressive banner, began to challenge the merchants, land traders, and rail barons who dominated civil society in Los Angeles. The well-heeled wives faced these same men at the dinner table, as debate over common schooling, family degradation, and "Americanizing" working-class Angelenos bubbled up in polite circles.

Early Progressives stopped short of questioning the core tenets of capitalist expansion or racially arranged schools and suburban housing (a few would join socialist clubs in the 1920s). Still, these assertive women aimed to build a more inclusive city, spearheading California's own Progressive movement, which eventually contributed to first-wave feminism and universal suffrage. "Real civil societies are contradictory and fragmented," as sociologist Jeffrey Alexander argues. "These dynamics create the conditions for suppressing the very existence of the civil sphere. They also create the possibility for its civil repair."[27]

At the top of the Progressive agenda: growing the town's count of public schools. These women argued that Christianity should firmly stand for mercy, fairness, and inclusion. Indeed, the model of "secular" common schools—taxpayer financed and pressing Protestant ideals—was already familiar to the New England ministers and midwestern wives who had come West. Common schooling was to hammer on "chastity, mercy, continence, patience, modesty," to civilize all Angelenos. This ideological pitch stemmed directly from the original Protestant theologians, Martin Luther and John Calvin.[28]

In Europe, the popular spread of literacy and civilizing institutions had aimed to incorporate disparate social classes into a uniform moral framework, emphasizing material progress within a civilized society held together by Protestant virtues and the secular state. Luther had argued for a modern era of tolerance of differing sects (proto-pluralism) while urging secular authorities to expand common schooling, that small-scale institution imbued with Protestant notions of merit, hard work, and individual achievement. Certain sects had already broken with their Puritan brethren, in part over the predestination issue. The Unitarians arriving to Los Angeles, for instance, believed that "the religious duty of human beings lay not in fearful subservience, but in working to achieve, through ever-increasing demonstrations of love, piety, and philanthropy."[29] Fast-forward to the late nineteenth century, and we see modernizing towns like Los Angeles defining schools as *public* works, seeking to incorporate all strangers into a hegemonic cultural and racially arranged framework.

Early on, the Protestant project intended to displace a Catholic spiritual order, originally carried north from Mexico by Franciscan padres, who first built Mission San Gabriel in 1771, eight miles east of the rudimentary plaza then established in Los Angeles. These Spanish-speaking settlers also brought hard labor, disease, and subjugation to the native peoples of California. Yet, Catholicism offered the cultural fabric of Californio society for the subsequent century, prior to the arrival of Protestant Yankees. The early Progressives wanted to head off any resurgence of Catholicism as the count of immigrants from southern Europe and Latin America continued to climb throughout the 1920s.

After all, Los Angeles was to become a different kind of city, pious Protestants promised, one free of the grime, degradation, and ethnic strife that had swamped industrializing cities like Chicago and New York. This imagined, bucolic city would be pitched as the "white spot of America" by city boosters and land speculators, including Harry Chandler, who inherited the *L.A. Times* dynasty.[30] He published full-page ads in broadsheets across the nation displaying a map with a magnified white circle that marked the beating heart of Southern California. Chandler and fellow elites reached out to investors and companies across the nation, promising a rural-like metropolis drenched in sun, where labor agitators, immigrants, and racial troublemakers could be avoided. (The young Chandler, a strict Congregationalist, abstained from alcohol, even from driving, a heretical stance in Los Angeles.)

Collis Huntington commissioned a shameless puff piece by journalist Charles Nordhoff, titled *California for Travellers and Settlers* (1873), urging easterners to move west, to stake a claim and till the soil, "where the grass is green all winter," where the "semi-barbarous habits" of working-class heathens had been avoided.[31] Charles Loomis boasted in 1897 of how Anglo-Protestants now dominated this California paradise. "Our foreign element is a few thousand Chinese and perhaps five hundred native Californians [of Mexican descent] who do not speak English." (The census had counted about 13,500 European immigrants, along with more than 30,000 Mexican and Asian laborers.)[32]

This nirvana-like White Spot required the vigilant monitoring of moral behavior. Members of the San Gabriel Orange Grove Association, a colony established by growers from Indiana, told of how Nordhoff's book had inspired their migration West.[33] Long Beach enthusiast William E. Willmore acquired four thousand acres from the Los Cerritos rancho in 1880, coaxing fellow Methodists to move westward. He worked for the California Immigrant Union, a spinoff owned by the Southern Pacific Railroad, which aimed to stem the inflow of Chinese laborers, replacing them with midwesterners who would protect "the homogeneity of our people and perpetuate our system of political liberty."[34]

Another Methodist colony from New York established a summer camp that promised Midwest churchgoers a climate that was "curative of nervous, dyspeptic, and bronchial disease . . . [where] everlasting spring abides, and never-withering flowers."[35] Willmore was "determined that the Devil should be kept out of his own settlement" in Long Beach. Its city council later imposed six-month jail sentences on women who frequented the beach in bathing suits that failed to hide their armpits down to "one third of the way [covering] the knee joint." Christian societies pitched Los Angeles as a place reflecting the "prevailing moral standards of an agrarian small town." Ditto for Pasadena, which hosted twenty-five churches and six schools as early as 1895. "Its founders, like the soldiers of Cromwell, were men who had the fear of God before them and made some conscience of what they did."[36]

Early Progressives drew from the Protestant-inspired synergy between religious piety and publicly financed schools. After all, Luther himself had championed state-run schooling for all children in Europe, not Catholic education for the privileged few. "It is the duty of the temporal authority to compel its subjects to keep their children in school," he wrote.[37] By temporal authority, Luther meant civic agencies, certainly not the Roman Catholic church. Public schools were to embody the Protestant virtue of self-achievement, reifying the lone individual's obligation to advance material development.

The Protestants that flocked to L.A. in the latter third of the nineteenth century were not uniform in their religious convictions. Congregationalists and Presbyterians stuck close to the Puritan endorsement of predestination, that God has designs on each of us at birth. But it remained impossible to know of one's eventual fate. "That edge of uncertainty only made believers redouble their efforts to purify their own lives and society as a whole . . . gaining greater reassurance of salvation."[38] The father of Methodist thought, John Wesley, rejected this dark view of predestination in the mid-eighteenth century, instead comparing God to a loving parent who nurtured and disciplined one's child to take a pious and virtuous path, to build a better life here on earth. For the Wesleyans, salvation is available to all, and good works for the poor, for the broader collective boosts one's favorable odds.[39]

These spiritual convictions informed the nation's wider "millennial ideology by which nineteenth-century Americans . . . blended their religious and political faiths and which provided a potent unifying force for collaborative action," Stanford sociologist John W. Meyer writes, along with the late historian David Tyack.[40] This millennial mission "was to be located in individuals . . . saved individuals, freed from the chains of sin and tradition and ignorance," animated by faith in "rational investment, technology, and free labor."[41] Or, as essayist Rodriguez puts it: "The comedy of California was constructed on a Protestant faith in individualism . . . a world where youth is not a fruitless metaphor, where it is possible to start anew. A Protestant conquest."[42]

Modernity arrived in Los Angeles as these Protestants nationwide took aim at the perceived cultural threat stirred by European immigrants and native Roman Catholics. One Republican senator, Henry Wilson, argued in 1871 for "an educational system that would transform 'the emigrant, the freedman, and operative' into proper citizens in accord with the desirable traits of New England and American character."[43] The *Catholic World*'s editorial board promptly hit back, claiming that Wilson's forms of public schooling aimed to mold all Americans "into one homogenous people, after what may be called the New England Evangelical type . . . [unable] to tolerate any diversity of ranks, conditions, race, belief, or worship." Pious sects, especially the Baptists and Methodists, were enjoying steady growth in membership, rejecting hierarchy and liturgical rituals, opting to weave Protestant notions of sin and upright behavior into secular civic institutions, starting with schools. The contest over pluralist tolerance and which groups exercised political influence was on.

A Telling Polarity: Progressives versus Profiteers

As Los Angeles grew and diversified along economic and demographic lines, Protestant Angelenos began to worry about cracks in their cultural-spiritual edifice. How to preserve their own conception of civilized society, moral piety, and racial purity? And which groups could legitimately be incorporated into the white Protestant rendition of polite society?

The population of L.A. rose to some 103,000 residents by 1900, spurred by rising citrus output and growing tourism, then unexpected oil discoveries just a short ride from downtown. (New York City by comparison had surpassed one million residents a decade earlier.) Economic expansion lifted the white middle class into comfortable suburbs, like Pasadena, which had been transformed from "an indifferent sheep pasture . . . the [old] San Pasqual Rancho," one writer

1890. The Arcadia Hotel, situated behind the Arcadia Bath House on Santa Monica Beach. Reprinted with permission of the Los Angeles County Library, Security Pacific National Bank Collection

noted in 1893, to "a city of palatial homes, paved streets and massive business blocks, the wonder of the tourist and the paradise of the health-seeker."[44]

Yet, over two-fifths (41 percent) of all elementary school pupils came from homes with at least one foreign-born parent by 1920, according to census figures. The arrival of automakers and tire manufacturers, steel plants, and film studios attracted rising numbers of Midwest laborers and failed farmers, southern Blacks, and skilled craftsmen from Northern California. Mexico's struggling economy, then its political revolution, drove tens of thousands to L.A. The foreign-born white population—mainly Britons, Germans, and Russians—climbed tenfold, from 14,000 in 1900 to just over 140,000 in 1930, as building crafts and factory jobs grew exponentially. The count of Mexican-heritage residents increased from fewer than 1,000 to more than 53,000 during the period; the count of Black Angelenos climbed from 2,000 to nearly 39,000.[45]

Hoping to cool off tensions sparked by demographic variety and income disparities, tepid Progressives like Caroline Severance, wife of a successful L.A. banker, moved to invite certain racial groups and lower classes into white civil society. The profiteers need not set the rules of the game, Severance argued. The best angels of Christian leaders must exercise their voice as well. Common schooling was the main institutional device through which they hoped to incorporate peripheral "strangers" into the Protestant mainstream.

Step one required convincing their well-to-do husbands and L.A. taxpayers that expanding school enrollments would "eradicate harmful habits . . . to [recognize] such moral tendencies as inimical to the community and provision must be made to combat these."[46] Severance also mobilized women's literary groups to wage "civic betterment" activities, from battling prostitution and drunkenness to exposing corrupt city officials. Their Civic Association created a "penny lunch" program for poor children in 1899. They got busy "improving schools, arranging for suitable luncheon for school children . . . instituting free baths, starting traveling libraries, and opening public playgrounds."[47] Severance's comrades donated picture frames to decorate classrooms and helped "tint the blackboards green."

Not exactly radical agitators, these early Progressives. Yet, their mission was deeply cultural in character, infusing Protestant piety and Yankee social forms within public institutions. They were preoccupied with moral cleansing. Progressives lobbied municipal officials to tear down "unsightly billboards," convincing the city council that "obscene or objectionable pictures and advertisements [be] removed." Severance won public funding for home-visiting teachers and English classes in foreign neighborhoods, "to make this the most beautiful, intellectual, moral and sanitary city in the land," as reported by Mrs. M. Burton Williamson, a fellow Progressive.

Los Angeles was to be "a city where slums may never enter, where it may never be said that its youth are over-educated in books but wanting in common sense."[48]

By "ruralizing"—enshrining Protestant virtues in greening suburbs—L.A. would become "a city without tenements, a city without slums," Dana W. Barlett, a Protestant minister, wrote in his 1907 book, *The Better City*. The poor and destitute would one day enjoy the "possibilities of social beauty, utility, and harmony of which they had not been able to even dream," journalist Henry Demarest Lloyd wrote. "No such vision could otherwise have entered into the prosaic drudgery of their lives."[49]

The Protestant faithful looked askance at pioneering filmmakers, moving West from the moral morass of New York City. Upstart director David Wark Griffith arrived in the rural outpost of Hollywood in 1910, just thirty-five years old, already having completed more than two hundred silent movies. But moving pictures manifest déclassé values as seen through pious Angeleno eyes. Film "remained a pastime of the inner-city working class," writes Gary Krist, "often immigrants who couldn't afford a ticket to the legitimate theater and for whom silent films presented no language barrier."[50] Known thespians at first refused to appear on camera for melodramatic shorts, projected in seedy nickelodeons, not wanting to sully their reputations. "This town [Los Angeles] full of culturally conservative midwestern transplants hardly saw itself as a future movie capital," Krist reports. Signs appearing in the windows of L.A. boardinghouses declared: "No Jews, actors, or dogs."[51] One early nonprofit calling themselves Conscientious Citizens gathered ten thousand signatures in a failed effort to expel who they viewed as disreputable filmmakers.

Nor would civic leaders tolerate defiance of Protestant norms. The arrival of five thousand Molokan immigrants from Russia early in the twentieth century revealed the cultural intolerance commonly exercised by city leaders. Austere to the core, Molokan parents instructed their children to read the Bible but little else. At first, they refused to send their children to city schools. Families pooled their income and lived collectively, settling across the river in Boyle Heights. One Progressive described the Molokans as "strange peasants . . . industrious, dignified, preoccupied with their own affairs."[52] Education officials prohibited Molokan girls from wearing head shawls at school, an indigenous practice meant to signal feminine modesty. Molokan leaders pushed back by asking the school board for separate facilities where their language and culture could be taught. This was followed by similar petitions from French, German, and Italian communities—typically rejected by Yankee-Protestant authorities.

But the tables were turned on Progressives in the early twentieth century. They were heavily criticized for turning a blind eye toward the racial segregation and material inequities that already marked city schools and suburban housing developments. Writer Frank Norris exposed the corruption and excesses embraced by California's rail barons in *The Octopus*, published in 1901. Carey McWilliams detailed horrific conditions faced by Mexican farmworkers in his

1895. Chinese and white Progressive teachers and benefactors at the Chinese Mission School, sponsored by the Congregational Church. Photo courtesy of Seaver Center for Western History Research, Los Angeles County of Natural History, and the University of Southern California Digital Library

book *Factories in the Field.* As late as 1916, more than one in three infants of Mexican heritage did not survive in L.A., an infant mortality rate four times higher than for whites.[53] A vile blend of profit-seeking and social anomie washed over the city's identity, along with a scent of political decay. This erosion of basic civility stemmed from municipal corruption, along with the dark cultural image expressed in L.A.'s noir literary tradition.

Labor guilds protested loudly in 1913 after the Los Angeles board overseeing high schools recruited a production expert from Chicago to teach courses in "mercantile efficiency." This prompted the Central Labor Council to oppose the curriculum unless the board would "include a section on the debilitating effects of factory work."[54] Resistance to cultural uniformity was arising in racial enclaves as well. Mexican-heritage residents rioted outside the San Juan Capistrano mission in 1910, sending filmmakers in retreat, after they attempted to film a faux holy procession, which real parishioners viewed as sacrilegious. The tacit view of civil society held by white Protestants—who defined what moral behaviors were deemed sacred—was giving way to alternative cultural forms, widening awareness of injustice, and the first inklings of pluralist politics.

Without doubt, the Progressive Era in Los Angeles yielded impressive benefits early in the twentieth century, pulling up deep roots of corruption between business elites and municipal officials. The Committee of Safety in Los Angeles hired Pinkerton detectives in 1899 to work undercover, revealing payoffs to cops for protection or simply looking the other way. Good-government reformers secretly purchased a bordello to gather quite vivid evidence on scores of officers. The Southern Pacific's political operative, Walter Parker, was exposed by Progressives after he bribed the city clerk to approve a railroad right-of-way that would have bisected downtown. Progressives across California pushed through statewide regulation of the rail barons and brought direct democracy through ballot propositions put before all voters. Overall, these reformers helped shift the political balance between champions of capital and the wider public interest, defining a broader common good for all Angelenos. They articulated a critical framework that opposed the raw pursuit of private profit and worsening inequality. Progressive advocates even wrestled control of the city's water system from private hands—still owned by Prudent Beaudry—in 1902.

Deepening Lines of Race and Class

This prickly polarization between profit-seekers and Progressives would persist for most of the twentieth century—weakly challenged until the rise of contemporary pluralists. The two sides squabbled over taxes, the pace (and cost) of expanding public schools, and whether to lift poor families. Yet, both sides organized politically within the bounds of white Protestant tenets. The Progressives and profiteers agreed that strangers on the edge of civil society must be Americanized, made to comprehend basic moral virtues and norms of behavior, not to mention learning a single language. The goal of pulling disparate groups into a single melting pot was not in question. Contention did arise over which groups should be invited into civil society, how fast, and at what public cost. Maybe well-educated and assimilating families of Mexican heritage. But certainly not Blacks, Jews, or Angelenos of Asian heritage.

L.A.'s commercializing economy intensified disparities in wages and living conditions, arranged along somewhat fluid lines of race and class. One's membership in civil society was earlier defined under colonial rules of status, designations tied to Spanish, Indian, or mixed racial heritage, along with levels of school attainment and ties to the military or Catholic church. The state's first census, conducted in 1836, reported a handful of occupations among native Californios: "proprietor, *vaquero*, laborer, or servant." Next to the names of Americans and Spaniards, a section titled "*gente de razón*" (civilized people of reason), appeared the occupations of merchant, cooper, mason, hatter, and three "tramps *de Norte America*."[55]

A half century later, as the Los Angeles economy began to modernize, wage levels mirrored similar layers of class, designated by race and gender.[56] Seamstresses earned about $330 yearly in 1880, relative to $480 for the average wheelwright and $730 for watchmakers and repairmen.[57] The rise of public institutions boosted the odds of landing a better-paying job. The police chief earned more than $1,000 yearly, and teachers earned about $33 monthly when employed by schools receiving city grants. For comparative purposes, Catholic colleges in L.A. charged $54 in yearly tuition.[58]

Racial categories operated in stark fashion at first, becoming more flexible during the first half of the twentieth century. Chinese and Indian laborers initially earned about half the average manufacturing wage, according to one survey in the 1890s.[59] The racialized job structure set back Mexican laborers as well, especially after Chinese workers were expelled from the United States in 1882. The Pacific Electric Company, extending rail lines across L.A., paid Mexican workers about $1.25 per day, compared with $1.75 for white peers. Charles Crocker, who owned the Central Pacific Railway, paid nearly ten thousand Chinese workers $30 per month to lay the transcontinental rail line, finally connecting California to the nation in 1869.[60] (Crocker labored up north to turn San Francisco into his self-declared "Paris of the West.")

Yet, commercial growth, together with the spread of schooling, began to blur lines of class identity and who was permitted to assimilate into white society. Two-thirds of adult residents who reported at least $2,500 in property claimed they could read and write in 1880, compared with one-fifth of those owning less than $1,000 in property.[61] School attendance grew unevenly as Progressives pushed to build more schools: two-thirds of white, primary-age children were enrolled by the final decade of the nineteenth century, compared with just one-third of Mexican-heritage children.[62] Literacy levels of young African Americans climbed early in L.A., as detailed by J. Max Bond in his 1936 sociology thesis at the University of Southern California. By then, literacy rates ranged up to 88 percent among Black Angelenos, 10 to 54 years of age.[63]

The city of Los Angeles grew to 1.2 million residents by 1930, the wider county hosting nearly twice the population. The harbor south in San Pedro now shipped out thousands of cars each day, along with countless barrels of oil, even as the nation's economy faltered after the financial crash of 1929. The US Rubber Company had arrived in 1919, erecting its first West Coast factory. Goodrich, Firestone, and Samson Tire and Rubber followed suit by the 1920s. Modern factories stretched more than twenty square blocks south of downtown, once verdant pasture lands, in places like South Gate, near Watts. By World War II, Los Angeles had become the nation's ninth-largest manufacturing hub. Investors aggressively pursued New York movie producers, delivering ever-bright sunshine and inexpensive land for expansive back lots. Some fifty-two studios arose adjacent to the Hollywood hills, employing more than fifteen thousand workers by the 1920s.

The late-coming Industrial Revolution created tens of thousands of well-paying factory jobs for arriving Black workers and failed farmers from the

Midwest. The rising structure of wages lifted nonwhite Angelenos into a widening middle class. The magnet of manufacturing boosted the Black population to 64,000 by the start of World War II, accounting for nearly one-third of the city's demographic growth in the preceding decade.[64] Labor leaders would slowly embrace the growing count of Black factory workers but exclude Mexican-heritage laborers until the 1950s. Overall, the diversity of L.A.'s burgeoning middle class—still segregated across separate housing developments—was beginning to erode the cultural and moral tenets, along with the assumed political dominance, of white Protestants.

Novel class distinctions were emerging among white subgroups as well. The Great Depression and failing farms in the Dust Bowl drove hundreds of thousands of poorly educated Arkies and Oakies to Los Angeles in the 1930s. Even though of Protestant stock, they weathered intense ridicule and discrimination. "They were white, native-born Americans whose rural backgrounds and evangelical religion placed them in the same cultural ballpark," writes historian John Laslett. Some came to call L.A. the "Iowa coast." Yet, these ex-farmers were defined as "not quite white . . . seen as violent, stupid, and inferior by many of the existing working-class residents." After a large count was hired at the Cal-ship factory close to the San Pedro harbor, they were taunted by a urinal labeled the "Oakie Drinking Fountain."[65]

Civilizing Strangers in Uniform Schools

The spread of common schools—uniform in their moral message, skilling youths for a commercializing economy—was central to the Progressive agenda. This modest institution promised to temper the pursuit of private gain, endorsing a wider, less utilitarian common good, a benevolent L.A. that aspired to become more inclusive. J. J. Ayres, publisher of the *Evening Express*, complained in 1872 of a town where "purses rule and not the cultured mind." Yet, he remained hopeful that "our school [will] build above the vulgar plane of sordid streets," celebrating the opening of Central School on Poundcake Hill, an institutional haven in an otherwise heartless world.[66] Whether such tolerant and integrating ideals would win out, pitted against the sharply bounded circles of white communities, remained a festering question for the coming century, animating the rise of contemporary pluralism.

In 1868, about half the 3,131 children of Yankee or white parentage attended school in fledgling Los Angeles, with one-third enrolled in small private or Catholic schools.[67] The Common Council financed four new grammar schools that year, employing another nineteen teachers, providing instruction mostly in Spanish. But from the first inkling of Protestant modernity, educators in Los Angeles did not see all children as created equal, as sharing the same unbounded opportunity that city boosters so earnestly promised. The offspring of Chinese,

1888. Students with their teacher, Mary Crawford, at the Lankershim School, located in present-day North Hollywood. Reprinted with permission of the Los Angeles County Library, Security Pacific National Bank Collection

Black, and Mexican laborers, even non-English-speaking Europeans, were kept on the periphery of civil society, destined for low-level jobs. One grammar school was erected atop Bunker Hill in the 1870s, "the only building upon it being a little public schoolhouse devoted to colored children," Ayres wrote.

Command, Control, and Conformity

Progressives aimed to confront the gross disparities experienced by the widening variety of groups that characterized Los Angeles in the late nineteenth century. But these good-government advocates also pushed to expand common schooling out to the proliferating suburbs. So, to spread the word institutionally, Progressives pressed for the "scientific management" of schooling. This modern approach to public administration stressed centralized control of regimented curricula, moral lessons, and didactic pedagogy—all codified and regimented by education managers downtown.

This institutional form—rejecting the inefficient one-room schoolhouse—became the "one best system" of public education, as historian Tyack infamously called it. Larger schools with age-graded classrooms would deliver greater efficiency, administrative Progressives argued. School organizations became more differentiated, sorting children along "scientifically tested" measures of intelligence, naively ignoring differences in family background and home language. "We are getting toward the next step in the development," one L.A. analyst declared in 1909, applauding this rationally managed system: "what is better than non-partisan—a non-personal administration of public school affairs."[68] These Progressives "maintained that irrationality in politics, greed, and corruption could be replaced by scientific and objective bureaucrats," as Charles Kerchner wrote. "Pure politics guided by selfless experts."[69]

Public schools sprouted across settlements and tiny districts adjacent to the city of Los Angeles, operating just one or two schools. This diffuse localism came to be seen as unfair and inefficient in the eyes of Progressives—since teacher salaries and quality levels were necessarily tied to a neighborhood's property wealth, and L.A.'s school boards (one for grammar schools, the other for high schools) could raise comparatively more revenues. So, between 1896 and 1932, Los Angeles educators bullishly annexed more than forty-one neighboring districts, reaching way beyond the city limits, incorporating schools in Hollywood, Huntington Park, and Watts.

As early as 1910, the territory run by the tandem school boards stretched across four hundred square miles. In this way, education planners fed the now-infamous suburban sprawl of Los Angeles, the drift of white Angelenos out to tree-lined streets and their segregated suburbs.[70] "The district's administrative headquarters on North Hill Street has grown into a sort of junior Pentagon," *Daily News* editor Robert Harris wrote. He warned of hypercentralization, where the syllabi and "methods of instruction are ground out by the ream . . . through the administrative chain of command to the teaching rank and file."[71]

Most civic leaders viewed this hyperuniformity, enforced by a centralized regime, as the modern way of expanding an imperious school *system*. But it masked contention arising in Progressive circles over the fundamental aims and social agenda of schooling. Even back in the late nineteenth century, some Progressive activists emphasized what they saw as the unbounded curiosity and potential of children. They harked back to Enlightenment philosophy rather than Calvinist skepticism regarding the innocence and capacity of young children—if raised in proper environs. These mostly female activists challenged standardized didactics as dampening children's desire to explore and construct their own understanding of their world. Meanwhile, the administrative Progressives claimed that centralized control would ensure classroom uniformity, moving all children toward Yankee-Protestant conventions of moral behavior, language, and literacy.

The arrival of Horatio Stebbins to Los Angeles stoked early on this divisive debate within Progressive circles. A Unitarian minister from Massachusetts, Stebbins immigrated to San Francisco in 1864. This was the era of California-based writers like Bret Harte and Samuel Clemens, who romanticized the unbounded West in their portrayals of amusing ruffians and jumping frog contests, untethered from East Coast stuffiness. Stebbins joined forces with Phoebe Hearst, the wife of mining magnate George Hearst (and mother of William Randolph Hearst) to press the cause of kindergarten, a novel institution that was spreading across Massachusetts and New York, promising to nurture children in enlightened, nonutilitarian ways.[72]

Severance, the Progressive leader and fellow Unitarian, invited Stebbins to visit L.A. to aid her press to extend free kindergarten to all families.[73] She would soon succeed in creating kinder classrooms inside Protestant churches, often situated in poor sections of the city, offering learning activities in English along with periods of play and lessons in personal hygiene. It was a notable victory for the humanist wing of Progressives, moving the monied class to raise taxes for working-class children in the 1890s. At the same time, Progressives were confidently reaching into the daily practices of non-Yankee populations, guiding how these foreigners should properly raise their children. "The private world of the family would be enhanced by the ministrations of a nurturing professional," as historian Judith Raftery put it, "as institutions entered the private world."[74]

Mary Gibson, wife of city school board president Frank Gibson, similarly argued that civic clubs should engage in "constructive social work" that advanced "social purity."[75] She helped found the town's first Protestant orphanage and raised money for the new city library and the Unitarian church. Gibson raised $10,000 in 1911 to finance a campaign for women's suffrage, and backed Hiram Johnson, the victorious Progressive Party candidate for California governor.

Gibson worried about the fate of the city's rising count of poor and immigrant families, convincing Johnson to create the Home Teacher Act, an effort to didactically instruct immigrant mothers. "It shall be the duty of the home teachers to work in the homes of the pupils, instructing children and adults in matters relating to school attendance," her report read, "in sanitation, in the English language, in household duties such as purchase, preparation and use of food and of clothing and in the fundamental principles of the American system of government."[76] Her state commission ranked groups on a scale of moral superiority in 1910: "The Italian with his love of industry and frugality, whose adaptability makes him quickly assimilated . . . [compared] to the Mexican with his lack of initiative, whose roving temper increases the difficulty of adjusting him."[77] Without decisive action, California would "pay the penalty of social disorder," Gibson argued.[78]

Segregated Schools as Suburban Amenity

Meanwhile, the school institution kept seeping outward, keeping pace with L.A.'s suburban sprawl. Pupil enrollment grew steadily to 30,909 by 1903, as families continued to arrive from the Midwest and the American South, Canada, and East Asia.[79] By 1909, the grammar school board employed 1,306 teachers. Two world wars and the Great Depression merely slowed demand temporarily. The downtown schools office ran 164 schools by 1913, enrolling just over 87,000 pupils (figure 1.7). By 1928, almost 330,000 students attended one of 364 public schools.[80] Nearly half of all students were born to parents of nonwhite heritage, and one in eight of Mexican heritage.[81] Demographic diversity and deepening segregation were overtaking the Protestant press for moral and cultural conformity.

Education leaders did not welcome L.A.'s ethnic variety with pluralist hurrah. Instead, they conspired with home builders and local officials during the first half of the twentieth century to assign Black, Latino, and Asian-heritage children to racially isolated schools. Aspiring middle-class whites—seeking their segregated slice of paradise—sought out subdivisions with good schools and affordable property taxes. Developers attracted the expanding middle class by putting up small cottages in school districts that kept taxes down and minority groups out.

As one housing developer, anonymously named Mr. Borg (by sociologist Charles Spalding), said in 1939: "We looked around and discovered that

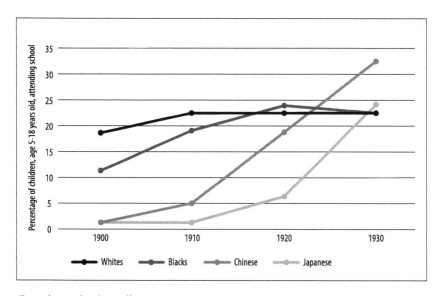

Growth in school enrollment, 1900–1930

Montebello had the lowest tax rate of any nearby district, so we went into it."[82] His firm carved out nearly two thousand lots from the pasturelands of Bell Gardens, twenty minutes south of downtown. As Blacks were excluded from whites-only housing tracts, schools grew more segregated. Back in 1890, less than one-third of all Blacks lived in any single ward of the city and another third were scattered across three other wards. By 1930, seven in ten Blacks resided in a single area south of downtown: the area known as South Central, including the Watts District.[83]

Builders such as Los Angeles Suburban Homes donated lots on which Protestant ministers founded churches and school districts erected schools. The city of L.A. kept stretching out to unincorporated towns, annexing endless tracts of pasturelands and citrus orchards. One educator, Arthur Gould, complained in 1920 that schools were being scattered out to "sparsely settled" hinterlands, "spread out over an area that is sixty miles in length from north to south and about eighteen miles wide." He emphasized how this propagation of standardized schools was "exceptionally rapid . . . practically all available income has had to be devoted to expansions in lines already established without giving great support to innovations."[84]

City boosters promised new arrivals a classless nirvana, where even the "poor live in single cottages, with dividing fences and flowers in the front yard," as Barlett, the Protestant cleric, boasted in 1907. He foresaw manufacturing plants growing in "the country . . . [amid a] wealth of climbing vines and roses."[85] This Disneyesque fantasy spread to the architectural design of factories. The Samson tire plant, the largest physical structure west of the Mississippi in 1929, mimicked an Assyrian castle, replete with griffins perched above crenellated battlements. "Instead of the suburb fleeing to the edges of the city, the suburban ideal could colonize the city," argues urbanist Graham.[86] New arrivals were "surrounded by pleasant fields and faithful friends" into the 1930s, as historian Becky Nicholaides writes, "in houses covered with vines and clothed with flowers, looking from the open window upon rustling fields."[87] Transplants from midwestern farms knew how to live off the land marked by unpaved streets, and "rabbit hutches, chicken pens, and even tethered goats proliferated in these communities."[88]

Amid this suburban paradise, housebuilders found profits in protecting the white-Protestant frame. "Homeowners as a class are universally considered to be thrifty, law abiding, religious, public spirited, good workmen, desirable citizens," one developer promised potential buyers.[89] Builders and municipal leaders enforced housing covenants that prohibited selling one's property to Blacks or Angelenos of Mexican descent, a practice upheld by the state courts in 1919. One local editor put it more directly in 1925, that South Gate was "the ideal residence for people of moderate means. The only restrictions are racial—the white race only may own property here." Chamber of Commerce publicists wrote that this budding suburb was "directly in the path of Southern California's industrial development . . . where 90 percent of the residents own their own homes . . . of the better class, 100 percent American."[90]

Housebuilders in Glendale advertised the exclusion of Black children from local schools in the 1920s. Booker T. Washington Jr. fought a long battle to retain a house he bought in the San Gabriel Valley, adjacent to Pasadena. According to one resident, many Blacks "had come to Los Angeles with ready cash. "Even though many of the residential sections then occupied by the whites were nothing to brag about, these communities were veritable Edens to some of the Negroes," wrote Bond, the USC sociologist.[91] When educators in Watts proposed $128,000 in local financing to boost school quality, one Home Gardens resident squawked. "There are too many people from Oklahoma, Texas, Arkansas . . . to support an issue for schools in Watts where the Negro pupils outnumber the whites."[92]

School boards in Los Angeles played along with this Protestant penchant for racial purity, eager to acquire more territory, acquiescing to white parents'

1920. Children in a Chinese kindergarten. Photo courtesy of the Seaver Center for Western History Research, Los Angeles County of Natural History, and the University of Southern California Digital Library

preference for segregated schools. Housing segregation predictably led to un-evenly funded schools, what became a flash point for the new pluralists a half century later. The middle-class northwest section of South Gate, for example, attached itself to the Huntington Park City School District in the 1920s, where stronger property values buoyed higher spending, equaling $32 per pupil. Home Gardens—literally on the other side of the tracks, hosting a rising count of Black families—could only raise $8 per student from local property taxes.

Plural Forms of Resistance

The deepening segregation of schools did not go unnoticed. But those speak-ing out against racial or economic disparities risked retribution from business leaders. Two Progressive school board members up for reelection came into the crosshairs of Harry Chandler, the *L.A. Times* publisher. Most objectionable in Chandler's eyes was G. Bromley Oxnam, pastor of the Church of All Nations, who had appeared on the podium with socialist writer Upton Sinclair. The nov-elist had questioned the values of police chief Louis Oaks, a barely closeted member of the Ku Klux Klan. Returning fire, Chandler attacked Oxnam as being tied to "disloyal Americans" like Sinclair, who purportedly opposed US involvement in World War I. The Merchants and Manufacturers Association sided with Chandler, and they convinced voters to remove Oxnam and a fellow Progressive serving on the school board. Such episodes of contention served to cement the polarizing duel between downtown business leaders and more equity-minded Progressives, a tension that also would later fuel a more plural-ist politics.

Political resistance began to surface in Black and "Mexican" communities well prior to World War II. Mutual aid associations first appeared in the 1870s among Angelenos of Mexican heritage. Members of *La Sociedad de Hispano Americano* paid monthly dues, allowing them to borrow small sums to invest in their business or improve their households.[93] Bond, the young sociologist, de-tailed the ameliorative work of self-help associations and local organizers surfac-ing in South Central L.A. by the 1930s. He described sixty-six Black churches that served this blue-collar community, including Baptist and African Method-ist Episcopal congregations. Sustaining southern faiths, the so-called Sancti-fied and Holiness denominations ran nine Black churches; "the chief element of this type of religious expression is spontaneity . . . love of excitement, drama, and a ready response to the spoken word," Bond wrote. Churches offered a va-riety of services for African American families. "Me and my old man come to Los Angeles without a dime," one woman reported. "We went to [the] Brother's church . . . he made an appeal from his pulpit and we got a room. Some kind soul found us a job."[94] Plural nodes of ethnic solidarity and political authority were quietly taking root.

1945. Unidentified jazz musicians, as Los Angeles became nationally renowned in the jazz world. Photo from collection of Walter L. Gordon Jr., a Black attorney born in Santa Monica; used with permission of the Los Angeles County Library, Shades of L.A. Collection

Mexican American youth, two decades before the Watts riot, also fought against the racism to which upstanding Protestants turned a blind eye. In 1943, many soldiers trained on a small base located close to Chavez Ravine. These hills, northeast of downtown, were home to hundreds of Mexican-heritage families (later evicted to build Dodger Stadium). White soldiers frequented pubs and eateries in nearby Chinatown and adjacent blocks populated by Latino families. These young Chicanos donned long coats and baggy wool pants, the style popularized by Lalo Guerrero, a revered guitarist and farmworker activist. The War Production Board had ordered a cutback of most fabric production, including this stylized costume worn by young Mexican Americans. White soldiers took offense, or they simply aimed to pick a fight. After a series of street skirmishes, full-scale rioting broke out that summer, as soldiers swept into Latino parts and proceeded to trash stores and theaters, beating many of the so-called zoot-suiters with "sadistic frenzy," as journalist Cary McWilliams reported.[95] The police allowed the fighting to continue, then arrested more than five hundred Latino youths.

Maturing civil rights activists began to challenge segregated and poorly funded "Mexican schools," officially sanctioned by school districts across Southern California. These legal activists won the celebrated *Mendez* case in 1947, ordering Orange County officials to desegregate their schools. It was the nation's first successful challenge in a federal case of the US Supreme Court's "separate but equal" doctrine established in 1896. Fred Ross, trained under Saul Alinsky in Chicago, then helped organize Mexican American parents to upend similarly isolated schools out in Riverside County.[96]

In 1961, Mary Ellen Crawford, a Black teen, attempted to register at L.A.'s South Gate High School, a campus hosting enrollments that were 98 percent white, serving families that enjoyed the uptick in factory jobs and middle-class aspirations. But Crawford's parents were told she must attend Jordan High, situated just one mile away, where enrollments were 99 percent Black. The American Civil Liberties Union filed a lawsuit arguing that the L.A. Unified School District (now run under a single administrative roof) had violated Crawford's constitutional right to equal protection. As the civil rights movement gained steam across America, equity-minded advocates had coalesced to confront the past century of residential segregation of L.A.'s widening variety of families, and the perpetuation of equally segregated schools.

The old political regime—this persisting dialectic between efficiency-minded business leaders and pro-education Progressives—had never encountered such rough weather. A political storm was gathering in Los Angeles. A barrage of novel forces were gaining steam: judicial challenges to school segregation, the public revelation of economic disparities, a vocalized yearning for civic respect and identity heard from Black and Latino communities. The amiable political center could no longer hold. A fresh crop of activists, well educated and impatient, surfacing from within communities of color, was climbing onto the civic stage, talking of ethnic pride and cosmopolitan inclusion. Aging civic leaders had little to say in response, whether rooted in business, labor, or the aging Progressive circles. This century-old political dialectic and its unrelenting press for cultural hegemony held little appeal to the diverse insurgents. It was giving way to a festive politics of pluralism.

Then came 1965.

1965

A momentous year for Los Angeles, setting in motion telling forces that would play out through century's end. Most relevant for our story, though, are the demographic and economic upheavals that would open a novel political space, virgin terrain previously unexplored. A maturing rainbow of civic activists surfaced in the wake of urban unrests—first within L.A.'s Black communities, then joined by the Chicano movement, seeking its own ethnic identity and pursuit of cosmopolitan respect and political power. They were soon joined by litigators pressing for civil rights, advocates focusing on school reform, even wealthy benefactors and young Jewish leaders. Still, a pair of seismic shifts in 1965—the Watts riot and federal immigration reform—catalyzed the transforming complexion of Angeleno families and the schools their children attended. Ironically, these tandem quakes shook Los Angeles as it basked in postwar prosperity, reaching its ideological and material apex on the eve of going bust.

The East Coast media in 1962 had discovered California once again. The Golden State was surpassing New York as the nation's most populous, with 1,500 new residents arriving each day. The television networks first descended to report on this sunny nirvana's return, followed by journalists from *Newsweek* and *Life* magazines. Governor Edmund G. Brown trumpeted the latest newcomers as "the greatest mass migration in the history of the world."[97] *Look* magazine's senior editor, George B. Leonard, declared that California provided "a window into the future . . . the most fertile soil for new ideas in the U.S. . . . an increasingly egalitarian society, with unprecedented opportunities for personal pleasure and fulfillment [where] the shackles of the past are broken."[98] Leonard would soon go native, helping to establish Esalen, the out-there human potential haven at Big Sur.

Defense industries situated in Los Angeles would surge during the Cold War as well, creating abundant jobs at firms like Lockheed and Douglas Aircraft. The Jet Propulsion Lab in Pasadena was attracting the nation's top scientists and engineers, who literally sent Americans, like John Glenn, into orbit. Governor Brown pushed for his own aqueduct, a channel that ran nearly four hundred miles from Sacramento to Southern California. Even the Brooklyn Dodgers had moved to Los Angeles in 1957. Tom Petty, looking back on the rise of folk-rock music that became known as the "L.A. sound," put it rather simply: "People were dreamers who believed you could do something that was not ordinary."[99]

But California's golden moment and its sunlit innocence vanished instantly after one murderous week of civil strife in 1965. The mostly Black swath of Los Angeles known as Watts was suddenly engulfed in flames. Deepening segregation and family poverty, bubbling to the surface, unleashed unmitigated fury in this once-booming manufacturing center. It had become the industrial sump that Progressives once feared: a vast and economically depressed ghetto that manifested staggering crime rates, family dissolution, and starkly unequal schools.

On the wide and sparse boulevards of South Central, simmering with summer heat, a routine traffic stop by police turned into a minor shouting match, then full-scale brawl, as scores of officers swarmed the scene. Six days of looting followed, along with violent assaults on fellow Blacks, Korean shop owners, and equally poor whites. Left in smoldering ashes: 34 dead, almost 3,500 arrests, and tens of millions of dollars in decimated property. Hundreds of stores were picked clean. More than 10,000 people had participated, a show of collective rage, torching homes and retail outlets over a stretch of 46 square miles. "What struck the imagination most indelibly were the fires," a young writer, Joan Didion, reported. "For days one could drive the Harbor Freeway and see the city on fire, just as we had known it would be in the end."[100]

Watts brought into plain sight the grinding poverty felt by Black and Mexican-heritage families in that other Los Angeles, no longer invisible to white residents tucked away in comfortable suburbs. The McCone Commission, investigating the uprising, pointed to poor schools, dreary housing, and joblessness as root causes. "The whole point of the outbreak in Watts was that it marked the first major rebellion of Negroes against their own masochism," activist Bayard Rustin wrote in 1966. "Carried on with the express purpose of asserting that they would no longer quietly submit to the deprivation of slum life."[101]

The violence shook—in this moment—the century-old foundations of civil society in Los Angeles. It also spurred a new alliance between Black activists and left-leaning Jewish leaders on the affluent Westside, most long excluded from civic clubs and elite country clubs. Latino activism and the rising Chicano movement soon followed, emanating out from L.A. and across the American Southwest. These young activists united around efforts to desegregate the schools, as one key front to blast open the confined structuring of opportunity. It was a crusade that the old polarity—pitting champions of capital against labor and education leaders—had refused to tackle. Nor could withering Progressives contain or adequately respond to the wider battles now being waged by this militant and racially charged array of organizers, pressing on multiple economic and cultural fronts, attacking the staid politics of white Protestant leaders.

Yet, this roiling cauldron of political contention, leading to court-ordered busing of children into foreign ethnic lands, frightened middle-class Angelenos. These direct descendants of midwestern farmers and Protestant Yankees pulled up stakes again, often moving a few miles to smaller school districts just outside L.A. Unified, areas that still hosted predominantly white schools. As Democratic politicians got behind anti-poverty and civil rights initiatives, anti-tax whites across California mounted a devastating backlash. Proposition 13, approved by voters statewide in 1978, capped property taxes and set out to starve local governments, including public schools, in the subsequent three decades. Conservatives wouldn't stop there, going after immigrant families, welfare recipients, and the perceived incursion of the same urban strangers who had been stigmatized by L.A.'s business leaders and earnest Progressives nearly a century earlier.

As if civil unrest and racialized conflict were not enough, the deindustrialization of Los Angeles began to unfold with equally devastating force. The global economy was growing flat, and factory operations began moving south to Mexico or east to Asia. Imported cars deluged the US market in the 1970s,

1965. A member of the national guard helps a woman on Wilmington Avenue and 103rd Street following the Watts Riot. Photo by Bruce H. Cox; used with permission of the *Los Angeles Times*

built in far-off nations by less expensive workers. When General Motors closed the graveyard shift at its South Gate plant, union leader Sal Astorga told his members: "Don't worry, it will open up again when sales improve."[102] He was dead wrong. The factory closed for good in 1979, followed by the exit of Ford from its Pico Rivera plant the next year.

As factory jobs disappeared, middle-class aspirations evaporated as well. "Working at GM gave me a chance to own a home," one worker told scholar Eric Mann. A once-reliable job provided "enough to support my family, enough to send my kids to the state university, enough to allow me to be a good father."[103] But these opportunities imploded just as the political Left was struggling to integrate schools and narrow economic disparities among L.A.'s diverse families. All told, the L.A. and Long Beach metro area lost more than two-fifths of its manufacturing jobs between 1990 and 2005, a loss of 335,700 jobs paying union wages.[104] Those left behind included Black workers who had migrated to Southern California over the past two generations, now without a job, living amid eerily vacant factories, gritty stretches dotted with soiled strip malls and fast-food restaurants.

Another trembler shook more gently in 1965, at first causing little political upset and no broken glass. It drew scant public attention at the time. President Lyndon B. Johnson, standing before the Statue of Liberty in New York, offered poetic yet understated comments before signing legislation to liberalize immigration rules. Earlier immigration rules violated "the basic principle of American democracy," Johnson said, "the principle that values and rewards each man on the basis of his merit . . . untrue to the faith that brought thousands to these shores even before we were a country."[105] Nearly seven in every ten newcomers in the 1950s had come from Europe. But US allies in Latin America, along with newly liberated nations in Asia and Africa, sought open borders, wider opportunity in America. Heartfelt sentiments of civil rights had seeped into foreign affairs. Perhaps seeking to avert the blowback that was to come, Johnson added: "This bill that we will sign today is not a revolutionary bill. It will not reshape the structure of our daily lives."

The legislation, of course, would radically alter the complexion and daily lives of most Angelenos, and spark a demographic revolution across the land. In 1965, just 12 percent of Los Angeles County residents were of Latino heritage. This share climbed to 49 percent by 2016.[106] Resulting implications proved huge for the children served by the public schools—more than four-fifths of Latino origin in 2020. This brown revolution, combined with a deindustrializing economy, would upend which civic leaders could authentically speak for the chromatic mosaic of families that now inhabited contemporary Los Angeles. The Watts riot fostered a fresh generation of Black activists, many soon elected or selected into high positions of government. They would ally with Chicano activists to advance stronger financing of central city schools, better teachers, and civic respect for the languages and social mores expressed by L.A.'s novel kaleidoscope of families. The old political center could no longer hold; the seeds of cultural and political pluralism were taking root.

Next, let's meet the new pluralists, these next-generation Black and Latino leaders who arrived on the civic stage in Los Angeles nearly two generations ago. Ideological and literal offspring of the 1960s vanguard, these political youngsters gained from newfound access to college, along with lessons learned from failed desegregation efforts and the unrelenting backlash by white suburbanites. As

1965. Smoke rises from burning buildings during the Watts riot on Central Avenue, south of 43rd Street. Photo by Ray Graham and reprinted with permission of the *Los Angeles Times*

Ronald Reagan's conservative era gave way to President Bill Clinton's election in 1992, this spectrum of young activists would ally with civil rights attorneys, anti-poverty groups, and a growing circle of school reformers. Well-heeled foundations and wealthy Democrats signaled they were ready to join the cause of remaking public schools.

Chapter 2 details *who* makes up this diverse array of civic pluralists, *what* ideals and interests motivate their novel politics, and *how* they devise inventive policies to jostle and enlivened moribund institutions, especially public schools.

This coalescing network of activists rekindled progress on perennial issues, such as economic justice and financing schools fairly inside poor communities. More deeply, they took aim at the century-old foundations on which modern Los Angeles had been built. The new pluralists rejected the monochrome cultural norms and racialized morality enforced by white Protestants. These new activists sought to enrich and empower families inside Black and brown neighborhoods, not encourage flight to suburban hinterlands. Public works were meant to foster stronger ties and institutions in their communities, not to fuel sprawl and private gain. Nor did the new pluralists trust a centralized regime that protected bland and ineffective schools, reproducing rather than disrupting the inheritance of poverty from one generation to the next. The *ancien régime*—preserved by corporate leaders, union chiefs, and cautious Progressives—had dodged serious dialogue over inequality and recalcitrant public institutions. This old normal and the spent politics of Los Angeles had become intolerable for these rising young activists.

Many of these Black and Latino activists—emerging on the cultural Left—saw little meaning in any civic or spiritual mainstream, instead pursuing a politics of recognition and ethnic identity, "a dignity inseparable from [one's] right to distinct attachments," as sociologist Todd Gitlin once wrote.[107] This sprawling metropolis was moving from mostly white to predominately brown. Industrial forms of organization survived greatly diminished, further exposing the archaic features of L.A.'s old economic regime. By the final decade of the twentieth century, even corporate leaders had formulated "different touchpoints," as Nicholas Lemann wrote. "Innovation, mass empowerment, cultural tolerance, and the overturning of existing arrangements." These shifts conspired to subvert fading tenets, like "Christianity, order, obedience . . . ," Lemann argues.[108] Even elites in Los Angeles were shifting their gaze from the American East or Midwest to across the Pacific and Far East—the agents that now animated fresh trade, cuisine, high-tech workers, and cultural variety.

The polarized incumbents of the old regime—whether aging corporatists or staid labor leaders and graying Progressives—could no longer accommodate the intensity of social pluralism, identity politics, and the sharp-edged pursuit of social justice taking shape in Los Angeles. The new pluralists steadily united with reform-minded educators and eager donors who cared about, and expected more from, the city's diverse array of students. Most fundamentally, the new pluralists endeavored to craft a democratic politics on a more expansive and inclusive civic stage. Their shared vision was to decenter who controlled schools across the city's breathlessly diverse neighborhoods, then create alternative forms of education that nurtured caring and effective relationships inside. Let's meet these inventive activists, learn of their policy ideas, and discover how they organized to shake a deeply entrenched institution—urban public schools.

Palace Revolt

The graying dawn was doused in that "calligraphy of lights on the night freeways of Los Angeles," as poet Gary Snyder once put it. Endless rows of headlights, seen by arriving organizers from the asphalt knoll above, streamed along like disciplined fireflies trailing along the 110 downtown. Then, a startling sight came into focus, lit by the rising sun. A sea of empty desks, nearly four hundred cold Formica tables fused to small plastic chairs, stretched out in tidy columns, filling the street outside the towering education bureaucracy. A crisp spring morning in 2014.

Muscular members of the Los Angeles Rugby Association neatly adjusted each desk in silent solidarity with local activists. Photojournalists began arriving, snapping shots in the early morning light. Police officers closed off the busy street, now filled by this huge outdoor classroom. "We had found out how many students drop out each week," Ryan Smith, the United Way education chief who devised the riveting photo op, said. "I told my staff we needed to find hundreds of desks to represent the push-out of kids. They looked at me like I was crazy."

The eye-catching display was timed for a day of protest, as the L.A. school board inside began debating how to distribute an $820 million infusion of new dollars from the state capital. Hundreds of parents and teens poured in, adorned in brightly colored T-shirts that read "Schools We Deserve" and "Equal Funding Is Social Justice!" Bryant Villegas, a senior from Maya Angelou High School, took the microphone, shouting to the lively gathering: "Who better than students, who go through the education system every day, to address these issues?"[1]

The boisterous crowd—delivered by United Way and four dozen allied nonprofits—demanded passage of an "Equity Is Justice" resolution, which if passed would send these new dollars to schools in poor parts, hoping to narrow racial gaps in achievement. Maria Brenes, the head of Inner City Struggle in Latino East L.A., held up maps pinpointing school locations where these energized groups hoped to target funding. This political coalition—calling themselves the Communities for Los Angeles School Success (CLASS)—urged the board to hire additional tutors to lift Spanish-speaking pupils, along with more college preparatory courses and counselors to boost graduation rates.

Board members voiced support for these priorities later that day, voting to focus resources on the remedies put forward by Smith and Brenes, even aligning larger chunks of the district's $6 billion budget with an "equity formula." Schools chief John Deasy threw his weight behind the civic insurgents, gaining political ballast against a teachers' union that preferred to evenly distribute new monies across all schools, and thus union members, whether campuses were located in rich or poor neighborhoods. Video of "this graveyard of desks" appeared on the nightly news across Southern California, then went viral on social media. "What made the last few months historic and unique is that the community has risen to the occasion and really weighed in," Brenes told me at the time. "Our concerns have been considered."[2] Largely working *within* the system was yielding pro-equity gains for this array of nonprofits and school reformers, now powered by a wider democratic politics.

This chapter introduces this fresh generation of activists, rising up in the 1990s, who devised inventive policies aimed at shaking the massive institution of public schooling in consequential ways. These *new pluralists* formed a fluid network of civic players, staking out a third political terrain—corners of the civic stage rarely visited by staid business leaders or union officials.[3] This wave of small "d" democrats includes civil rights lawyers, social justice nonprofits, ethnic leaders, reform-minded teachers and city officials, advocates for charter schools, philanthropists, and dot-com donors. One wing descends from the Black and Chicano pioneers that led desegregation and anti-poverty efforts in Los Angeles, winning initial respect and political savvy in the wake of 1965. But now, these younger activists, like Brenes and Smith, advanced a variety of novel fronts, nurturing schools that mirrored the city's diverse cultural groups and languages, creating alternative forms of schooling run by principals and site councils (not from downtown) and fostering social relations inside that motivate all children.

This chapter begins by describing the moderate wing of the pluralist movement in L.A., those I dub *loyal insiders*. These ethnic leaders and local nonprof-

2014. Three hundred and seventy-five school desks placed by United Way organizer Ryan Smith and the Los Angeles Rugby Club, blocking the street in front of the L.A. Unified School District headquarters. Photo by Al Seib and reprinted with permission of the *Los Angeles Times*

its retained faith in the Los Angeles Unified School District (L.A. Unified), the nation's second largest education authority, one that corrals and cajoles nearly one thousand separate campuses and employs more than 33,000 teachers. This chapter details the roots of these upstart activists, who they are, why they surfaced in the 1990s, and how they accumulated political strength. Chapter 3 turns to the radical wing of the new pluralists—the *civic challengers*—those activists and well-heeled donors who lost faith in the dominant institution. These agitators went rogue, coming to believe that only a competitive challenge from insurgent charter schools could dislodge the old politics of education. Other civic challengers preferred to mobilize parents and students, building a participatory politics while never hesitating to hammer L.A. Unified from the outside.

Few could have predicted how the confluence of racial uprisings, demographic transformation, and industrial collapse in Los Angeles would stir this realignment of school politics. The emergence of new pluralism has not been unique to L.A. Many Black and Latino leaders had grown impatient with the pace of educational change across the United States by the late twentieth century. Their likely allies in the labor movement resisted efforts in Chicago and New York to decentralize who runs neighborhood schools, preferring centralized control and labor rules that work to preserve the status quo. Union officials resisted efforts to progressively fund schools enveloped by poor neighborhoods. And labor chieftains were protecting mediocre teachers, even when concentrated in predominantly Black or brown schools. By 2001, Senator Edward Kennedy and President George W. Bush had coauthored No Child Left Behind, a centralized federal effort to hold educators' feet to the fire and narrow disparities—legislation drafted by civil rights groups and initially opposed by teachers' unions.

Back in Los Angeles, Antonio Villaraigosa was elected mayor in 2006, the first mayor of Mexican heritage since the Yankee conquest a century and a half before. He surprised his old allies by breaking from labor, flipping his allegiance to the same social justice nonprofits and pro-charter advocates demonstrating outside the L.A. Unified skyscraper. Villaraigosa appealed to disenchanted parents who hungered for better schools, families populating the kinds of blue-collar neighborhoods in which he had been raised by a single mother. This fertile period attracted "an increasingly broad set of actors . . . engaging in decisions around public schooling and changing the nature of educational governance," writer Julie Marsh of the University of Southern California.[4]

Los Angeles would become a microcosm of political shifts at the national level. "Democratic Mayors Challenge Teachers Unions in Urban Political Shift," read the *Washington Post* headline, as mayors in Chicago, DC, and New York fought for similar reforms, to "replace the uniform pay scale with merit pay . . . expand public charter schools . . . lengthen school days."[5] By 2009, another inventive Democrat, Barack Obama, would borrow elements of Villaraigosa's reform agenda. Let's turn to the individuals and groups that make up these loyal insiders in L.A., how they accumulated political credibility and clout. I will then describe their core policies strategies and review what is known empirically about the effects of their reforms. The timeline on page 57 shows the past half century of school politics and reform in Los Angeles, a guide to the narrative that follows.

Los Angeles Turned Upside Down

Pluralist politics sprouted through the concrete rather slowly, fed by the shifting metropolitan conditions that followed 1965, along with the hindered capacity of education officials to comprehend and respond to the magnitude of change being demanded. The bracing cascade of events citywide—repeated civil unrest, white flight from the central city, the collapse of manufacturing, the inflow of families from Mexico and Central America—all conspired to radically transform Southern California. Nor could the old political dialectic—that rather polite tit-for-tat between business elites and proper Progressives—contain the rising force of ethnic identity, rejecting the white Protestant cultural frame, along with a frank attack on racial isolation and gross economic disparities.

Watts had been the worst urban riot in Los Angeles history, until the LAPD officers who struck Rodney King fifty-two times—lying facedown on the street

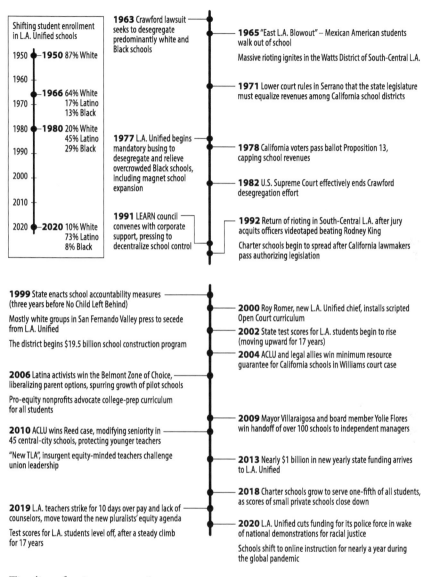

1963 Crawford lawsuit seeks to desegregate predominantly white and Black schools

Shifting student enrollment in L.A. Unified schools

1950 — **1950** 87% White

1960

1966 64% White
1970   17% Latino
   13% Black

1980 — **1980** 20% White
   45% Latino
1990   29% Black

2000

2010

2020 — **2020** 10% White
   73% Latino
   8% Black

1977 L.A. Unified begins mandatory busing to desegregate and relieve overcrowded Black schools, including magnet school expansion

1991 LEARN council convenes with corporate support, pressing to decentralize school control

1965 "East L.A. Blowout" – Mexican American students walk out of school

Massive rioting ignites in the Watts District of South-Central L.A.

1971 Lower court rules in Serrano that the state legislature must equalize revenues among California school districts

1978 California voters pass ballot Proposition 13, capping school revenues

1982 U.S. Supreme Court effectively ends Crawford desegregation effort

1992 Return of rioting in South-Central L.A. after jury acquits officers videotaped beating Rodney King

Charter schools begin to spread after California lawmakers pass authorizing legislation

1999 State enacts school accountability measures (three years before No Child Left Behind)

Mostly white groups in San Fernando Valley press to secede from L.A. Unified

The district begins $19.5 billion school construction program

2006 Latina activists win the Belmont Zone of Choice, liberalizing parent options, spurring growth of pilot schools

Pro-equity nonprofits advocate college-prep curriculum for all students

2010 ACLU wins Reed case, modifying seniority in 45 central-city schools, protecting younger teachers

"New TLA", insurgent equity-minded teachers challenge union leadership

2019 L.A. teachers strike for 10 days over pay and lack of counselors, move toward the new pluralists' equity agenda

Test scores for L.A. students level off, after a steady climb for 17 years

2000 Roy Romer, new L.A. Unified chief, installs scripted Open Court curriculum

2002 State test scores for L.A. students begin to rise (moving upward for 17 years)

2004 ACLU and legal allies win minimum resource guarantee for California schools in Williams court case

2009 Mayor Villaraigosa and board member Yolie Flores win handoff of over 100 schools to independent managers

2013 Nearly $1 billion in new yearly state funding arrives to L.A. Unified

2018 Charter schools grow to serve one-fifth of all students, as scores of small private schools close down

2020 L.A. Unified cuts funding for its police force in wake of national demonstrations for racial justice

Schools shift to online instruction for nearly a year during the global pandemic

Timeline of major events, 1963–2020

with video rolling in 1992—were deemed innocent by a jury, sparking a second firestorm. Police chief Daryl Gates took little action in the opening hours of the Rodney King riot, according to credible reports, letting South Central burn once again.[6] The return of urban chaos would redouble the pace of white flight from L.A. Unified, along with a rising Latino middle class that aspired to find safer neighborhoods and better schools. One article in the *Los Angeles Times* talked of white Angelenos "who fear violence growing out of integration." Another headline read, "Threats of Race Riot Likely to Continue." On the other side, Roy Wilkins of the NAACP told a reporter that he supported "tearing up the school district . . . the only thing some people understand is public disturbances."[7]

A variety of new civic players arose from this terror and ugliness. The revitalization of downtown L.A.—fueled by construction of the massive Staples Center, a walkable expanse that hosts restaurants, hotels, convention-goers, and the Lakers basketball team—stemmed from positive campaigns led by labor, along with young Black and Latino organizers, as sociologist Manuel Pastor Jr. has detailed.[8] They advocated for affordable housing and green spaces for downtown residents. A group calling itself the Mothers of East Los Angeles blocked construction of a proposed state prison, then a trash incinerator, both slated for Latino parts of East L.A. These early successes signaled the rise of assertive nonprofits by the 1980s, rooted in neighborhoods of color, led by a new generation of careful and deliberate activists. But could these various organizers gain traction in altering a massive and thick-skinned institution like the public schools?

The most visible revolution sweeping across Los Angeles was demographic in nature. The metro area, along with L.A. Unified, was shifting from white to brown in the blink of an eye. More than 18 million immigrants entered the United States legally after President Lyndon B. Johnson's immigration reform. Mexico was the leading sender, accounting for 4.3 million legal immigrants, and Los Angeles a leading destination.[9] L.A. County hosted just over 6 million residents in 1960, some 9 percent of Latino origin; over four in five Angelenos were of Yankee-Caucasian stock. By 2016, the county was home to 10.1 million residents, of whom 49 percent were Latino, now just 26 percent white.[10] One-third were foreign-born arrivals.[11]

The city of Compton, not far from Watts and the birthplace of Black rap and hip-hop, became two-thirds Latino during the same half-century. Aging factory towns twenty minutes south of downtown, like Cudahy and Huntington Park, went from hosting white and Black autoworkers to becoming home to predominately Latino immigrants. Meanwhile, the macro economy was crumpling. In 1970, income per capita in the L.A.–Long Beach area ranked fourth highest in the nation, falling to twenty-fifth among metro areas by 2009.[12]

By the 1990s, schools in these Latino enclaves were packed to the gills. L.A. Unified operated two or three sessions of classes each day and during the summer. Thousands of students were bused from South L.A. north to the San Fernando Valley (an hour in traffic each way) to middle-class neighborhoods that enjoyed spacious campuses. Sociologist Jeannie Oakes cited the example of Cahuenga Elementary School in Koreatown west of downtown, where seven hundred Latino kindergartners rode buses for hours each day in 2002.[13]

The return of Latino demographic dominance by the 1980s, along with the emergence of well-educated activists, prompted novel advocacy for civic respect, bilingualism, and economic fairness. The Chicano movement had surfaced two decades before, marked in 1968 when some 22,000 high school students walked out of classrooms, protesting unequal school funding and police brutality. Cesar Chavez, a physically slight yet lion of an advocate, had founded the National Farm Workers Association in 1962. Equally youthful peers across Southern California were taking on segregated schools. "Before the walkouts, no one cared

1968. Chicano activist Freddie Resendez rallies students at Lincoln High School to protest underfunding of central-city schools and racial injustice. Photo by *Los Angeles Times* staff and reprinted with permission of the *Times*

that substandard schools made it all but impossible for *Chicano* youths to find strength and pride in their culture, language and history," David Sanchez, founder of the Brown Berets, recalled a half century later.[14] Latino activists by the 1990s held little illusion that a melting-pot model of society would respect their heritage and language, or bring an equal share of resources to their schools.

The steady exit of middle-class whites from L.A. Unified further spurred the new politics of education. In the wake of Watts, the city lost one-fifth of its white residents, while the count of Latino residents grew by three-fifths. L.A. Unified reported in 1966 that just over 396,000 white children enrolled in district schools, nearly two-thirds of all pupils. By 1980, the count of white students had fallen to about 127,000, one-quarter of total enrollment. The share of pupils of Latino heritage district-wide jumped from 17 to 45 percent in less than 15 years, from 1966 to 1980.[15]

Berkeley economist David Card, tracking rising shares of nonwhite pupils, found a tipping point at about 20 percent. That is, once a school's enrollment became more than one-fifth Black or Latino in L.A., white enrollments fell.[16] The rapid spread of charter schools then arrived in the 1990s. These publicly funded yet independently run campuses attracted white and Asian-heritage students at first, then soon drew many Black and Latino families looking for safer, human-scale schools. Declining fertility rates and middle-class Latino flight have conspired to further undercut pupil enrollment in conventional schools. The figure below displays enrollments for L.A. Unified over the past

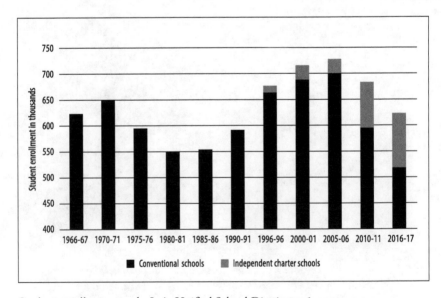

Student enrollment trends, L.A. Unified School District, 1967–2017

half century, tracing its peaks and valleys in demand for traditional and charter schools.

Meanwhile, school enrollments swelled outside L.A. Unified, nearly doubling in Ventura County (just northwest of Los Angeles) in the 1970s. Even when remaining in Los Angeles County, many parents pulled up roots and moved to one of seventy-nine other districts located near to L.A. Unified, ironically helping to integrate nearby cities.[17] Other young families moved east to Riverside or San Bernardino, drawn by job growth and cheap housing, growing by two-thirds in the 1980s. This migration, fed by affordable mortgages, fueled a construction boom. Tens of thousands of "starter homes" went up, many built by KB Homes, the "B" signifying Eli Broad, the late billionaire proponent of charter schools. A quarter century later, deep in economic recession, the so-called Inland Empire ranked fourth nationwide in home foreclosures.

As class aspirations and educational attainment climbed in the late twentieth century—now shared among white, Latino, and Black families—those who could, departed from L.A. Unified. When my team isolated higher-achieving students—the top one-fifth on state tests—we found the share of students with a parent who had completed some college fell from 62 percent in 2002 to 48 percent in 2012.[18] This was not attributable to a more equal distribution of high achievers; it stemmed from the exit of better-educated white and Latino families. Since 1990, the count of Black Angelenos has dropped by one-fourth to about 364,000 at the time of this writing.[19]

The Los Angeles economy began showing signs of life by the late 1990s, a force that helped energize the rise of pluralist politics. Up north in Silicon Valley, the digital revolution was generating enormous wealth. California would soon become the fifth largest economy on earth. This began to swell the state treasury, as dot-com investors recorded skyrocketing capital gains. Equally notable, Southern California voters were shifting to the political center, as rising counts of Latino and well-educated whites voted Democratic. This helped L.A. Unified and state lawmakers win voter approval of five revenue bonds, yielding a $19.5 billion surge in new funding to build and renovate schools. As the economic weather began to clear, the surge in public investment, along with rising spending from philanthropists, provided rich grist for the work of L.A. nonprofits, ethnic organizing, and reform-minded educators.

Harvard sociologist Robert Sampson began tracking L.A.'s economic rebound, drawing on data first collected in 1990 from representative households. He found that just over two-fifths of all adults had failed to attain more than a high school diploma; less than a third had completed a four-year degree program.[20] The county's pyramid of income correlated tightly with racial membership: three-fourths of households earning between $150,000 and $200,000 were of white, Jewish, or Asian heritage, one-tenth were Latino.[21] But the economic status of working- and middle-class families also began to rise with California's economy in the late 1990s. Less than one-fourth of all Latinas had completed any college courses in 1990. Two decades later, nearly one-half of the adults in the same neighborhoods had made headway through a two- or four-year degree program, led by young Latina women.[22] The hollowed-out portion of L.A.'s middle class was filling back in.

Educational attainment climbed across immigrant generations as well, as sociologist Frank Bean has detailed. One-point-five-generation females of Mexican descent—foreign born but raised in Los Angeles—achieved 12.2 years of schooling early in the twenty-first century. More acculturated third-generation peers attained 14.2 years of schooling, including two years of college on average. Yet, these gains held bittersweet consequences for L.A. Unified, as fertility rates began a long and steady decline, markedly so among young Latinas. The number of babies born in Los Angeles County fell from just over 200,000 in 1990 to roughly 130,000 in 2010, driving down school enrollments. Educators had become a victim of their own success.[23]

The Plot Thickens: Student Learning Climbs

Then, inexplicably, children's achievement began to rise across Los Angeles in the opening years of the twenty-first century. These welcomed gains first appeared in elementary schools. Multiple barometers soon revealed collateral gains in learning and student engagement inside high schools. These upward trends in achievement—the first bump observed in 2002—would persist for the subsequent generation, finally leveling off in 2019. Let's first consider several indicators of progress, then return to how policies advanced by the *loyal insiders*—the moderates among the new pluralists—likely contributed to this buoyancy in student success.

One story line credits achievement gains to the onset of school accountability—tough-love provisions for teachers enacted by California policy makers in 1999. This included clarifying learning objectives (what students were to learn at each grade level), then assessing their acquisition of easily tested bits of knowledge. California began to rank each school in their ability to raise exam scores, what became known as *standards-based accountability*. Rather mechanical in operation, the testing and standards movement had shown results by the early 1990s in Massachusetts, North Carolina, and Texas—at least in raising children's basic literacy and math skills. President George W. Bush, spurred on by civil rights groups, spread the model nationwide in 2002 through his No Child Left Behind legislation.

This seemingly elegant way of tightening up the work of teachers inside schools drew support in Los Angeles from many loyal insiders, especially social justice advocates who aimed to shine a brighter light on learning disparities among racial groups. Gross inequalities in the results of public schooling had for many years been swept under the rug. One accountability enthusiast, Roy

Romer, became superintendent of L.A. Unified in 2000, after serving as Colorado's governor, then chair of the Democratic Party. Romer was a contemporary of Bill Clinton, fellow architect of the centrist agenda pitched by so-called New Democrats, which included holding educators' feet to the fire.

Romer began by regulating the work of elementary school teachers— specifying learning aims, then matching textbooks and weekly lesson plans to proscribed competencies that all children were to learn. It resembled nineteenth-century common schooling while adding centralized monitoring and a precise testing regime. Romer purchased the lockstep Open Court curriculum from publishing giant Harcourt Brace. Teachers were to post each week's required proficiencies on classroom walls, to follow the daily script with unwavering fidelity. Romer hired monitors to verify that teachers were following the script, inquisitors known as the "Open Court police." Romer was armed with "well-traveled displays depicting six years of rising bar graphs and upward squiggly lines," as journalist Howard Blume put it.[24] Echoing many civic activists on the political Left, Romer said he was tired of moving budgets around, arguing over decentralized governance without tackling the life and pedagogy found in classrooms.

Many loyal insiders felt elated the morning of October 10, 2001, when they woke up to a euphoric headline in the *Los Angeles Times*: "First-Graders' Scores Surge on Reading Test." Less than two years after installing Open Court in four-fifths of all kindergarten and first grade classrooms, pupil scores were on the rise. The average first grader was now reading at the fifty-sixth percentile, unheard of since the white exodus and accumulating arrival of Latino immigrants to L.A. schools. "The proof is in the pudding," Romer celebrated, "and this is the first taste of the pudding."[25]

But Open Court added insult to injury for many teachers, who were already suffering from flat salary levels due to Proposition 13 and struggling to serve a rising count of Spanish-speaking students, who were increasingly being crammed into overcrowded schools. Now, Romer was insisting on conforming to a regimented script, instructing children in didactic fashion. "The system is very totalitarian," one second grade teacher told a reporter in 2000.[26] "Children in Russia learned to read, but at the expense of creativity, at the expense of questioning." Open Court required teachers to administer diagnostic tests every six to eight weeks, then adjust content to fill revealed gaps. At the same time, some rookie teachers praised the set structure. "As a first-year teacher it's very practical to have a program where everything is laid out for you," said Erika Cornejo, a first-grade teacher.

Labor leaders squawked loudly: top-down accountability, as animated by Romer's team, was deskilling classroom teachers, union chiefs argued. Civil rights groups and those demanding better teaching in central city schools were mixed over the Open Court initiative. Reform-minded nonprofits that preferred more complex forms of teaching and deeper learning sided with the union, including the Small Schools Support Network and the humanities-focused L.A. Education Partnership. They opposed shrinking pedagogical practices down to easily tested facts, claiming this would drive curiosity and joy from the classroom (reminiscent of the Progressive split a century earlier over the humanist nurturing of curious children versus skilling them in utilitarian fashion). Skeptics claimed that instructors were simply teaching to test.

Yet, then student gains appeared in the rigorous National Assessment of Educational Progress (NAEP) conducted in L.A. Unified by the federal education department. This barometer is more widely generalizable and impossible to directly manipulate by mimicking test questions in one's classroom teaching. A few pictures illustrate this uplifting, though ultimately bittersweet, story. The next figure plots mean NAEP reading scores among fourth- and eighth-grade students from 2002 to 2019. The performance of fourth graders proved most impressive, rising about fourteen scale-score points over the seventeen-year period. This equals a gain of more than one grade level (pegged to national norms) in reading proficiency. Eighth graders displayed remarkable progress as well, finally dipping a bit in the 2019 assessment of L.A. Unified students.[17] Parallel scores on state tests—in synchrony with California's curricular aims—began to rise one year earlier and continued their upward trajectory as well.

Good news for sure. But at the same time, a troubling subplot emerged over this two-decade-long story. Most ethnic and social class groups displayed marked progress, including white and Asian-heritage students. But gaps in learning

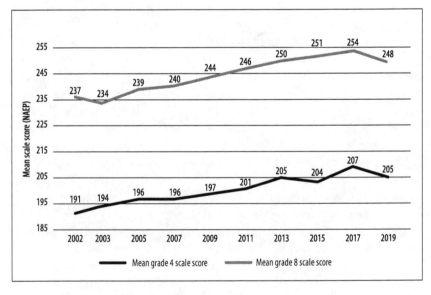

Mean reading scores for Los Angeles students, 2002–2019

among racial groups barely budged. In addition, absolute pupil performance remained low in Los Angeles, compared with the learning curves of pupils nationwide, even those attending schools in other urban districts. The performance of Black students drifted lower in L.A., relative to the gains enjoyed by white, Asian-heritage, and Latino youngsters.

Measurement gurus translate test scores into four levels of pupil learning: below basic, basic, proficient, or advanced. The figure below illustrates how the share of students proficient or advanced in reading skills has more than doubled since 2002. But only one-fifth of all fourth graders in L.A. were proficient or advanced in reading by 2019. This share falls five percentage points below students in Boston and New York City, and far below San Diego, where nearly two-fifths of fourth graders perform proficiently.

The biggest worry from an equity standpoint—plus how we weigh the efficacy of policy remedies mounted by the loyal insiders—is that achievement gaps narrowed ever so slightly for Latino and white children, and not at all for Black youngsters. Learning curves climbed sharply for white students. White fourth graders gained nearly a grade level between 2003 and 2019 (figure on page 66). That's good news for their parents and strategists inside L.A. Unified who read the city's political economy, eager to retain middle-class families, but it's bedeviling for pro-equity activists who hope to equalize the benefits of public schools among racial groups. Latino fourth graders displayed the most robust jump in reading. Their mean scale scores rose twelve points over the sixteen-year period.

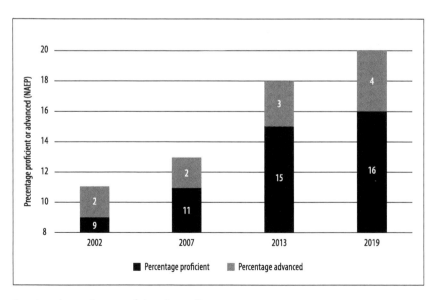

Los Angeles students proficient in reading, 2002–2019

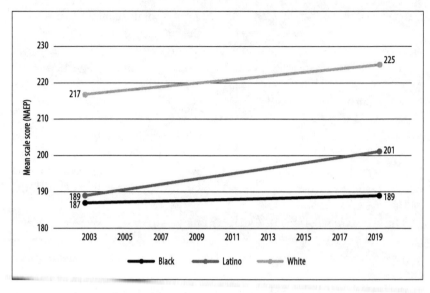

Gains in reading proficiency by race and ethnicity, 2002–2019

Average scores for Blacks remained flat. Mean disparities actually grew larger between Black and white pupils: equaling thirty points in 2003 (nearly three grade levels) and widening to thirty-six points by 2019. The question remains: How to spark civic politics and institutional reforms that work to narrow disparities, rather than simply lifting more advantaged students?

Upbeat signs did appear across L.A. Unified's high schools as well. This included a bevy of smaller campuses built under Romer's ambitious construction program: magnet schools and decentralized pilot schools, the latter hosting social justice curricular themes, along with proliferating counts of dual-language programs, mirroring the city's cultural pluralism. In turn, the share of secondary school pupils graduating in four years climbed from 62 percent in 2010 to just over 80 percent in 2017.

Modest gains in the share of students taking Advanced Placement (AP) courses—rigorous classes with externally assessed results—signaled progress as well. Enrollments in AP courses moved upward, from 24 to 29 percent of all tenth-to-twelfth-grade students, 2013 to 2015, for those attending conventional L.A. high schools. These AP rates for charter schools equaled 29 to 35 percent, respectively, over the period. Students acquire college credits in high school when scoring 3 or higher on AP exams run by the College Board. The share of pupils scoring at this level (as a percentage of AP test takers) remained static over the period at about 33 percent for youths attending conventional high schools and 42 percent among charter school pupils.[28]

These results seemed to back claims by the loyal insiders that pushing for organizational change *within* the educational institution could yield palpable gains for students. So, let's back up to ask which new activists advanced what policy reforms, animated by differing ideological positions and strategies for institutional change. How did these loyal insiders gain political traction and shake this recalcitrant institution, all the while laboring under the L.A. Unified umbrella? And how might empirical evidence point to specific policy devices that elevated student learning over time?

Loyal Insiders Reframe the Debate

Nancy Meza remembers back in 2006, when just one-third of her classmates ever graduated from Roosevelt High. A sophomore at the time, Meza wanted to somehow right this obvious wrong. She joined a youth organizing effort led by Inner City Struggle (ICS), the Latino nonprofit based in East Los Angeles, headed by Maria Brenes (the young Harvard graduate who helped lead the "Equity is Justice" protest). A decade earlier, Meza and hundreds of fellow students were demonstrating outside L.A. Unified's board chambers chanting, "Give us life prep, not a life sentence."

They succeeded at convincing skeptical board members in 2005 to expand the count of college-preparatory courses, the so-called A-G listing recognized by the University of California for admission. This signaled more rigorous course content, intending to shift teachers' own mindset about the potential of all students, as earlier detailed by UCLA's John Rogers and Ernest Morrell.[29] The A-G victory marked the widening influence of the new pluralists, the end of a politics that had long been "dominated by professionals and civic elites," Rogers and Morrell argued. Influential civic players were no longer limited to corporate do-gooders or labor-allied progressives. Now, a fresh set of civic players were assembling data, identifying school-level fixes, then mobilizing parents and students to advance their persuasive case. "It is great to see parents and students work together to demand these courses," school board president Jose Huizar told a reporter at the time.

Leaders at ICS had come together with the multiracial Community Coalition (Coco) and nearly twenty other nonprofits two summers earlier to plan a strategy that would elevate expectations and courses for disadvantaged teens. ICS leaders aimed to change "the power relations between the people and the schools . . . by building civil society in East L.A.," Brenes told Rogers. Acting in concert, these small-scale community groups—who neither contributed to political campaigns nor held union-bargaining power with the district—could turn out hundreds of heartfelt protestors at board meetings or march in the streets. These loyal insiders often had to overcome the tepid reaction of labor leaders to pro-equity reforms. "A coalition gives you power," said Alberto

Retana at the Community Coalition. "And it is more democratic . . . you have a greater impact if you can show you have a citywide alliance that crosses geography and race."[30]

Their eventual victory in spreading college-prep courses across high schools in the poorest parts of Los Angeles did not come overnight. It took a decade to appreciably raise the percentage of courses that met rigorous standards. Implementation remains a work in progress. First, a central office was created downtown at L.A. Unified to lead the effort. But a culture change was required inside many urban campuses. Teachers needed to shift their expectations and respect for students, along with the content and pace of their teaching in math, biology, English literature, and so on. The old racialized assumptions about the potential of differing students had to be set aside, replaced with caring and respectful relationships.

Then, as implementation took root, rising shares of students began completing A-G classes. Just 18 percent of all high school graduates in 2005 had completed these demanding courses with a grade of C or better, improving their odds of entering a four-year university. This share rose to 57 percent for the graduating class of 2017. Fully 79 percent of all charter school graduates completed A-G courses at the same performance level by 2015.[31] These trends likely contributed to slight gains in the share of graduates who entered college, the largest bump for those matriculating into two-year colleges.[32]

2016. Parents and students demonstrating in support of wider access for college-preparatory courses. Photo courtesy of Sara Mooney

The college-prep campaign showed how the new pluralists could win on issues that struck to the institution's core: the quality of pedagogy and underlying expectations held by teachers about student ability. For the loyal insiders, they had achieved proof positive. By pressing the education bureaucracy, while not alienating board members and district managers, these activists could foster political support and guide implementation on the inside. And this plural array of agitators was establishing credibility and organizing skills independent of corporate moderates and labor leaders, the aging blocs that often showed little interest in altering the everyday work of schools.

Looking back fifteen years later, Maria Brenes at ICS emphasized that "A-G was foundational to the work advanced after that time, like smaller and innovative learning environments, the dismantling of the school-to-prison pipeline." Yes, the discrete policy change proved consequential. But this widening array of civic activists was framing a novel civic "debate about the purpose of schools . . . the first time in decades that LAUSD was forced to confront racial disparities in student outcomes," Brenes told me. "We revealed with data that LAUSD didn't expect very much from Black and Latinx students." These young activists had joined with UCLA scholars, Rogers and Oakes, to vividly map how "if you attended a school on the Eastside or South L.A., you were far less likely to have access to courses that give you a pathway to college," Brenes recalled.

"At the community level it was shocking . . . how this had been allowed to go on for so long. It was really a debate about the moral high ground that we forced in public . . . the fact that for decades these had been centers for failure, perpetuating structural racism," Brenes said. "We envisioned schools to humanize students, to support them holistically . . . schools that acknowledge who they are and where they come from." And this required "a broad-based alliance to serve as a force to escalate public pressure for this change." ICS and allies transported more than a thousand students and families to attend board meetings at L.A. Unified. Their "unheard stories were brought to the forefront . . . of their dreams for the future and what barriers they faced in getting these college-prep courses." Once the board approved A-G courses for all, the next question became how to foster richer learning environs for teens and teachers alike. "It created the terrain for other reforms, such as small learning communities, pilot schools, [fostering] positive school climate," Brenes said.

A Civic Rainbow Rises

It is instructive to step back and sketch this widening landscape of activists and nonprofits that had surfaced by the 1990s. The economic reach of L.A. Unified is eye-opening, an institution that spends more than $7 billion each year and remains the second largest employer in Los Angeles County. Stakeholders include no less than twelve labor unions representing various slices of the district's labor force, from teachers and tens of thousands of support staff to classroom aides and warehouse workers.

You have already met leaders of key pro-equity groups, such as Brenes at ICS and Ryan Smith at United Way (who afterward moved to EdTrust West and then the Partnership for L.A. Schools). The American Civil Liberties Union (ACLU) has led efforts to progressively finance schools since the 1970s, along with the Advancement Project, created by a pair of wealthy attorneys, and the Community Coalition, based in South Los Angeles. Forty members of equity groups and teachers networks joined the CLASS coalition's efforts to direct new state dollars to the most challenged schools. Additional local and national groups with L.A. offices focus on teacher quality or inventive pedagogies, such as Teach for America, Educators for Excellence, and the Small Schools Support Network (later renamed Center for Powerful Public Schools).

This breathtaking number and variety of civic players—advocating for differing forms of institutional change in L.A. schools—must be recognized before generalizing about these new pluralists. They are best distinguished by their aims and organizational logics for reform, which typically depart from low-tax and efficiency-minded business leaders, or the preservationist instincts of labor leaders. This loyal-insider wing of the pluralist movement, by the 1990s, had gained traction on two intertwined issues. The first—a sustained campaign to *fairly distribute dollars* across schools and communities—was pursued by legal aid groups and social justice nonprofits. The second—*enriching classroom quality* and *fostering engaging relationships* inside schools—would then build from the college-prep victory, as Brenes describes, uniting with reform-minded teachers to create smaller, hopefully more effective, schools. This generation-long effort to build magnet, pilot, and dual-language campuses occasionally borrowed from the playbook of charter school proponents. Yet, the loyal insiders held limited faith that market competition alone would foster caring and efficacious schools.

The more radical wing of shock troops—the militant advocates for charter schools—stormed over the horizon in the 1990s as well. California's legislature became the nation's second to send public funding to separately run charter schools in 1992. The civic challengers then argued that L.A. Unified bureaucrats and recalcitrant union leaders would forever stonewall true institutional change. Only head-to-head market competition for students and families would force novel and effective ways of organizing schools. These outside challengers pulled into their ranks wealthy, mostly Democratic donors—who often echoed the priorities of loyal insiders: build diverse forms of schooling that proved effective and responsive to L.A.'s colorful array of families.

The California Charter Schools Association, early in the new century, was raising millions of dollars to support allied candidates for the L.A. Unified school board. These pro-charter advocates include Netflix founder Reed Hastings, Doris Fisher, cofounder of the Gap, and former builder Eli Broad (who passed away in 2021). Business leaders also take great interest in the district's construction and renovation program, financed through facilities bonds, approved by voters, and equaling nearly $20 billion since 1999. These concentrated sources of private dollars—including the coffers of major labor unions—grease the campaigns of widely varying candidates for the school board. This includes young politicos rising from new-pluralist ranks in the 1990s, such as Mónica García and Yolie Flores, who drove parental choice reforms examined below.

Funding Schools Fairly

Atop this crowded civic stage, loyal insiders have mounted a variety of reforms to equitably finance schools. Legal activists, like the ACLU and Public Advocates, have pushed to distribute new school spending to poor communities, going back to the desegregation era. Middle-class interests, business moderates, and labor leaders have shied away from progressive financing, instead backing additional state funding spread evenly across all schools and union members.

The landmark finance case in California remains *Serrano v. Priest*, initially filed in 1971, prompted by gross disparities in how residents were taxed to support highly unequal schools. *Serrano* revealed that Beverly Hills was spending $2,200 per pupil, based on a lower property tax rate than L.A. Unified, which could only afford to spend $1,206 for each student.[33] A string of court victories required the legislature to equalize per-pupil spending across the state's nearly one thousand districts. It was a huge win for the young coalition of finance activists, led by the ACLU and law professors at Berkeley, convincing the state court that local revenues for education should not be set by a neighborhood's wealth or poverty.

Yet, the progressive *Serrano* decision also contributed to the white backlash following the Watts riot and subsequent moves to desegregate L.A.'s schools. This pushback by suburban white voters resulted in passage of California's ballot Proposition 13, the anti-tax measure, in 1978. This sent L.A. Unified into a fiscal tailspin for nearly two decades. The district could not expand its budget to accommodate growing counts of students in heavily immigrant communities, under revenue caps imposed by Proposition 13, nor adequately serve pupils with disabilities.

Central city schools became severely overcrowded. South Gate Middle School, built for 800 students, housed 4,200 pupils in 2002, as kids attended one of three shifts and during summer months. Miles Elementary became one of the most densely packed schools in the nation, enrolling more than 4,000 children. Some 95 percent of families in the southeast cities, minutes from downtown, were of Latino heritage and most poorly educated. They kept arriving as factory jobs continued to move overseas. Doing fieldwork in Washington Middle School, scholars Jeannie Oakes and John Rogers reported that only two-fifths of teachers were credentialed. Science labs lacked running water. Pupils sat watching movies while an army of substitute teachers struggled to maintain order.[34] Teacher salaries sank lower and lower. Even in tony communities, like Laguna and Newport Beach, parents complained that revenue caps were forcing drastic cuts in their neighborhood schools.[35]

To relieve grossly overcrowded campuses, by 2005 L.A. Unified was busing more than 25,000 kids from East and South Los Angeles each morning, kids who rode north to spacious facilities in better-off communities. "The whole school cannot fit in the multi-purpose room," one teacher told my research team back then. "So, we have to have three lunch periods to fit all students at tables." Public health became a key worry. "Whatever germs we got seem to stay here," one principal said. "Whether they got into the AC, it's hard to say, but . . . the health of the population here has been much lower."[36] When federal test scores for L.A. students came out in 2002, the district displayed the lowest reading proficiency of any city nationwide, tied with pupil performance in Washington, DC.[37]

New Schools, Rising Achievement

Two policy strategies—championed by the loyal insiders—helped Los Angeles and its public schools emerge from this dark hole. First, L.A. Unified embarked on a massive program to renovate or construct entirely new schools, led by Supt. Roy Romer. This long-awaited return to public works stemmed from shifting politics statewide, a rebounding economy, and the widening legitimacy of the new pluralists. Silicon Valley benefactors campaigned for revenue bonds that financed school construction, moving beyond their focus on charter schools. Then, in 2013, Governor Jerry Brown achieved a dramatic redistribution of education funding, as California's economy lifted out of the Great Recession. Brown moved nearly $23 billion in yearly spending to urban districts, like L.A. Unified, which served large shares of disadvantaged students. These tandem finance wins stemmed in part from the maturing influence of the loyal insiders, whose state-level affiliates lobbied mightily for these cash infusions that benefited schools in Los Angeles. Meanwhile, many corporate elites and union leaders remained on the sidelines.[38]

The most resolute dot-com donor remains Hastings, the Netflix founder, who initially pushed the California legislature to authorize taxpayer support of charter schools. Hastings, a former Peace Corps teacher in Africa, would eventually lose faith in L.A. Unified, opting to hammer the district from the outside via market competition. But the stark overcrowding of urban schools moved Hastings, along with venture capitalist John Doerr, to help politically. Doerr, after joining Intel at age 23, would become one of the wealthiest hundred individuals in the United States. Doerr, Hastings, and L.A.'s Eli Broad financially backed the ballot proposition, approved by voters in 2000, that lowered the plurality required for local voters to pass revenue bonds. This soon brought $19.5 billion in fresh construction dollars to L.A. Unified, aiming to relieve overcrowding by building 130 new facilities in the subsequent two decades.

The high-tech moguls became potent allies of legal activist Steve English as well. English cofounded the Advancement Project in 1999, a forceful civil rights organization based in downtown L.A., along with his wife, Molly Munger. She is the daughter of Charles Munger, the billionaire vice-chairman of Berkshire Hathaway, which has owned Dexter Shoes and See's Candies, along with a major stake in GEICO insurance. Warren Buffet is the elder Munger's longtime financial partner. The well-resourced Advancement Project operates among and often leads coalitions of advocates to lift central city schools and families. English quietly leads the charge—technically and politically—on gaining civic support of school construction bonds.

These contemporary progressives enjoy independent wealth and influence. They are neither beholden to labor nor to the city's earlier champions of capitalist expansion. Nor do the likes of Munger and English seek a uniform and regimented "system" of schools, as did their Progressive forbearers a century

2018. Maria Brenes, executive director of Inner City Struggle, leads a rally for progressive funding in front of Los Angeles school board chambers.

earlier. Instead, they contribute to the new pluralists' push for a nimble and diverse array of urban schools. They are quite willing to work inside the conventional system, or challenge it politely (as does English in understated fashion) or with unabashed bravado (Hastings). They add cash and strategic thinking, mostly for the loyal insiders who prefer to organize politically under the institutional umbrella of L.A. Unified. Still, I would like to return to the question of whether the political girth and gravitas of these wealthy benefactors contributes to, or tacitly undermines, the democratic rules of engagements preferred by the new pluralists.

By 2002, as scores of new facilities—early-learning centers for young children, small high schools, equity-oriented pilot schools, and dual-language campuses—were being erected across Los Angeles, I began meeting with the district's chief of facilities, Guy Mehula. He was asking our team, led by Berkeley's Jeff Vincent and Mary Filardo, a Washington-based expert on school construction, a key question: Does moving thousands of students into new and spacious facilities work to lift their learning curves? Mehula asked us to get to the bottom of this empirical issue, tracking pupils over this first decade of the new century.

A decade into L.A. Unified's ambitious construction program, we did estimate robust gains in student achievement, especially for pupils raised in poor communities who migrated from overcrowded campuses to brand-new schools. Learning gains were most striking for elementary-age children who exited the most densely packed campuses. Gains in math and reading after two years in a new facility equaled about one-fifth of a standard deviation, or one month of additional instructional time, relative to children's prior growth curves. This bump in achievement was twice the magnitude resulting from large reductions in class size, while reaching gains associated with attending quality preschool for one year.[39] The benefit for students moving into new high schools, while significant, ranged lower: one-sixth of a standard deviation in reading and English language arts.

A more extensive analysis, completed in 2019 by Berkeley economists Julien Lafortune and David Schönholzer, tracked students for additional years after switching into pristine facilities. These scholars employed more robust techniques to estimate achievement effects. They essentially replicated, then extended, our earlier results.[40] (Their study also found that property values climbed in neighborhoods in which new schools were erected.) Still, why or through what social mechanisms these benefits occurred remains a mystery. We observed that many poor children moved to much smaller high schools, staffed with young and more often Latino teachers, compared with their earlier, overcrowded school. The seriousness and caring found in human-scale schools may have contributed to gains. "I don't feel like I'm in a ghetto school," one student told our colleague Greta Kirschenbaum. Her interviews showed how moving into clean and elegant campuses made many teens feel like the adults finally cared about their future.[41]

As this huge construction effort began to wind down, Governor Jerry Brown's finance reform delivered another $1.1 billion in yearly operational funding to L.A. Unified, under what became known as Local Control Funding. The measure boosted spending on public education by two-fifths across California, or $21 billion yearly, relative to earlier levels.[42] The new pluralists once again proved to be the mothers of civic invention, backing this pro-equity initiative in the state capital, then closely tracking its implementation in urban districts like L.A. Unified. Seasoned policy thinker Michael Kirst at Stanford, along with Berkeley law professor Goodwin Liu, had sketched a simple formula that would allow more dollars to be distributed to local districts serving large shares of poor children. This appealed to Brown, who was eager to offload central government responsibilities to local authorities, citing his favored decentralizing principle of *subsidiarity*.

Governor Brown intended to move civic debate over school funding down to local communities; budget priorities would no longer be hammered out in the state capital. "We are bringing government closer to the people, to the classroom where real decisions are made," Brown promised in signing the new funding bill.[43] The concept of subsidiarity derives from ancient debates over the Vatican's historical tendency to centralize in ways that dis-incented local initiative, according to earlier advocates of decentralizing governance.[44] Brown preferred that budgets be crafted at the lowest level of civic action: local school boards. So, he shifted fiscal authority back to the districts, unheard of—especially among liberal Democrats—since the centralization of the education sector after the Great Society. Yet, it all played into the new pluralists' hands back in L.A., bolstering their democratic theory of institutional change.

The 2013 state finance reform arrives late in our L.A. story, a decade after sagging achievement levels began to climb. But passage of Local Control Funding, along with its contested implementation in Los Angeles, confirmed the growing influence of the new pluralists. The redistributive feature of Brown's reform was enthusiastically supported by the ACLU, Citizens for Justice, and allied pro-equity groups. These influential nonprofits then worked hard to move new dollars to the most challenged schools.

School spending in L.A. Unified had grown since the desegregation era, from just over $4,600 per pupil (for operating costs) in 1975–76 to $10,800 per student forty years later in 2015–16 (inflation-adjusted 2016 dollars).[45] But the school board was not legally compelled to send new dollars to classrooms, nor were they required to report which schools benefited most under Governor Brown's reform.

Going back to the 1950s, the board had approved labor-friendly benefits for teachers, including ripe pension plans and lifetime health coverage. Fully 27 percent of the district's operating budget went to pension and health care costs in 2018—rising to more than *half* of the budget by 2031 unless the board adjusts employee packages before then.[46] Meanwhile, the district had been hemorrhaging students for some time due to middle-class flight and a declining fertility rate, with student counts falling from 676,000 to 501,000 since 1975.

Findings soon emerged showing how L.A. Unified officials were redirecting $450 million from legislated beneficiaries (mostly poor children), under Governor Brown's reform, to offset the rising cost of special education services. In addition, the district had sent equal dollars out to all elementary schools, whether they served high or low concentrations of disadvantaged pupils.[47] The ACLU and Citizens for Justice went into superior court and appealed to the state Department of Education. The Community Coalition of South Los Angeles and ICS advised, then joined, the ACLU litigation. The state education department soon issued two regulatory rulings, largely concurring with the advocates' complaint. ACLU attorneys Sylvia Torres-Guillén and Victor Leung would settle out of court in 2017. The school board, dodging any admission of culpability, agreed to another $151 million for fifty schools serving the largest shares of poor students or English learners.[48] The district then approved an equity formula, designed by Advancement Project staff, tying future spending to the most challenged schools, consonant with the ACLU settlement. This coalition convinced the board to tie another $700 million to this Student Equity Needs Index in 2021, as L.A. Unified began recovering from the pandemic.

Brenes at ICS was determined to move new state dollars to the most challenged Black and Latino parts of L.A. She still labored to implement the college-prep initiative, altering teacher expectations for children of color. Her nonprofit also helped win the Belmont Zone of Choice. "We need smaller, more personalized schools, and we need more autonomy for our schools, our teachers," Brenes told me in 2009, "being able to control the curriculum [at school sites], staffing in terms of teachers and budgets."[49]

By 2014, Brenes was directing a network of activists dubbed the Los Angeles Forum for Equity (LA-FE, or *the faith* in Spanish). That same fall, Smith at United Way expressed his organizing genius, lining the avenue in front of L.A. Unified with the 375 classroom desks.[50] In alliance with these networks, along with the ACLU's legal prowess, they would win the designation of hundreds of millions of dollars for middle and high schools in the poorest communities. The Student Equity Needs Index was crafted by leaders at Coco and the Advancement Project, driving the distribution of nearly $300 million out to schools in the most impoverished parts of Los Angeles.

New Pluralists Challenge Labor

The loyal insiders took up the nagging issue of teacher quality as well, beginning in the 1990s. They worried initially over high turnover among young teachers, often of Black or Latino heritage, working in central cities schools. Union chiefs had long defended "must-hire teachers," mediocre instructors purged by one principal, then reassigned to another school, campuses typically situated in poor neighborhoods. Resembling aging athletes who are constantly traded late in their careers, the policy was not curbed by the L.A. board until 2019, at the behest of pro-equity advocates. It was reminiscent of the "rubber room" in New York City, where unacceptable teachers still assemble each day, far from children, while collecting their paychecks. Back in Los Angeles, union contracts held seniority rights as sacred as well, allowing experienced teachers to flee poor schools for the suburban edges of L.A. Unified. During the Great Recession, post-2008, this "last hired, first fired" provision emptied urban schools of young and committed teachers. District leaders refused to push back on seniority rights or cull mediocre teachers, further alienating pro-equity advocates.

In 2010, the ACLU sued the district to suspend seniority in forty-five schools located in poor sections of East and South Los Angeles. This litigation was joined by the Partnership for L.A. Schools, a nonprofit spin-off by then mayor Antonio Villaraigosa. This coalition won the so-called *Reed* case, which protected central-city teachers with little seniority from being laid off. John Deasy, the pro-equity school chief at the time, testified in support of the ACLU suit, even though his office was being sued. The United Teachers of Los Angeles (UTLA) did eventually cooperate to improve working conditions and reduce teacher turnover. Deasy's support endeared him to equity-minded pluralists, signaling his willingness to take on the teachers' union. He aptly read the democratizing politics of education emerging in Los Angeles, embracing these dissonant pluralists to offset the conserving instincts of labor leaders.

Meanwhile, reform-minded educators—not necessarily tied to ethnic leadership or pro-equity lobbies—pushed for schools that would host committed, high-quality teachers. Education theorists such as Jeanne Fauci pressed the district to create small high schools, originally financed by the Gates Foundation and allied donors. She joined Karen Hunter Quartz at UCLA and renegade district official Richard Alonzo to create the Belmont Zone of Choice in 2004. This allowed low-income parents, for the first time, to choose from among differing schools, rather than sending kids to an assigned school nearby (the same demand pressed by desegregation advocates a generation earlier).

District superintendent Ramón Cortines—and, after him, Deasy—urged inventive teachers and nonprofits to also create site-managed *pilot schools*, small campuses at which principals hire and fire their own teachers. This is similar to how charter schools, shaking free of voluminous labor rules, operate. A cluster of pilot schools with diverse curricular offerings was built in Latino East L.A., along with small high schools that emphasized themes of social justice. Pilot schools, new preschools, and the district's expanding count of magnet schools by 2010 formed an aggressive offense against the charter school threat, while borrowing the charter model of flexible, school-level control.

Taken together, these reforms bolstered the legitimacy and influence of the moderate pluralists. These loyal insiders—such as Brenes, Fauci, and Smith—did not hesitate to criticize the glacial progress of L.A. Unified in retaining quality teachers or lifting learning. But they remained faithful that, when allies could be found inside the district edifice, discernible gains were achievable. We also see by the late 1990s a maturing and inventive political network that displays racial and cultural sensitivities, along with varying pedagogical strategies hosted by a proliferating count of magnet, pilot, and dual-language campuses—aiming to mirror the city's cultural and political diversity. The old model of common schools had become a dusty artifact of the past. Instead, plural interests—whether defined in cultural, linguistic, or ideological terms—were animating the spread of diverse forms of schooling. Each campus, while still under the banner of L.A. Unified, must now boast a distinct curricular mission, from theater arts to computer science, and echo the curricular and socialization priorities of particular ethnic and linguistic communities.

Did Progressive Funding Lift Students?

In political metrics, these reform episodes buoyed the credibility and influence of the loyal insiders. Their inventive policies served to establish the growing presence of new pluralists on the civic stage. But did their strides in progressively funding schools jolt the school institution in ways that elevated student achievement? When Governor Brown swiftly decentralized budget decision-making, for example, he shone a bright light on local deliberations. But did it work?

My efforts to trace the impact of new dollars on L.A. schools, conducted with Joonho Lee, a University of Alabama professor, reveal a bittersweet story. First, L.A. Unified officials did progressively allocate Governor Brown's fresh funding to L.A. *high schools* that hosted larger percentages of poor children and English learners.[51] On these campuses, pro-equity advocates largely succeeded—via legal filings, street protests, lobbying board members, and influencing decisions made behind the scenes—by moving new dollars and staff slots to the district's most challenged campuses. In turn, principals hired additional teachers, counselors, and tutors for language learners.[52]

In contrast, superintendents Cortines and Deasy distributed new monies evenly across *elementary schools*. Cortines preferred to restore librarian and assistant principal posts lost after the nation's financial meltdown in 2008. These district leaders were motivated to hold on to a declining count of middle-class families, as flight to charter schools and neighboring districts persisted. For whatever reason, the uniform layer of new monies out to elementary schools ensured almost no progressivity in the financing of elementary schools: those serving middle-class or well-off students received near-identical augmentations relative to central-city schools hosting impoverished kids.

At the same time, the potential benefits of progressive financing for high schools was tempered by a heavy reliance on young and inexperienced teachers. As new funding arrived in 2013 and principals surged into the labor market, they mostly hired rookie or less experienced teachers. Many, holding little seniority, were then assigned to courses dominated by English learners. Such is the entrenched structure of status in American high schools: the newbies get the most challenging students, and teachers with seniority enjoy higher-achieving pupils. In addition, the share of courses offered that were college-prep under the A-G class reform declined in schools receiving larger infusions of new funding. These campuses could now build out elective courses, hurried by the collapse of accountability pressure under No Child Left Behind (which was gutted by Congress in 2015). Better-funded high schools were able to lower class sizes and reduce the count of teaching periods assigned to instructors, thereby improving working conditions.

The good news is that pupil performance in math and reading climbed in better-funded high schools, compared with those campuses gaining less from Governor Brown's cash infusion. The finance reform seemed to rekindle L.A. Unified's earlier momentum in raising test scores. But racial disparities in proficiency levels failed to narrow, despite all the new funding. This may have stemmed from assigning less experienced teachers to pupils who have farther to travel to clear state proficiency standards. It accents the paradox facing the new pluralists: their inventive reforms have lifted all ethnic groups since the 1990s while failing to reduce inequality. We did find that students from poor families did better when attending schools with larger shares of middle-class peers, compared with similarly poor youths in campuses situated in beleaguered neighborhoods. This finding mirrored the argument made by desegregation advocates a half century earlier.

Moving Inside Schools—Quality Teachers and Human Ties

These youthful activists remaining loyal to L.A. Unified settled on another policy strategy by the late 1990s. This reform logic was simple in design, though difficult to implement: undo teachers' racialized assumptions about student ability, improve pedagogical practices, and invigorate the curriculum to boost the percentage of graduates entering college. We introduced Superintendent Romer's imposition of a clear and regimented didactics earlier in this chapter. The Open

Court initiative had kick-started children's gains in basic literacy and math, at least for elementary school youngsters. But the mechanical, command-and-control nature of Romer's policy could not be sustained politically. His classroom regimen would not outlive his retirement in 2006.[53]

Devising a more complex curriculum, while enriching respect and social relations inside high school classrooms, would prove more daunting. This deeply institutional question would divide the loyal insiders, this moderate wing of the new pluralists. Civil rights advocates continued to lobby for precise and regimented learning standards, as pressed by the Clinton, George W. Bush, and Obama administrations. Yet, this appeared to dumb down the curriculum and rewarded didactic teaching, artificially lifting test scores, critics claimed. In contrast, other education reformers opted for organizational diversity, creating schools that hosted complex pedagogy and deeper learning, typically pegged to inventive curricular themes, from digital technology to theater arts, or small pilot schools focusing on social justice. All this, so reminiscent of the split among Progressives in Los Angeles a century earlier: those pushing for efficient control of a uniform curriculum, against a humanist caucus that advanced deeper and critical thinkers, students nurtured by thoroughly engaging teachers.

Teacher Quality, Rigorous Learning for All

The task of improving teacher quality was taken up by John Deasy soon after he took the helm at L.A. Unified in 2011. He arrived with a reform pedigree rooted in the Gates Foundation and neoliberal circles, led by those who viewed labor leaders and education bureaucrats as impediments to reform. The core task, as Deasy saw it, was to jolt this moribund institution in ways that might narrow racial disparities in learning. Impatient and critical of established interests, he soon allied with social justice activists, kindred spirits on the anti-poverty front. These new pluralists also provided a counterweight to what Deasy saw as the conserving drag of union chieftains. "What had been missing" before Deasy's arrival "was a sense of urgency from the top . . . a willingness to brook excuses or delays," the *L.A. Times* editorial board wrote.[54]

Deasy's rather brief and contentious rule remains difficult to sum up. He certainly enriched the credulity and influence of the loyal insiders. Raised in Providence, Rhode Island, by parents "who had their own struggle," he told me, taught him that "you do good for others no matter what you have." Short and muscular in build, he typically speaks to multiple issues (and frustrations) all at once, animated by a rapid-fire mind. Deasy met his future wife, a young immigrant from Syria, on the first day of high school. At age 24, Deasy joined New York City's teaching force, then became a school principal. He attended the Broad Academy, created by the late L.A. developer Eli Broad, where educators learn about the virtues of charter schools and parental choice. Take no names, take no prisoners, shake the institution's resilient foundations.

Deasy shared the pluralists' concern with how to enliven classrooms, how to better motivate teachers and students alike. "We had long since moved from direct instruction [under Romer], [and] I believed that teachers really know best, so we focused on outcomes," Deasy recalled. His in-your-face personality signaled firm and centralizing control. But he argued that caring and inventive teachers would be served by school-level autonomy. "I was watching remarkable work where teachers wrote their own rules . . . wrote how their school would work," he said, moving to expand pilot schools newly negotiated with the union. To empower inventive teachers, new forms of schooling and decentered management were necessary. So, Deasy lent voice to a coalition of equity advocates, charter school enthusiasts, and rebellious teachers—seeking to lift teacher quality and motivate closer relationships inside schools.

Social justice advocates had long pressed to purge lousy teachers, many stashed in politically weak inner-city schools. The Gates Foundation had begun sinking hundreds of millions of dollars into measuring the "value added" of teachers—that is, how much each instructor advanced the growth of students. Kati Haycock, head of the pro-equity Education Trust in Washington (the parent of Ryan Smith's former shop in Oakland), had trumpeted the magic of value-added estimates in testimony before Congress in 2001. Deasy soon embraced the value-added cause. He hired a gaggle of young technicians to devise a procedure for observing the district's some 33,000 teachers, aiming to identify bad apples while diagnosing how to enrich everyday pedagogy.

Yet, the *Los Angeles Times* soon enflamed the debate, even before Deasy could devise a credible protocol for assessing classroom teachers. The paper's editors decided to publish estimates of effectiveness along a five-point scale—publicly appearing for each reading and math teacher by name. "In the past, too often we've just gone with gut instinct and haven't been careful about whether those things are important," said Richard Buddin, a RAND economist paid to run the *Times*'s controversial analysis.[55] The ethics and validity of publishing a single score, often estimated with considerable error, struck many as troubling. One low-ranked teacher died by suicide.

The value-added strategy enflamed opposition from many civic activists, not simply from union leaders.[56] Inside schools, the piloted assessment tools aimed to give teachers formative feedback on how to improve their pedagogy. It was not intended as a "gotcha exercise" to weed out incompetent staff. But many defined the value-added strategy as overly corporate, even bordering on surveillance of teachers, who presumably acted as reflective professionals. In Deasy's mind, he aimed to "fundamentally reform human capital with strong teacher quality to ensure high quality choices for every parent," he told me. But this short-lived reform undercut Deasy's credibility with the school board. He also opted to film a promotional clip for Apple Computer while negotiating a $1.3 billion contract, intending to provide a free iPad for every student in L.A. By fall 2014, the board nudged him to resign.

Still, Deasy's grasp of the shifting nature of metropolitan politics, especially his alliance with the new pluralists, became a lasting legacy. It was "city-wide organizations like ICS, United Way, Educators for Excellence that worked with us," Deasy said, "including the [Catholic] diocese and 23 mayors of cities, trying to weave together a stronger coalition, a youth movement for social justice." He saw how the new activists, nonprofits, and reform-minded educators offered novel policy ideas and authentic voices for working-class families. Together, they were willing to challenge the sluggishness of labor and the soul-crushing nature of L.A. Unified's central bureaucracy. Deasy sensed the pluralists' rising influence, along with how their third political ground could foster inventive policy options. Deasy had welcomed all-comers onto the civic stage, provided they join his cause for equity and teacher quality.

Respecting and Motivating Students

Loyal insiders also pressed to decriminalize student discipline, another way of fostering respect and caring relationships inside high schools. In 2012, new federal data revealed that suspensions and expulsions were being disproportionately meted out to Black pupils in L.A. Unified, at a rate exceeding three times their enrollment share.[57] "Disciplinary policies are racially profiling African American students," said Marqueece Harris-Dawson, president of the Community Coalition. "It is not that African American students are lazy, unmotivated or not smart, [they] are being pushed out of schools."[58]

Half of these suspensions stemmed from the district's zero tolerance for "willful defiance" by students, which covered everything from "mouthing off to wearing baggy pants." One senior at Garfield High, Joshua Ham, confessed to being "very active as far as talking in the classroom, you know, the class clown," who was suspended less than a month before graduation.[59] CADRE, a parent group in South L.A., joined with Coco leaders to advocate the repeal of willful defiance, eventually approved by the school board in 2013, along with a Student Bill of Rights that nudged principals to build a positive climate, nurturing respect and dialogue between teachers and students. The district also began funding so-called restorative justice practices, where aggrieved parties come around the table to resolve conflicts, fights, and fissures that open up between students or that may involve a teacher. The odds of being suspended from high school declined from one in every eleven students to one per ninety students between

2005 and 2015.[60] Yet, as suspensions declined, calls to the police department or probation officers climbed, still exceeding 4,700 referrals in 2016.[61]

In 2019, Students Not Suspects, an allied set of advocates led by the ACLU and Black Lives Matter (later joined by the UTLA), convinced the school board to prohibit the district's police from randomly checking pupil backpacks.[62] "It's contradictory to the values of this organization . . . of trying to make every student feel welcome at our schools to continue random searches," said board member Kelly Gonez.[63] This coalition of new pluralists won several reforms not only regarding discipline procedures but also measures constraining the authority of L.A. Unified's sizeable police force. The debate grew larger after the death of George Floyd in 2020, his neck crushed beneath the knee of a Minneapolis police officer, sparking massive protests nationwide. By late June, the board was deadlocked over whether to eliminate the district's police unit, cut its budget, or further constrain its allowable actions on middle and high school campuses. Equity advocates focused on decriminalizing misbehavior urged phasing out the police within three years, an effort led by board member Mónica García, a close ally of ICS and Coco. She aimed to defund the force, then send the savings out to largely Black schools.[64]

But union leaders, led by the UTLA, urged piecemeal action, worrying over the safety of its members. The Service Employees International Union (SEIU) agreed with teachers on this question, since the children of many members attend L.A. schools. Some recalled a spate of local school shootings in the 1990s. "I have high hopes . . . that labor partners will be a part of the conversation," said Juan Flecha, chief of the administrators union.[65] Jackie Goldberg, reelected to the board with UTLA's backing, advocated a go-slow approach, banning the use of pepper spray and shaving back the police budget. After a second board hearing—lasting thirteen hours with testimony from dozens of community groups and ICS-organized students—members voted 4-3 to cut $25 million from the police department's budget and lay off 65 of the 471-member unit. The savings were to be redirected to predominantly Black schools. "The fight for real school safety has only just begun," said Melina Abdullah, parent and cofounder of the L.A. chapter of Black Lives Matter.

Looking across these policy successes, the new pluralists—especially this moderate wing of loyal insiders—firmly established their popular credibility and political clout between the early 1990s and Deasy's departure in 2014. This fluid network of pro-equity nonprofits, civil rights lawyers, and reform-minded educators had staked out novel political ground, gaining distance from devotees of capital and stubborn labor leaders. They had achieved policy wins in three arenas, at times embracing strange political bedfellows to form potent coalitions. Finance reforms included the creation of additional magnet schools, dual-language schools, and pilot schools—efforts to remake that uniform set of common schools once set in stone a century earlier. Their victories were not simply episodic; the moderate pluralists were pursuing long-term change inside the institution of schooling.

The pluralists also succeeded in moving the reform discourse across Los Angeles, shifting teachers' racialized expectations of student potential and expanding access to college-prep courses. And these youthful insurgents were showing how grassroots organizing—delivering thousands of parents and students to board meetings or marching in the streets—could move the often intransigent institution of public education. These loyal insiders displayed agility in pressuring officials from the outside while crafting remedies with reform-minded officials inside. "Scientific and technical arguments have a limited capacity to resolve matters that reach so deeply into cultural values and political contention," Oakes and Rogers observed, which "turn more on the power of grassroots advocacy groups than on any finding of fact."[66]

The new pluralists were at loggerheads with union leaders in the opening years of the twenty-first century, as children's achievement began inching upward. Few civic players could have foreseen how the pluralist spirit—seeking fair, effective, and culturally sensitive schools—would seep into a collateral, yet equally sluggish institution, organized labor. Let's turn next to this unexpected episode, another curious twist in the L.A. story: how a young generation of union leaders arose, then borrowed the sentiments and policy inventions of the new pluralists.

Labor Goes Pluralist

Our tale of political realignment, thus far, features an amicable divorce between organized labor and many of the new activists and diverse nonprofits that surfaced in the 1990s. It's remained a rocky romance, with the new pluralists at times coming together with labor on specific issues, especially as L.A. Unified recovers from the fifteen months of shuttered classrooms during the Covid-19 pandemic. Yet, the loyal insiders continue to challenge labor when union chiefs deny shortfalls in teacher quality or the progressive funding of central-city schools. At the same time, L.A.'s unions are not uniform in their ideological foundations and policy priorities, nor does their leadership remain static over time. Indeed, labor must adapt to the same political ecology that gave rise to new pluralism in Los Angeles. Pluralist impulses—centered on a renewed focus on fairness and nurturing responsive institutions—would visit labor associations as well.

A. J. Duffy, president of the UTLA, had long battled with great bravado to win higher pay and fringe benefits for his members. But his abrasive style and protectionist posture were isolating his once powerful organization from reform-minded groups. His vociferous opposition to charter schools was understandable, as market principles aimed to erode pro-social norms of labor. But Duffy also refused to acknowledge to social justice advocates, when pressed to reconsider seniority or purge mediocre teachers, often warehoused in mostly Black or Latino schools. Duffy failed to see the opening of this third civic territory, pioneered and settled by the new pluralists.

By 2010, an insurgent movement was gaining members inside the UTLA, calling themselves the New TLA. These dissidents pressed for new pilot schools and managerial freedom from the L.A. Unified bureaucracy, then pushed Duffy to focus squarely on gross resource disparities among schools.[67] The insurgents campaigning inside the union soon secured one-third of all seats in the legislative council. Leaders of the New TLA established ties with the new pluralists, like Maria Brenes, pushing the union to negotiate a flexible contract under which pilot school principals eventually won authority to hire and fire their own teachers.

Then in 2014, Alex Caputo-Pearl, a high school teacher with pro-equity *bona fides*, challenged Duffy's aging regime, winning his own campaign to take over the UTLA, as its new president. He promised to take "a leadership role . . . in supporting immigrant students, challenging racism, advocating for affordable housing [the district is one of the county's largest real estate holders], and creating green space at our schools."[68] He promised to return labor to its social reform roots, not simply build a protective moat around conventional schooling.

After serving in Teach for America in 1990, Caputo-Pearl had taught at Crenshaw High School in Compton, where nine in ten students grew up in poverty after the shuttering of auto plants and aircraft factories. He and fellow teachers took charge, running the school as a democratic cooperative, raising millions of dollars to split the sprawling campus into human-scale "academies." One cluster mentored students in the history of civil rights, delving into how youths could advance racial equity (an applied precursor to critical race theory). Reform for Caputo-Pearl was about nurturing and mobilizing students, not simply tinkering with the official curriculum or raising test scores. Duffy, ever the stalwart unionist, claimed that Crenshaw's curricular reform was being led by a bunch of "leftist crazies."[69] But graduation rates began drifting upward at Crenshaw, as student engagement and motivation reportedly climbed.

Still, measurable progress was unfolding too slowly in the eyes of the new superintendent, John Deasy. He announced in 2012 that no incumbent teacher would be guaranteed a job at Crenshaw. This high school was to be turned upside down. Deasy drew on his ties with the Community Coalition in South L.A. to support reconstituting the entire staff at both Crenshaw and Fremont High. Caputo-Pearl was asked to leave.[70]

This did not deter Caputo-Pearl. He promised a more militant form of "union power," arguing that Duffy's successor, Warren Fletcher, was too timid in combatting charter school growth and extracting richer benefits for UTLA members, even "letting billionaires take over the public schools," a reference to growing campaign contributions from the likes of Broad and Hastings. Caputo-Pearl would exercise "a far-more-aggressive stance against the spread of charter schools, standardized testing . . . and Deasy," one analyst wrote, along with killing off the district's value-added strategy for evaluating the quality of teachers.[71]

A Widening Agenda

Caputo-Pearl watched the spread of teacher strikes across the United States in 2018, igniting in states where Republican governors had slashed funding for public schools. National politics had swerved Right with the election of Donald Trump as president. The Supreme Court ruled against mandatory dues in the *Janus* case, striking to the financial heart of public sector unions. The Red for Ed movement, sparked by tech-savvy teachers, mobilized massive protests in states like Arizona, Oklahoma, and West Virginia, winning pay raises and re-kindling a common concern over the health of schools, even in these otherwise conservative parts of the country.[72] Arizona even flipped to the Democrats in the 2020 presidential election, reflecting a renewed faith in public institutions.

Caputo-Pearl, moving with the militancy of Red for Ed, rallied his members into an eleven-day strike in January 2019. Teachers marched downtown protesting California's relatively low investment in public education, compared with other states, and stridently opposed the school board's embrace of charter schools. The UTLA campaign became more than just a battle over bread-and-butter interests. This was "a struggle over the future of public education," Caputo-Pearl argued. He kept returning, during our three interviews together, to his desire to pull from the pro-equity heritage of the labor movement. "The district does not have nearly enough counselors, psychologists or librarians to give students the support they need," he said. "Eighty percent of schools don't even have full-time nurses."[73] He borrowed such humanist and economically progressive goals from the new pluralists—focusing on how to nurture and challenge all children inside L.A.'s public schools.

The union won a modest pay raise in the end. L.A. Unified leaders agreed to slightly lower class size in central-city schools. Caputo-Pearl stayed honest to his commitment to fairness, shifting newly negotiated dollars, counselor posts, and holistic social services to schools and neighborhoods most in need. Equally telling, Caputo-Pearl had drawn from the pluralist playbook, centering on the felt experience and support often denied students inside L.A.'s schools, moving way beyond basic trade union issues. He had echoed the voices of Black and Latino leaders: schools must be fairly financed, teachers must respect and lift all students, attending to their broader well-being—not simply aiming to raise test scores. Caputo-Pearl soon backed targeting new dollars on the most impoverished parts of L.A., a position not seen since *Serrano* in the 1970s. In short, Caputo-Pearl enhanced his own legitimacy by visiting and borrowing policy innovations from that third political ground.

This nimble union chief then joined with yet another nonprofit founded in the 1990s—the L.A. Alliance for a New Economy—to document the ideological and institutional shifts that had occurred inside the UTLA, leading up to the 2019 strike. It's a remarkably candid report, displaying eye-catching photos of protesting teachers filling the streets of downtown Los Angeles in bright red T-shirts, telling of how Caputo-Pearl led "a complete reorganization of the union."[74] The UTLA's first step under Caputo-Pearl was to win "the support of dozens of grassroots, civil rights, and immigrant advocacy organizations, as well as other labor groups and academic organizations across the city," this official chronicle reads. Here, too, the union drew from pluralist strategy: new staff were hired to "reach out and organize community-based groups . . . seeking to build deeper, mutually respectful relationships." Left unsaid was how these ties with local nonprofits had been severed long ago, going back a generation. Yet, now Caputo-Pearl intended to mend that political wound.

Labor organizers reached out to "activate unorganized parents," precisely what Coco and ICS had been doing over the past generation, as prior union leaders ignored. "He [Caputo-Pearl] hired people we knew and had worked with," said Roxanna Tynan, director of the L.A. Alliance for a New Economy. The new unionists even appropriated *La Posada* from the Latino cultural tool kit, how Mary and Joseph searched for lodging in Bethlehem (old Protestant elites turning in their graves). Under UTLA's rendition, high school students crashed a fundraising party attended by Austin Beutner (now the L.A. Unified chief) in a swanky Pacific Palisades neighborhood. A band of teachers enacted their posada by visiting Netflix's Hollywood studio, demanding to meet with Reed Hastings.

Caputo-Pearl's demands during the teacher strike centered on inventive forms of schooling as well, pressing to extend preschool to additional young children and create additional dual-language campuses and so-called community schools hosting health care and social services for families, a reform borrowed from New York City. While Caputo-Pearl cast charter schools as part of an evil empire, his new forms of schooling stemmed from the same pressures driving charter growth: parents demanding safe and effective schools, linguistic and cultural diversity, and diverging organizational logics over how schools might work better.

A Union of Color

The UTLA has long occupied a privileged position in the pantheon of California labor organizations. Its rising power and financial strength since the 1970s had come to eclipse the interests of other worker associations. But emerging contention within L.A.'s labor movement helped bolster the growing influence of Black and Latino leaders and social justice groups, unfolding during the early twenty-first century as well. Lester Garcia teaches us much about the forces motivating this realignment.

Garcia, a teenager raised in East Los Angeles, had never felt such "tremendous respect, being valued and trusted," as he did one afternoon in 1999 when Luis Sanchez, founder of ICS, handed Garcia an extra set of office keys. "The prom was coming up" at Roosevelt High, Garcia told me. "I needed some money and had applied for a job at MacDonald's [*sic*]." Recognizing young talent, Sanchez instead offered Garcia a job. It would become a "cliché moment . . . the first day of the rest of my life," Garcia said. He had met Sanchez at a student walkout, where they had rebelled against poorly funded and overcrowded schools in the barrio. More than 5,400 students attended overcrowded Roosevelt High at the time, and few ever graduated. Garcia had joined Movimiento Eotudiantil Chicano de Aztlán (MECHA), the Chicano group that emerged in the wake of the 1968 "blowouts," when thousands of teens took to the streets for the first time, protesting racial segregation, expressing a proud Mexican-heritage identity.[75] As a child, Garcia had traveled by bus out to Beverly Hills with his mother to help clean houses. By his teenage years, "images were swirling around me," Garcia said. "Friends leaving school, helicopters flying over the neighborhood."

He moved on, politically seasoned at age 24, to become chief of staff for Mónica García, the L.A. Unified board member who represented the heavily Latino east side. Here he learned of the challenges of moving a sluggish, deeply entrenched institution. "Bashing the district was not enough," Garcia said. Around the table inside L.A. Unified, "these were the people who could implement or obstruct" any new initiative. He learned how to buy a sharp suit, to arrange a necktie with precision. "If you wear a tie in my neighborhood," he smiled, "you are either going to court or a funeral."

Then, Garcia caught the attention of Courtni Pugh at a United Way luncheon in 2013. Pugh served as deputy to the chief of SEIU Local 99 before taking the helm at 41 years of age. And Pugh "didn't want to be a leader that just filed grievances day after day," she later told me. Local 99 represents more than 35,000 service workers inside L.A. Unified: modestly paid secretaries, classroom aides, janitors, and warehouse clerks. Pugh represented another 5,000 childcare and preschool staff, even a smattering of support workers inside charter schools. The broad goal of Local 99 in the eyes of Pugh and Garcia was "to allow our members to enjoy an improved quality of life," and this meant "supporting quality public education." When Garcia, now SEIU's political director, surveyed members in 2014, "the number one priority for upcoming contract negotiations was to improve the schools." It's "unlike any institution," Garcia said. "It's where they [SEIU members] feel safe."

So, Garcia and Pugh began strategizing with leaders of ICS, United Way, and the Community Coalition, organizations that now shared the ideals and policy options already blooming in L.A.'s third political terrain. These pro-equity impulses from within the SEIU were not altogether new. Originally dubbed the Building Service Employees, the union long labored to foster a more inclusive association, organizing Black and Mexican-heritage janitors in Chicago, San Francisco, and L.A. after World War I. The crafts and building trades, especially those situated in the American Federation of Labor, had allowed only white Yankees into their union, as detailed by UCLA historian Ruth Milkman.[76] And recall that Irish and allied labor leaders in California had railed against Chinese and Japanese workers going back to the nineteenth century. By 1950, just 2 percent of all teamster drivers were Black, and only 3 percent of unionized painters were Black. But two in five janitors were Black in Los Angeles, and they were joining the SEIU.[77]

Given this institutional heritage, it was natural for Pugh and Garcia to build ties with pro-equity nonprofits. And John Deasy, who ably read this shift in the political landscape, recognized SEIU's interest in lifting schools. They came together to back the "15 by 15" campaign, pushing the L.A. Unified board to guarantee a minimum wage for the district's service workers by 2015. Pugh and Garcia also fought to ensure that every child in the district would benefit from a free breakfast at the start of each school day—an initiative that UTLA leaders vigorously opposed. Many SEIU members belong to L.A.'s ranks of the working poor, Garcia said. Deasy eventually agreed to hire more staff to organize morning breakfasts, served in regular classrooms during first period. "This was a win-win for us," Garcia reported. "It created more union jobs and fed the kids." But teachers complained of yet another chore, one that soiled their classroom and cut into instructional time. UTLA leaders testified before the school board, hoping to kill the school breakfast initiative. But the board sided with Deasy and SEIU, and approved the new program.

The ethnically diverse, blue-collar profile of SEIU members only enriched the economic justice agenda of many new pluralists. "There's a certain level of arrogance, even racism from teachers [who say], 'we have degrees'," another labor organizer told me under condition of anonymity. "Well, we have a bunch of guys sending teachers their supplies down at the Pico Union warehouse, and they're telling us their kids still can't read."

Pugh would leave Local 99 in 2014, but she had left her mark after four years at the helm. The UTLA was not happy with her alliance with Deasy, along with the pro-equity agenda she had devised. Yet, SEIU had crystalized a forceful counterpoint to the teachers' union, revealing the limits of static schools and exposing the preservationist instincts of UTLA. Soon, this once-dominant labor group began listening carefully to the new pluralists, punctuated by Caputo-Pearl's arrival. He now situated public education within wider inequalities and spoke to the well-being of students, enriching social ties and raising the efficacy of conventional schools. When it came to questions of institutional change, the new pluralists had become widely respected authorities. And a youthful generation of labor leaders was following suit.

Lessons Learned from Loyal Insiders

No decisive battle marked the civic revolution waged by the new pluralists. Yet, a palace revolt of sorts did unfold over the past quarter century. These moderate activists formed a loyal opposition, confident that alliances with leaders inside thick-skinned L.A. Unified could yield lasting institutional change. Their coalescing strategy—animated by the likes of Maria Brenes, Jeanne Fauci, Lester Garcia, and Ryan Smith—emphasized tandem fronts. First, they carved out that novel civic terrain, a proving ground distinct from efficiency-minded corporatists and recalcitrant labor leaders. They devised a series of inventive policies, aiming to progressively fund schools and foster social relations inside to motivate students and teachers, drawing from the best of humanist ideals. Second, they organized with allies inside the belly of the beast, especially Romer and Deasy, to deliver vivid wins for their diverse constituencies. The loyal insiders had been altering the reform discourse since the 1990s. Their organizing efforts went far beyond policy talk. This wing of plural groups chalked up policy victories on several fronts while carrying out discernible change inside the guts of this stubborn institution.

Not all policy wins proved to be empirically predictive of gains in student achievement. But several did, in spades. Recurring waves of school finance reform, pressed by the ACLU, Public Advocates, and the Community Coalition, spurred voter support of the district's $19 billion construction splurge. Two analyses have discerned sharp gains in learning among students who migrated from overcrowded to brand-new, and often smaller, campuses. This same network of pluralists helped push through Governor Brown's vastly progressive finance reform in the state capital, then jammed district leaders in court to ensure the new dollars would be moved to the students who generate fresh funding for L.A. Unified. Our five-year tracking study revealed gains in student achievement in high schools that won the largest funding increases.

The second policy front—advocating crisp curricular goals and strong teacher quality—has yielded less definitive results in recent decades. Superintendent Romer's early drive to clarify learning proficiencies for students, then enforce a didactic pedagogy, met with a blizzard of political resistance. But it did kick-start children's initial gains in basic literacy and mathematical skills. Romer was in sync with a variety of civil rights groups a generation ago, those eager to shine a bright light on the learning curves of disadvantaged students. His controversial regimen appeared to lift test scores, at least among elementary school children. The pluralist agenda in high schools became more ambitious and subtle: aiming to alter teachers' racially arranged expectations of student potential while widening access to rigorous college-prep courses. This goes to the institution's beating heart, as loyal insiders fostered motivating relationships and humanized discipline inside schools, along with propagating a garden of human-scale campuses, including pilot, magnet, and dual-language programs.

We saw how, as the loyal insiders gained allies and private funders, the established players adjusted their positions in this fluid political field. Romer drew on the push by civil rights activists, including the ACLU and the Education Trust, to specify learning standards and routinize pedagogy. Deasy embraced the new pluralists, as counterweight to union stalwarts, pressing for progressive school funding and pruning pallid teachers. The social justice wing of pluralists would motivate Mayor Villaraigosa to split from labor and hand off scores of schools to decentralized managers, an episode that is detailed in the next chapter.

We saw how young activists carved out the third political terrain, gaining distance and crafting inventive policy options, separating from old capital, aging labor leaders, and tame Progressives once so enamored with cookie-cutter schools. But these established groups—whether protecting material interests or testing their own reforms—also shifted ground like soccer stars repositioning, adjusting to their opponents' play. When unsettled by economic or institutional shocks, metropolitan fields prompt novel realignments of key players, as sociologists Neal Fligstein and Doug McAdam have described.[78] When under political fire or rocked by ideological or political shifts, established players ally with the insurgents, even borrow from their novel quill of policy tools. So, we saw how once protective labor leaders began to reach out to the pluralists, trumpeting their goals of economic justice, seeking more nurturing relations between teachers and students inside schools. And the loyal insiders began to define the policy discourse that other groups must echo to rekindle their own legitimacy within this fluid institutional field.

Next, I turn to the radical wing of plural and nonaligned activists—those who concluded in the 1990s that L.A. Unified was hopelessly captured by mid-level "edu-crats" and union chieftains, who together would repel any serious effort at institutional change. These civic challengers, more skeptical than the loyal insiders, viewed this organizational behemoth as hog-tied by standardizing routines and labor rules meant to protect the adults, rather than elevate students and families. L.A. Unified had become a political economy unto itself, generating tax dollars to fund a vast administrative and teaching staff, and dole out steady salaries and ample pensions, these challengers argued. So, charter school warriors and grassroots organizers rallied behind a direct remedy: hammering L.A. Unified from the outside. Without competitive pressure or in the absence of a radically democratic politics of education, this urban institution would never change.

CHAPTER 3

Outside Agitators

WITH MALENA ARCIDIACONO, CAITLIN KEARNS,
AND JOONHO LEE

The cry of flower power echoes through the land. We shall not wilt. Let a thousand flowers bloom.

—Abbie Hoffman, 1967

Caprice Young shares no ideological chops with Abbie Hoffman. She does enjoy disrupting institutions. Young won a seat on the Los Angeles school board in 1999 at the ripe age of 32, then helped spread charter schools throughout the land, taxpayer-financed yet independently run campuses. "We grew the charter school movement as a conscious movement of dismantlement," she told me.

Handpicked by Republican mayor Richard Riordan, Young and her pro-market insurgents ascended to power as labor leaders fell from grace, unable to reelect a pro-union board. The radical disruptors had given up on the system, breaking from loyal insiders who insisted that reform could percolate from within the central bureaucracy. Young, along with unexpected allies inside Black and Latino enclaves, argued instead that building a network of charter schools, waging head-to-head competition with conventional public schools, was the only answer to L.A. Unified's intransigence. This combative strategy would best yield lasting institutional change, Young and her comrades claimed.

This chapter chronicles the rise of these *civic challengers*, those opting to attack the education edifice from the outside. Early pioneers of the charter school movement in Los Angeles had once been loyal insiders, polite civic leaders like Judy Burton and William Ouchi, who labored in the 1980s to decentralize control of neighborhood schools, granting principals the authority to hire and fire their own teachers. But these old-timers had been defeated, watching their governance reforms subverted by downtown managers and labor leaders. So, "we said screw it," Young proclaimed. "We are going to create a bunch of charter schools to prove to L.A. Unified that we can do it better . . . giving up on seeing the board or the district as a lever of change."

The radical wing of pluralists went about creating nearly three hundred charter schools by 2021, enrolling one-fifth of all students in L.A. and punching a huge hole in the school district's budget. The late developer Eli Broad, Netflix's founder Reed Hastings, and heirs to the Walmart retail fortune helped to capitalize the charter school campaign. They bankrolled local politicians who pledged fealty to the charter cause. These wealthy donors railed against the education system as being hog-tied by special interests. Meanwhile, the pro-charter caucus was buying its own political machine.

This (largely) neoliberal caucus among the new pluralists, emerging alongside the loyal insiders in the 1990s, was not so intent on building a democratic politics of schooling. The capital dished out by Broad and Hastings aimed to eclipse the voices of others, buying political clout in nonparticipatory fashion. Yet, the civic challengers did break decisively from the central education bureaucracy and organized labor, joining their moderate brethren on that third political ground. Nor were the forces animating the external challengers rooted solely in market ideology or corporate affection for efficiency. Left-leaning pluralists had long pushed for neighborhood control of schools, trumpeted in New York back in 1964, when Black and Puerto Rican leaders tried to secede from the city schools. And recall that loyal insiders pressed for the Belmont Zone of Choice in immigrant East L.A., borrowing notions of parental choice and liberating schools from the downtown bureaucracy (chapter 2). The two wings of this pluralist spectrum opened policy windows for each other. They also came to rally around shared principles, devolving who controls neighborhood schools, nurturing richer social relations inside classrooms, and attempting to narrow disparities in which children benefit from public schools.

Let's turn to the motivations animating these civic challengers: Why did they decide to swing a large club, banging on the hard-shelled education regime? What policy options emanated from their corner of the civic stage? Did their efforts to build diverse forms of schooling elevate—or further stratify—children and families in Los Angeles over time?

Civic Challengers Rise from Defeat

Like any dutiful graduate student, William Ouchi wrote a careful review of the academic literature. He was intrigued with how large firms often lost their capacity to motivate workers, no longer able to rally them around a shared mission. As their feeling of camaraderie faded, so did profits. Ouchi turned to successful Japanese companies as one inspiring alternative, firms that nurtured collaboration among frontline staff, problem-solving in small teams. After attaining his PhD, he published a best-selling book in 1981, *Theory Z*, in which he argued that by decentralizing shop-floor decisions, morale would climb, making workers feel efficacious in tackling their everyday problems.[1]

Ouchi turned to the public sector after becoming a business professor at UCLA, visiting school principals in East Asia and reporting on how site-level managers exercised authority over teachers and budgets despite highly centralized exams required of students. In Japan, "every principal was required to build their own budget tied to a five-year plan," Ouchi told me. "Once those were approved, principals could spend money however they wanted." This fusion of two concepts—decentralizing control and organizational innovation—soon motivated rising faith in charter schools among moderate Republican leaders in Los Angeles.

Ouchi was not alone in pitching a fresh theory of management. David Osborne and Ted Gaebler put out a book in 1993, titled *Reinventing Government*, in which they reported on nimble local governments that had centrally set performance goals—from pursuing clean water to affordable housing—then awarded local production units with the discretion for puzzling through how to achieve their objectives.[2] It became the model, dubbed *loose-tight coupling*, that Al Gore would trumpet during the Clinton administration, as he promised to "reinvent government." This yielded Democratic enthusiasm over funding charter schools. Three decades later, Netflix's Reed Hastings still echoed this logic. "If we could fix the schools we have, that's definitely the best solution, but people have tried for decades and decades," he told a civic gathering in Texas. Describing his own strategy for running a hugely creative firm, he said: manage with "as few rules as possible."[3]

Pluralists Back Neighborhood Control

Back in Los Angeles, a high-powered rump group convened in 1991, led by then ARCO president Robert E. Wycoff. They tackled the question of how to kick-start the performance of L.A. Unified, as student test scores remained stagnant. This new civic circle included former Lockheed chair Roy A. Anderson, record company executive Virgil Roberts (and before that an attorney prosecuting desegregation cases), and Riordan (elected mayor in 1993). This elite caucus would call themselves the Los Angeles Educational Alliance for Restructuring Now (LEARN). They dodged discussion of Proposition 13 and California's crumbling public infrastructure. Instead, they landed on inefficiency and the apparent sluggishness of the district's centralized regime. These starting points resonated with many pluralists on the political Left as well, who were eager to regain effective schools, devolve control out to ethnic neighborhoods, and shrink gaping disparities in achievement.[4] The LEARN caucus invited Helen Bernstein into the group, the reform-minded head of UTLA at the time. "She had the belief that we ate babies for breakfast, unfeeling people, dishonest people," Ouchi said. But "after sitting and debating with us for about a year, she concluded we were normal human beings."

Booz Allen, the corporate consulting firm, was asked to find decentralized school districts that showed concrete results. "We found something called the charter school movement" (arising first in Minnesota in 1991), Ouchi told me. But "we were not going to do the charter school thing." Instead, they settled on a model rooted in Edmonton, Canada, where principals were awarded resources based on enrollment counts, then given the reins to hire their own teachers and craft their own budgets. Inventive principals recruited stronger teachers, which would then, in theory, attract more families to their schools. A union chief from Rochester, New York, was flown out to certify the virtues of neighborhood-level control, how decentered management would cultivate warm and supportive relationships inside schools. Even the UTLA had backed a limited version of school-based management to help settle a strike in 1989.

By spring 1993, LEARN's leaders, armed with petitions containing more than ten thousand signatures that urged decentralizing control out to principals and teachers, were ready to make their case before the L.A. school board. William Anton, schools chief at the time, was ready to back the radical plan, although he warned that "restructuring alone will not solve our problems."[5] He emphasized that schools were becoming more crowded as the Latino inflow continued and white voters refused to address California's dire fiscal straits.

Sensing the rising credibility of Black and Latino leaders, the original LEARN council branched out, establishing a larger council. This included the Los Angeles Education Partnership led by Peggy Funkhouser, who worked with teachers to foster the so-called *humanitas curriculum*, emphasizing the study of social values and analytical skills. Bernstein began to negotiate with district officials over what site-based authority for principals would look like. The LEARN network was "no longer the province of private elites but a coalition of people who felt . . . the whole community was needed to fix the problem," as Charles Kerchner wrote.[6]

The school board voted to ratify the LEARN plan, agreeing "to create a decentralized network as a form of organization in place of its well-established command and control hierarchy." The LEARN organization became, for nearly a decade, the dominant civic movement aiming to shake the central institution, empowering principals and nurturing cohesion inside schools, following Ouchi's theoretical formulation. LEARN's leaders hired a former state senator, Mike Roos, to run the organization, then allied with UCLA's education school to train the principal and one teacher from each participating school. Each pair acquired skills in the "basics of accounting, how to manage small groups, to debate and be civil in working toward solutions," Ouchi reported. More than one hundred schools applied in 1993 to take part in this decentralizing experiment.

A War of Attrition

But the knives wielded by entrenched interests soon came out. The teachers' union brought in Willie Brown, the venerable legislative leader, to negotiate a provision requiring sign-offs by each school's union rep before changes could be made to campus budgets. This preserved typical elements of union contracts: seniority rights, protection of mediocre teachers, allowing experienced staff to flee central-city schools for the suburbs. Brown's clout proved key, as California's legislature would have to provide fiscal relief to L.A. Unified if opposition to decentralized governance was to be overcome. Meanwhile, Republican governor Pete Wilson, aligned with Riordan in Los Angeles, began pushing charter schools as a stronger remedy to what they saw as a hopeless education bureaucracy. Soon to run for president by bashing immigrant families, Wilson shied away from placing any limits on the neighborhood control of schools, as required under Brown's deal.

By the second year of school-level control, the union's rank and file had grown restless, voicing distrust in the LEARN strategy. It felt like a distraction from the deeper economic straightjacket that beset the schools. Principals had gained control of miniscule resources. And Bernstein's coziness with Riordan rattled union stalwarts. State legislators from the predominately white San Fernando Valley came together, conspiring to secede from the district. This threatened to obliterate the district's tax base, leaving behind mostly poor Black and Latino parts of the city. The racial undertones were far from subtle. Brown, the African American leader of California's assembly, worked hard to kill it. Yet, what began as a move to rein in the downtown bureaucracy had become a political free-for-all. Those battering L.A. Unified from the outside soon ranged from racist white leaders in the Valley to Black and brown activists who had lost faith in the bureaucracy. Both ends of this political spectrum were now fighting for neighborhood control.

Stories vary as to why the LEARN movement withered and died by the late 1990s. For Ouchi, it was largely political. "We can't change schools through political advocacy," he recalled. "They [the union] will out-advocacy us. They had the legislature bought and paid for." In addition, the big donors, such as the Ford Foundation and Walter Annenberg (one-time publisher of *TV Guide* and *Playboy*), were folding their tents in L.A. The school reform circus was moving on. School principals complained of numerous meetings with LEARN organizers, required to draft annual plans, a new bureaucratic chore. The district's green-eye-shade guys downtown were picking away at budget details of each

LEARN school, quietly reexerting central control. Shifting funds to local principals meant unraveling bundles of fishing line downtown, the tangled snarl of budget formulae, position-by-position approval, and arcane accounting procedures. The LEARN initiative quietly succumbed.

Ouchi joined a meeting in 1998 at the NewSchools Venture Fund, a bundler of cash gathered from wealthy donors and foundations, eager to spread charter schools across the land. The fund—mimicking a well-adorned venture capital firm—was first headed by Ted Mitchell, a former UCLA dean. One speaker pitched how freedom from staid bureaucracies can free principals to devise a particular curricular mission in human-scale schools, now able to hire the best and brightest teachers. This theory of governance, pitched by charter school advocates, drew from Ouchi's logic as well, accented by a dose of Milton Friedman's faith in market competition.

"This light bulb went off in my head, ding!" Ouchi recalled.[7] Charter schools were beginning to sprout up across California, authorized by a 1992 bill authored by liberal Democrat Gary Hart. The increasingly frustrated core of LEARN—Burton; Riordan's wife, Elizabeth; and ARCO's Wycoff—would pull back, reset, and create their own charter firm, Alliance College-Ready Public Schools. This reform-minded cabal remained honest to their goal of lifting students in poor areas, opening a handful of charters in South L.A. Yet, these well-bred activists would no longer operate as loyal insiders: they threw in the towel. Ouchi and his comrades had been undercut by midlevel bureaucrats and labor chiefs, working doggedly to preserve their own power and ideology of control, as the disillusioned activists saw it. All reminiscent of what Steven Lukes calls the "third face of power," where the interests of labor chiefs and managers trump efforts to revive spent institutions.[8]

It was time for a radical revolt.

Plural by Design: Building Diverse Schools

The new civic challengers promised more responsive and effective schools. This pitch resonated with parents and activists across the racial and cultural mosaic that Los Angeles had become by the 1990s. Black and Latino leaders had earlier advocated for magnet schools—a mechanism for desegregating campuses while offering attractive curricular themes, from theater arts to digital technology. The desire of Mexican-heritage parents for discipline and proper comportment led many charter leaders to require student uniforms and tight behavioral norms. Many charter schools coalesced around cultural identity, a palpable feeling of belonging. Walk into many a principal's office and switch from English to Spanish, and you instantly feel trust from office staff—this guy's white but not a total outsider. Or, chat in Farsi, Korean, Mandarin, Yiddish—depending on where you shop, the cafés and pubs you frequent, and now the schools you choose. Of Armenian stock? Welcome to a new dual-language program in Armenian. The cosmopolitan diversity of Los Angeles, of course, seeps into its public institutions. Cultural pluralism begets organizational pluralism, and the charter movement operationalized this sentiment with great agility.

Melting-pot enthusiasts had long pitched Protestant-dominated common schools. Yet, by the 1990s no credible civic player was advocating the enforcement of plain-vanilla campuses run by a regimented bureaucracy. That had become heretical. Charter enthusiasts well understood the diversifying ideologies tied to how parents aimed to raise their kids—in what language, abiding by varying forms of respect and traditions of literacy or school attainment. Joe Nathan, a pioneering adherent of charters in Minnesota, called it a civil rights movement, what he saw as liberation for ethnic groups and families from a feckless state apparatus. A wider range of reformers began advocating for small, more intimate schools, run locally and sensitive to the particulars of ethnic neighborhoods. So-called mission-driven schools, essentially borrowing from the magnet model, aimed to attract strong students from across L.A., fostered by Jeanne Fauci, who created the Small Schools Support Network, along with school board member Yolie Flores. Bill Gates invested nearly $2 billion to finance inventive and human-scale high schools in the 1990s, campuses that were to focus on "rigor, relevance, and relationships."

Varieties of School Choice

Civic challengers highlighted the fact that just one-fifth of L.A.'s children were proficient readers entering the twenty-first century, or able to grasp basic math concepts. New forms of governance were required, they argued, where principals won authority to hire their own teachers and control site budgets. This logic was built from so-called school-effects research, emphasizing the role of strong principals and lead teachers in fostering a serious school climate. The unfettered power of principals was highlighted by John Chubb and Terry Moe in their 1990 book, *Politics, Markets, and America's Schools*.[9] It became a bible of sorts for pro-market civic challengers. The logic also fit the rise of neoliberal thinking: only market competition could overcome the self-preserving power of education bureaucrats and labor leaders.

President Ronald Reagan had spirited the cause of parental choice in the 1980s, pressing for school vouchers and tax credits, the latter policy tool heavily benefiting well-off families who enrolled their children in tony private schools. Conservative foundations supported a variety of voucher experiments, such as awarding low-income parents portable chits that could be cashed at parochial or independent schools. The US Supreme Court ruled in 2002—a 5-4 decision— that parental vouchers awarded to religious schools were permissible under the Constitution. The court selectively cited (still uneven) evidence that voucher forms of choice raised the achievement of poor children. In Los Angeles, charter schools became a moderate alternative to vouchers, the latter idea defeated twice by California voters. Charter schools staked out a middle ground in the debate over choice and organizational diversity, keeping taxpayer dollars in the public system while reaping the innovations and promised efficacy of these deregulated campuses, which advocates claimed.[10]

Let's take stock of this diversifying garden of schools before delving into the underlying politics advanced by the civic challengers. The figure below displays the rising count of charter and pilot schools in Los Angeles from 2002 to 2016, as well as the commensurate death of many private schools. Only a handful of charters operated in the late 1990s, yet they grew to more than two hundred campuses by 2016 within the bounds of L.A. Unified. The count of conventional elementary and high schools climbed as the district's ambitious construction effort took shape. Semiautonomous pilot schools were first created in 2007, after Superintendent Ramón Cortines imported the model from Boston, and Latino activists won creation of the Belmont Zone of Choice (chapter 2). The number of pilot campuses, mostly small high schools, grew to fifty-one during the same period.

The pluralist push for diverse forms of public schools killed off many private schools. The count of these mostly small campuses fell from 488 to 355 in L.A. between 2002 and 2016. This decline hit sectarian schools especially hard. Catholic schools lost one-fifth of their students over the period, while Christian

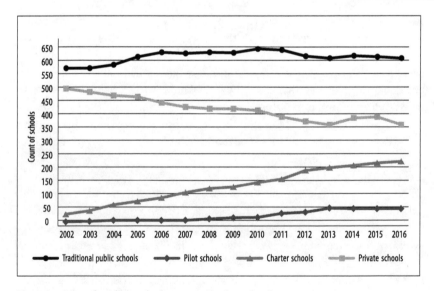

Changing mix of traditional, charter, and pilot schools, 2002–2016

academies and religious schools watched nearly half of their students disappear, families presumably migrating to tuition-free charter schools.[11] It proved ironic, given the religious Right's embrace of parental choice.

Overall, competitive pressure on conventional schools was growing across Los Angeles. After mapping the location of this diverse organizational array of schools in 2002, we observed four private high schools, on average, operating within a four-mile radius of each traditional public high school. By 2013, one-third of the competing campuses inside this radius were now charter schools, and another one-fourth, pilot schools. The total count of nearby competitors, by then, equaled six campuses on average.

This remarkable spread of nontraditional schools evolved in lumpy fashion. We can visualize the spatial arrangement of competitors—charter, pilot, and private schools—by mapping their locations relative to traditional district schools, as seen in the map on page 102. Each square locates a conventional elementary school, managed by the district. The size and darkness of the square indicates the count of competing schools located inside a two-mile radius in 2016. The average traditional elementary school faced three competing alternatives within this radius, the count ranging up to ten nontraditional schools in many communities.

Charter schools grew most rapidly in low-income parts of Los Angeles in the first decade of the twenty-first century. This countered worries that charters would exclusively serve affluent families, but it also put stiff market pressure on conventional schools in the poorest sections of L.A. We observed many competitors moving into the immigrant areas of Boyle Heights and East Los Angeles, and into the area bounded by downtown freeways, what Angelenos call the 5, 10, and 110 freeways. Rising competition can also be seen on the middle-class west side, close to Santa Monica (which runs its own district), as well as northwest of downtown, out to Koreatown, Hollywood, and the once Jewish section of Fairfax. Parts of the middle-class San Fernando Valley—now dotted with Asian, Latino, and white families—display high counts of nontraditional schools as well.

What political shifts, given life by the civic challengers, spurred this institutional diversity? *Who* were these movers and shakers, and *how* did they achieve such remarkable organizational change? Did this organizational variety lift the learning of students over time, or merely structure novel forms of inequality? These are the questions to which we turn next.

Magnet Schools: Place and Race

We begin with the rise of magnet schools. This organizational form was not invented by the civic challengers, but it hosted key features that charter school advocates would liberally borrow in the 1990s. Recall that magnet schools were first backed by the civil rights Left, as a device to desegregate public schools. Magnet campuses required the erasure of school attendance zones in which

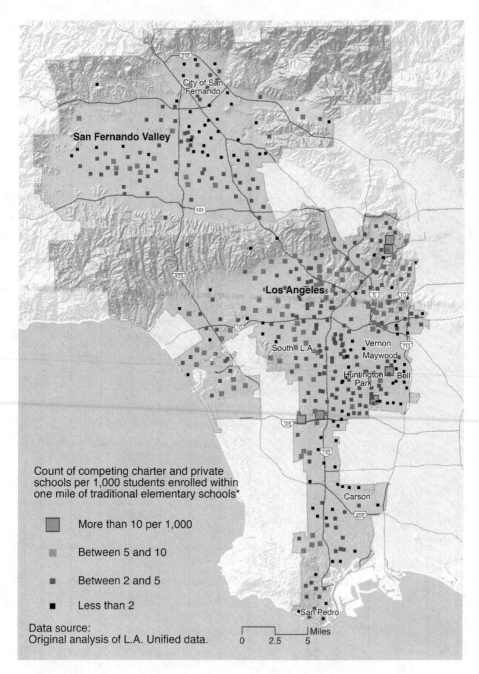

Count of competing charter and private schools per 1,000 students enrolled within one mile of traditional elementary schools*

More than 10 per 1,000

Between 5 and 10

Between 2 and 5

Less than 2

Data source:
Original analysis of L.A. Unified data.

Neighborhood competition among diverse schools, 2016

children were assigned to neighborhood schools. But this ensured that residential segregation was mirrored in the isolation of Black and Latino kids. Influential scholars at the time, such as James S. Coleman and Gary Orfield, urged liberalized choice for minority parents while hoping that white suburban families would stay put, accepting the integration of nearby schools.[12] Parental choice and crosstown transfer were viewed as necessary reforms to help achieve racial integration.

These curricular-themed campuses literally behave as magnets, offering such a compelling and rigorous climate for students that they attract a multiracial blend of families from across the city. Magnet schools have displayed impressive staying power in L.A. Unified. In 2020, more than 91,000 parents applied for half as many open slots across the district's nearly 300 magnet programs. More than 26,000 pupils attended magnets that focused on math, science, or digital skills. More than 7,500 studied music, visual art, or theater arts. Another 9,000 attended programs aimed to prepare students for service jobs: health occupations, child development, or tourism.[13] Magnets exemplify how a given institutional form can persist over decades, adapting to shifting contexts, even altering their raison d'être. These programs have long operated at the nexus of place and race, demonstrating how organizational variety allows the dominant form of schooling to mediate political conflict and diversifying preferences of parents.

Community Magnet Charter School, located a stone's throw from ritzy Bel Air, perched above the UCLA campus, offers a case in point. You can spot the school's rooftops from the Getty art center on the breezy west side of the city. Community Magnet enjoys autonomy from the downtown bureaucracy, granted "affiliated" charter status by the school board, meaning that teachers retain their health insurance and pension plan. Two-thirds of the school's enrollment is of white or Asian American heritage. Community Magnet accepted just 3 percent of all applicants in 2016; the waiting list stands at more than three thousand students.[14] Despite the comparatively privileged families it serves, remnants of institutional history persist. "Like all magnet schools in Los Angeles, admission is conducted through a priority point system based upon the Court-ordered reduction of the harms of racial isolation," the school's principal reports.[15] A bevy of buses heads east to downtown each morning, fetching pupils who come from low-income families, a two-hour round trip.

Magnet programs have proven to be chameleon-like, altering their aims and complexion to fit evolving demands. At first magnets stemmed from efforts of local civil rights leaders, white and Jewish liberals who pressed to desegregate L.A.'s racial checkerboard of schools. The desegregation case of *Crawford v. Los Angeles Board of Education* offered "the most spectacular litigation ever handled by a local county court," according to Orfield. "The largest effort to date . . . to adapt the common school ideal to a segregated and segmented city."[16] The trial court ruled in 1970 that L.A. Unified must desegregate, stemming from the ACLU's filing on behalf of Mary Crawford, who had been denied access to a nearby high school "for no reason other than the School Board's policy to ensure the separation of races," the court found.

It wasn't until 1978, after clearing the state supreme court on appeal, that Judge Paul Egly agreed to L.A. Unified's desegregation plan, which included creating magnet schools in largely white and Jewish areas of the San Fernando Valley, into which Black and Latino kids would be bused (the map in chapter 1 helps orient the reader geographically). The political firestorm that followed was fueled by the prospect of mandatory busing of white children from their attendance zones into predominately minority schools.

Groups like BUSTOP, led by Roberta Weintraub, vociferously opposed these efforts, kindling a stiff political blowback. Weintraub would be elected to the school board, then spearhead passage of ballot Proposition 1 in 1979, winning more than two-thirds of the vote statewide. This statewide ballot measure declared that district efforts to desegregate could not exceed the federal constitutional standard which "does not require integration, it only prohibits state-compelled segregation," said the appellate court in a ruling eventually upheld by the US Supreme Court in 1982.[17]

1970. The first Black students arrive by bus to integrate the Plymouth Elementary School in Monrovia, September 10. Photo by Fitzgerald Whitney and reprinted with permission of the *Los Angeles Times*

Meanwhile, magnet schools had gained widespread appeal among white parents in the Valley—provided they didn't serve *too many* minority youngsters and exercised selective admissions. Reflecting the adaptability of the magnet model, these campuses had become a way for white parents to better position their children relative to others. Since magnets were concentrated in the mostly white Valley, antibusing parents resolved to maximize the share of slots allocated for their own children. They had defeated mandatory busing. But voluntary integration efforts continued, especially with the spread of magnets: reaching eighty-six schools or programs by 1987 and retaining more than ten thousand families on waiting lists.

Earlier, the court had required that white students make up at least two-fifths of each magnet's enrollment to help meet desegregation goals. Now enrollment ratios approached 70 percent minority, 30 percent white. Weintraub, the antibusing warrior, fought a proposal before the school board that would have shifted the enrollment balance toward minority students. She preferred more slots for Valley kids, threatening to accelerate the pace of white flight from L.A. Unified. "I'm really tired of our Valley schools getting the shaft," Weintraub told fellow board members in 1987. If approved, "we will have a massive pullout of the middle class."[18]

A year later, Joseph Duff, an attorney for the National Association for the Advancement of Colored People, urged the district to create magnet programs inside Black and brown communities. "It's clear that magnets are so much better than comprehensive schools," he said. But the district believes that "magnets are too expensive and demand too much change in the system."[19] The institutional traces of magnets would eventually inform the rise of charter schools. They had gained widespread appeal, demonstrating that small-scale, mission-driven campuses often attracted a wide range of students.

Despite their institutional vitality, evidence remains sketchy on whether magnet programs lift student achievement, relative to conventional campuses. Magnet students in L.A. Unified outperform peers in conventional schools, yet this advantage is explained by differing family backgrounds and demographics, not necessarily by the value added of attending a magnet program, according to the district's own analysts.[20] Another recent study, drawing from waiting lists in a second urban district, found significant learning gains for both white pupils and students of color when they attended magnet campuses, relative to peers who lost in the admission lottery and remained in traditional schools.[21] Similar results stem from Connecticut's magnet schools.[22] Our research with Luke Dauter found that a student's geographic proximity to magnets raises the odds, on average, that they will not enroll in their conventional neighborhood school.[23] These schools hold magnetic power in attracting students, even when their relative efficacy remains weak.

Charter Schools

The civic challengers—after forsaking efforts at institutional change from within—began establishing charter schools in 1992. Newly financed by taxpayers yet run independently of central rules or labor contracts, these small and (at times) inventive campuses went head-to-head with L.A. Unified. To grasp the ideological heritage of these radical pluralists, it's instructive to visit Pacific Palisades High School. Opened in 1961, "Pali High" is nestled amid a green glade off Sunset Boulevard, a half-hour stroll to the beach or Riviera Country Club. The school had enjoyed a glamorous history prior to breaking free of the downtown district bureaucracy. Pali High was built atop the old All Hallows Farm, pastoral land owned by actress Virginia Conway, daughter of silent film star Francis X. Bushman. The spirit of the 1960s brought early fame to the campus, a blend of high-octane teens set against Vietnam protests and sexual adventure, prompting a *Time* magazine profile and television series.[24] Among its notable graduates are Christie Brinkley and Jeff Bridges. It's where producer George Lucas held auditions for *Star Wars* and the filming of *Modern Family* took place.

But the heralded campus had lost its luster by the 1990s. Soaring home prices had driven young families out of the Palisades. The superrich seemed too distracted to bear children. Remaining youths were migrating to pricey private schools. The resulting collapse in enrollment put Pali High on the chopping block for possible closure. Then, principal Merle Price and concerned parents advanced a heretical idea: take advantage of California's new charter school law and secede from the district. This ignited sharp debate inside Pali High, and among civic activists across L.A. If the school opted for charter status, would teachers keep their pension and health benefits and maintain seniority rights? "It frightens a lot of teachers frankly," history teacher Bill Winkes said at the time. The union was advising caution. Denise Rockwell Woods, vice president of UTLA, warned: "It looks good on paper, but how does it impact you—forever?"

Pali teachers decided to take the plunge, becoming L.A.'s first independent charter school network in 1993 (pulling its feeder schools into the charter fold) while retaining fringe benefits and seniority rights for teachers. The film giant DreamWorks funded the New Media Academy as a magnet program. Surfing became an option for physical education. Then, Pali High's leaders took another innovative turn, recruiting well-achieving Black and Latino kids from a wide region sweeping from downtown, west across working-class swaths of Los Angeles.

By 1994, 7 in 10 of Pali's 1,680 students were bused in from these sections of South or East L.A. Family demand for options like Pali was surging in low-income neighborhoods. (The district itself was busing 26,000 kids from overcrowded schools each day, prior to the district's new facilities boom.) This integration effort threw a lifeline to Pali High. "They're a little more strict here," 17-year-old Fernando Silva told an *L.A. Times* reporter. At Carver Junior High, his prior school in South Central, "the teachers let the kids walk out of the classroom, they didn't pay attention."[25] Two in every five students who attend Pali High today are Black or Latino.

Such contradictions and unforeseen twists marked this initial decade of charter school births. Reform-minded educator Yvonne Chan created a charter complex, pre-K to grade 2, in mostly Latino Pacoima, located at the north edge of the San Fernando Valley. Chan paid teachers 10 percent less than district peers, boosted attendance, negotiated a pass-through of state dollars, and ran a surplus of nearly $1 million in her first year, 1994. "It's really hard for me to imagine how they could do this," L.A. Unified's budget chief Mark Shrager said at the time. Yet Bob Scott, leading the Valley's movement to break free of the district, praised Chan's effort and allied charter activists. "It's not new to people in the private sector that you can be more effective with less bureaucracy."[26]

Charter Schools as Political Force

Richard Riordan, the incoming Republican mayor, would back pro-charter candidates for the school board and win big in 1999. Ouchi, aided by Harold M. Williams at the Getty Trust, had sketched a reform strategy for the new mayor. It involved deposing incumbent schools chief Ruben Zacarias, a veteran bureaucrat and popular Latino leader. Then, leveraging the new board majority, including new member Caprice Young, this bipartisan coalition approved scores of new charters, their count growing to 157 campuses a decade later.

Generalizing about the motivations or guiding ideology of charter advocates was proving difficult. Were they neoliberals bankrolled by corporatist reformers? Or, did these radical pluralists offer liberation for Black and brown families from a clumsy, even oppressive school bureaucracy? Green Dot Public Schools, for example, led by former Democratic organizer Steve Barr, aimed to create potent schools for poor kids in South L.A. In the fall of 2000, Barr opened Ánimo Inglewood Charter High School (Spanish for *spirited courage*), an "academically rigorous, few-frills school in rented classrooms," in the immigrant area of Lennox. Holding classes beneath the flight path into LAX, Ánimo proved hugely successful, boasting 99 percent attendance, laptops for kids, and soon boosted college attendance among its graduates. All this from kids whose parents were largely illiterate in English and first-generation Angelenos.[27]

Whenever prolabor members of the L.A. Unified board opposed a new charter petition, Barr mobilized marches by parents and teens, converging from poor sections of the city to protest downtown. He paid starting teachers more than the conventional system and encouraged the California Teachers Association to unionize his staff. Barr went directly to the statewide board of education to win approval for new charter campuses. He was aided by Reed Hastings, the Netflix founder, and now a heavy Democratic donor. "He's [Barr's] a lunatic, but in a good way," Young said in 2004. Riordan, by now Governor Arnold Schwarzenegger's education secretary, applauded Barr's militant efforts. "I think Steve's sensational, he's created some great schools."

Eli Broad gave $10.5 million to Green Dot in 2006, hoping that charter firms would assume management of conventional L.A. Unified schools. "This is not about a hostile takeover and throwing everybody off campuses," Barr said at the time. "It's about doing an assessment of what's working and what's not." Cortines, at that time education advisor to Democratic mayor Antonio Villaraigosa, was impressed by Barr's operation as well, and "very much open to partnering with Green Dot."[28] A majority of teachers at violence-ridden Locke High School voted in favor of being acquired by Green Dot in 2007, what proved to be a daunting challenge for Barr's organization.

To maintain social order, Barr's mostly white teachers, fresh out of Teach for America, issued "excruciating concrete instructions to students, telling them exactly where to put their pens and what to do," as Alexander Russo reports in his book *Stray Dogs, Saints, and Saviors.*[29] Teachers awarded points to students for good behavior or homework completion. Still, some students sat in the back and "pulled their hoodies up over their heads . . . snuck headphones into their ears," as Russo describes. Green Dot staff harped on orderly behavioral norms in the first year, then began to engage errant teens. Daily attendance climbed; fights and bullying incidents declined.

Wealthy Democrats, including Broad and Hastings, then consolidated their growing political power within EdVoice, a new civic group based in the state capital, which began channeling millions of dollars in campaign contributions to local candidates pledging support for charter schools. The maturing California Charter Schools Association advised parents and local activists on how to secure facilities and set up budget systems. In 2020, Bill Bloomfield—after growing rich on laundromats and internet servers—went after board members who opposed charter expansion. He sent $4.5 million to the association's war chest to defeat a prolabor candidate, falsely tying her to a child abuse scandal and defenders of gun rights.[30] These pro-market advocates among the new pluralists—once complaining about how entrenched interests had a stranglehold on public schools—were now buying their influence on the civic stage.

The wealthy civic challengers, gaining political strength and economic capital from the 1990s forward, did follow corporatist ideologies. These core tenets center on the alleged inefficiency of vast public institutions: taxpayers put more and more money into, say, public schools, which in turn display thin results and slight responsiveness to the client's demand for quality and accountability. Idealized market competition is often the knee-jerk remedy from this private sector perspective. Then, critics of this neoliberal position tend to clump dot-com donors, like Hastings and Broad, into this camp, along with those expressing antipathy toward government or white voters' disaffection with programs that fail to lift families of color.[31] Yet, the plot thickens in Los Angeles, where many pluralists on the equity-minded Left began to adopt neoliberal logics for challenging L.A. Unified, pressing to build diverse forms of schooling.

The Democratic Left Embraces Charter Schools

These civic challengers sensed a larger political opening when Antonio Villaraigosa decided to run for mayor of Los Angeles in 2005. Former legislator and leader of the state assembly, Villaraigosa had grown frustrated with the glacial pace of change inside city schools. He came with considerable street cred: raised by a single mom, authentically from the East L.A. barrio. This handsome and high-energy leader reached out to Latina leader Yolie Flores and Green Dot ally Ben Austin, a reform-minded operative who had worked for Mayor Riordan, then Hollywood director and preschool enthusiast Rob Reiner. Villaraigosa was drifting apart from old labor friends and moving closer to grassroots pluralists like Flores, Maria Brenes, and United Way's Ryan Smith. Villaraigosa began voicing support for liberalized parental choice and charter school expansion. Hefty campaign contributions soon began to arrive from the dot-com Democrats.

Villaraigosa's first job out of college was to organize teachers for the UTLA. "I cut my teeth working for the union," Villaraigosa told me in 2010. "I cultivated these young teachers who had come to these schools to change the world." But his affection for labor had turned sour, an estrangement that would dog Villaraigosa for years to come. (He lost a run for governor in 2018 to a prolabor Democrat, despite receiving another $7 million from Hastings.) His about-face shocked the California Teachers Association, which had spent millions to ensure his rise in the California legislature. Instead, Villaraigosa pivoted to broaden the coalition of new pluralists—uniting pro-equity advocates with big-money Democrats—then push the spread of charter campuses.[32] Villaraigosa continued to consult with Eli Broad. "The board is made up of political wannabes," Broad told me in 2009. "The only time we have seen dramatic change in urban education is when you have mayoral control."

But Villaraigosa's attempt to take over L.A. Unified—which was approved by Governor Schwarzenegger in 2006—was overturned in a court challenge spearheaded by the unions, who feared the mayor's pro-choice agenda. Villaraigosa quickly swiveled to pursue his Plan B: raising campaign dollars for board candidates who would back his reform agenda. "We have got to move away from a model where school boards are defenders of a failed status quo," Villaraigosa told me, "where the unions just control the board." Three fresh candidates, each aligned with Villaraigosa, won election to the board in 2008, thanks to the $3 million raised from Broad and his pro-charter allies.

Yolie Flores, the new petite and soft-spoken board member, proved to be a Latina Saul Alinsky of sorts. Flores told me she felt like "the house was on fire, walking around [the halls of L.A. Unified] not knowing whether to cry or scream." Meanwhile, the mayor urged appointment of his education aide, Cortines, as the new schools chief. Hollywood mogul Casey Wasserman added a cool $3 million to support a cadre of bright young architects of reform inside the bureaucracy. By the spring of 2009, the mayor's platform was taking shape behind closed doors. It accented the need to decentralize school management, letting a thousand organizational flowers blossom, run by school leaders with autonomy from the district bureaucracy.

Flores didn't fully anticipate the political blowback that would come from UTLA. At first she couldn't discern the chorus that was being shouted by an auditorium filled with second graders at Annendale Elementary School, situated in a middle-class area just west of Pasadena. But then she heard all too clearly, "Shame on you, shame on you," as the youngsters shouted with quizzical expressions, unsure of why they had been told to greet Flores this way. "I was shocked, I couldn't believe it," Flores recalled. Union activists had wound up these young children to deliver their opposition to budget cuts and Villaraigosa's reforms.

The sides were drawn, pitting youthful Latino leadership against the entrenched teachers' union, led by the hot-tempered Irishman, A. J. Duffy. He was furious in 2009 with what he saw as political opportunism. "Everybody around the city is asking the question, why has he [Villaraigosa] broken with his roots?" Duffy asked during our interview. "Maybe he feels he's got the support of enough billionaires." If only "the board fired some of the people who were in the way of reform," Duffy argued. Pointing his finger at "Arne Duncan and the president [Obama], pushing more and more charters, [while] virtually all the data is saying that charters are not better than regular public schools."[33]

Flores would gain the board majority needed to approve a radical plan to decentralize who ran schools in Los Angeles, passed in the summer of 2009. She aimed to transfer up to 251 schools—one-fourth of the district's campuses—to independent operators. Flowing from her earlier pitch to shrink the size of schools, Flores was now keen on liberalizing school choice, arguing it's "morally wrong to deny parents" options. Meanwhile, charter hawks like Austin were eager to take ownership of sparkling new campuses. "My thinking has been more aligned to Paul Hill's work on moving toward a portfolio approach to public schools," Flores told me. "I started moving in this direction with the Small Schools Resolution last year [passed by the board]," Flores said. She accented doing "something dramatically different to turn around failing schools . . . to engage parents and the community in the process," without relying solely on charter schools.[34]

Yet, a telling vote shifted when Flores's pro-choice proposal went before the board. Mónica García, politically rooted in Latino Boyle Heights, threw her weight behind neighborhood pilot schools, emerging from Inner City Struggle's earlier advocacy of the Belmont Zone of Choice. The legitimacy of charter firms had suffered in García's eyes, when they preferred to assume control of new facilities rather than fixing troubled schools. After succeeding in moving the board majority to back pilot schools, Maria Brenes at Inner City Struggle explained: "Some of our best teachers rolled up their sleeves and developed quality plans." As for charter schools? "A lot of folks out there were just not grounded in the community; [they] underestimated our organizing capacity in East L.A.," Brenes said. Mayor Villaraigosa took direct control of a handful of schools, forming a new nonprofit—the Partnership for Los Angeles Schools—which continues to run a charter-like network of campuses to this day.

Higher Achievement, Sharper Stratification

The *Los Angeles Times* headline rang out with upbeat news for the radical challengers in 2003: "Charters' Test Gains Higher, Study Shows." This early research had revealed that California's 372 charter schools largely served pupils from low-income families and lifted their learning curves, relative to peers attending traditional public schools (TPS). The results "show great promise for the future of charter schools," claimed Margaret Raymond of Stanford University.[35] But a few buildings away on campus, statistician David Rogosa soon added new test scores from the state, and instead found miniscule differences in growth rates.[36] The game was on: scholarly efforts to discover which sector—charter or conventional schools—best elevates student learning, net any prior differences in family attributes that likely explain achievement differences as well.

Raymond returned a decade later with thicker results specific to Los Angeles, after tracking the district's students from 2008 to 2012. By this time, more than 220 charter schools were in operation inside L.A. Unified, enrolling more than 82,000 youngsters. Nearly three-fifths of all charter students were of Latino heritage, and just under 70 percent qualified for free meals. These storefronts and humble campuses had sprouted up way beyond the privileged west side, as seen earlier at Pali High, popping up across stretches of South and East L.A. Raymond offered a methodological advance, matching charter attendees to children who had attended the same feeder schools and displayed nearly identical demographics and prior test scores. This was not a true experiment but did provide a quasi-experimental strategy to validly estimate differences in growth curves between groups.[37]

Raymond discovered modestly steeper gains among charter students, compared with peers attending TPS. The advantage in terms of calibrated effect sizes equaled just 0.07 of a standard deviation (*SD*) in reading scores and 0.11 *SD* in mathematics. Such differences are not usually worth writing home about. Yet, Raymond calculated that the math advantage equated to seventy-two days of additional instruction for the average charter pupil (without regard to grade level). She also found stronger effects for charter campuses run by a management organization, relative to mom-and-pop charter schools. The achievement advantage was strongest in math for students who remained in a charter for three years, moving up to 0.26 *SD*. This magnitude equals what 4-year-olds gain from attending a quality preschool, relative to stay-at-home children, or about three times the magnitude of lowering class sizes within affordable ranges. Importantly, Raymond found that Latino students from poorer families enjoyed the strongest benefits from attending charters, relative to matched peers remaining in TPS. Asian, Black, and white charter attendees displayed no achievement advantage compared with peers in traditional schools.

We decided to rethink Raymond's framing of the question, first asking whether charter schools in Los Angeles attract differing students, relative to those remaining in TPS. We had earlier uncovered how conversion and start-up charters were serving somewhat different students and attracted distinct kinds of teachers. Working with Doug Lauen at the University of North Carolina and Luke Dauter, my Berkeley colleague, we followed more than 53,000 L.A. Unified students as they moved through elementary school over six years, 2002–2008. About 1,500 of the student sample attended a charter school.[38] Among kids who moved into a charter, half came from families with parents who had not completed high school; almost three quarters were of Latino heritage.

These early differences between the sectors proved stark. The charters opting to affiliate with L.A. Unified downtown—so-called conversion charters like Pali High—hosted much larger concentrations of middle-class kids. White youngsters made up two-thirds of their enrollments, and 11 percent were of Asian heritage. Two-fifths of all affiliated charter enrollees reported that at least one parent held a graduate degree. Test scores in math averaged nearly one *SD* above the mean score for their TPS counterparts. While some affiliated charter high schools reached out to poor families, this did not occur for charter elementary schools. They mostly sealed off their borders, hoping to preserve their middle-class position in what was becoming a segmented field of diverse schools. Pupil growth curves varied wildly among individual charter schools. Raymond found that in just over half of all charters, students performed no better or worse than nearby peers in TPS.

We also found traces of charter schools admitting higher-achieving children, relative to the distribution of children in TPS. This inequity did fade in the study's fourth year as more new charters were established in low-income areas. In the first year (baseline), charter students early in the grade cycle (grade 2) already outperformed TPS peers by 0.14 *SD*. Overall, we found a significant yet declining level of skimming by conversion charters among elementary schools. Meanwhile, the civic challengers kept attracting political capital and popular appeal among L.A. parents through the 2000s. But these early findings suggested that the charter sector was further isolating high- from low-achieving children.

In a second study, we extended Raymond's analysis with more recent data, covering the 2007–2011 period and joined by Hyo Jeong Shin at the Educational Testing Service. This time we tracked 97,000 students spread over elementary, middle, and high schools. We distinguished between kids who began the period already enrolled in a charter school (*stayers*)—at grades 2, 6, or 8 to capture their achievement level as students began a grade cycle—versus peers who started within a TPS, then switched to a charter school (*switchers*). Estimates of the learning gains tied to charter attendance are most valid for the switchers, since we know their achievement level *prior to* entering a charter.[39]

Our findings proved consistent with Raymond's earlier results, revealing a modest charter advantage. This was empirically discernible for kids who switched from a TPS into a charter *middle school*, their gains in reading and math outpacing traditional peers by one-sixth to one-fifth *SD*, respectively. When middle schoolers switched into a charter *high school*, they displayed significant learning gains as well, although the magnitudes were quite small, about one-tenth of a *SD*. When Katrina Bulkley and colleagues followed achievement trends in "semiautonomous" campuses, including affiliated charters, L.A. Partnership, and site-managed schools (the latter under a separate contract with UTLA), they found a 0.40 *SD* gain in achievement between 2011 and 2015.[40] We do not know whether pupil composition changed during that period.

Equally consequential, we observed a tendency for charter educators to skim stronger pupils inside district-affiliated *and* start-up charters. Selection of this metaphorical cream surfaced among conversion elementary charters, which served a lower share of Latino students (65 percent) relative to TPS (84 percent Latino). Two-fifths of kids attending conversion charters were from middle-class homes, compared with just 16 percent in TPS. Selectivity was strong for charter high schools as well: pupils in eighth grade, *prior to entering high school*, already achieved 0.35 *SD* higher in reading when compared with TPS peers. Almost two-fifths of all pupils in start-ups came from families where parents had completed some college, compared with just one-fourth of TPS youngsters. Prior-year scores for students attending the four conversion charter high schools were 0.45 *SD* above the starting scores for traditional students, even after matching kids on feeder schools and child-level demographics.

Overall, this research details how charter schools in Los Angeles do serve many low-income families. But kids whose parents navigate the education market with greater agility are more likely to enter a charter school. One advantage of our analytics is the focus on how pupils are stratified along lines of prior achievement, not simply by race or social class. Evidence exists from outside Los Angeles that some charter operators also filter out kids that misbehave or those with learning disabilities, raising average performance in a rather heinous way.[41] Critics of our study, even discerning analysts at the California Charter Schools Association, argued that a portion of our baseline scores resulted from pupils' earliest years in charter preschools or initial grade levels, a point that requires further study.[42] We do not infer that charter staff intentionally discriminate against low-achieving students. Much of the skimming likely occurs through self-selection, animated by parents who seek out options and push to score a charter slot. Whatever the underlying dynamic, the unequal effects remain.

Profiles of teaching staff also differ between these competing sectors. We found that three-fifths of all teachers in conversion high schools in L.A. were of white ethnicity, relative to 45 percent in start-ups and 48 percent in TPS. Less than one-fifth of all start-up elementary teachers had gained tenure, compared with almost two-thirds of peers in conversion charters and 86 percent in traditional schools. Charter operators tend to hire younger teachers and provide little job security. Many arrive with slight teaching experience, coming from white, majority-culture backgrounds in a district where Latinos make up four-fifths of all students.

Expanding the count of charter schools represented the leading beachhead for civic challengers. The romance among strange political bedfellows grew deeper, uniting grassroots Latina activists, like Brenes and Flores, to wealthy Democrats, such as Broad and Hastings. One might cast this coalition as neoliberal. But agitators on the political Left, like Antonio Villaraigosa or Steve Barr, held little affection for markets or the lions of capitalism downtown. They did press to decentralize control of schools, weakening the central bureaucracy, in hopes of diversifying the forms and effectiveness of public schools. Few doubt that these radical challengers succeeded in creating a competitive force, one that increasingly jams L.A. Unified to innovate or scale back. Charter proponents also demonstrate how the state can reward parents who seek out what's best for their kids, as seen through their eyes. On the other hand, we find that charter enthusiasts have created a parallel sector that often isolates low- from high-achieving students—in an educational institution that was already severely segregated.

Pilot Schools: If You Can't Beat Them, Join Them

The charter school insurgency spurred an unexpected political shift: it opened up room for loyal insiders to advance novel forms of schooling while remaining under the L.A. Unified umbrella. The multiplying, plural nodes of civic authority began fueling *organizational pluralism*. Flores and Villaraigosa had led their own palace revolt inside the district, voting to transfer scores of schools to independent managers, from charter firms to progressive educators who remained inside the system. This also advanced Superintendent Cortines's earlier push for semiautonomous pilot schools. Feeling the competitive heat from charters, union leaders opted to cooperate with Cortines, then John Deasy, to expand this charter-like model of decentralized control. Principals of these small-scale pilot schools gained authority to hire and fire their teachers, along with (constrained) discretion over how to allocate their budgets. Yet, unlike charter schools, pilot teachers remained as district employees and union members, retaining health insurance and pension benefits.

Loyal insiders also swung toward pilot schools, given their roots in largely immigrant communities, small campuses often created by inventive teachers with social justice commitments to surrounding families. These youthful teachers told me how they mistrusted both downtown district bureaucrats *and* charter companies. Teachers emerged, like those at Garfield High School, arguing that smaller and personalized schools would better serve poor kids and their parents. These teachers were behind the formation of *New TLA*, the insurgent group that successfully challenged UTLA's stubborn posture. Garfield High's enrollment had soared above four thousand students. The school was home to Jaime Escalante, the inspiring Bolivian math teacher portrayed by Edward James Olmos in the 1988 film *Stand and Deliver*. But replicating Escalante's success proved difficult as enrollments skyrocketed and dropout rates soared.

Latino activists had long advocated for smaller, more caring high schools, harking back to the magnet school movement. By 1999, L.A. Unified's massive construction program yielded capital and political space to rethink the size and character of high schools. The Belmont Education Collaborative, led by Maria Casillas, arose to amplify the voices of other Latina leaders. "Powerful institutions . . . play a high-stakes game . . . with high-powered players," Casillas said at the time. But the "essential question" remained: "Who do the parents have as their voice?"[43] First- and second-generation Latino families had suffered from severely overcrowded schools and high teacher turnover during the prior decade. At the same time, planners sketched new campuses for the Pico-Union and East L.A. neighborhoods, prompting the opportunity to diversify the missions and teacher profiles for area high schools.

When I asked teacher Brian Fritch why the pilot school model was gaining steam in predominantly Latino East L.A., he simply said: "Because teachers are demanding them." A history teacher at Garfield, Fritch worked with colleagues to gain UTLA's support of this charter-like model. His youthful generation held few historical roots in the labor movement; they were more invested in winning equitable resources and raising students' social-historical awareness inside human-scale schools. He and others began speaking out publicly against UTLA's habit of protecting mediocre teachers and opposition to devolving school control. Fritch went on to help devise the cluster of pilot schools that opened in 2007 at the newly constructed Esteban Torres Complex, serving immigrant and second-generation Latino families.

The birth of pilot schools in Los Angeles illustrates how policy ideas and organizational models float across civic circles, gaining adherents in unpredicted ways. A potent mix of civic players had coalesced around the notion of small high schools, spearheaded by Jeanne Fauci, who you met in chapter 2. The Co-alition of Essential Schools, led by Ted Sizer at Brown University, formed ties with the L.A. group Civitas, along with UCLA's Karen Hunter Quartz, a teacher trainer and reform thinker. Sizer's group brokered ties with small-schools ini-tiatives in New York City and with Dan French in Boston, who was instrumen-tal in creating pilot schools there. Casillas, now director of Families in Schools in Los Angeles, yet another civic group, provided the missing piece of this organ-izing puzzle. She could gather Latino activists around the table, then advance the institutional reforms articulated by Fauci and Hunter Quartz.

Richard Alonzo, L.A. Unified's area director in the Pico-Union community, decided to work the inside game with the outside pluralists. "The community could have taken the easier route and turned to charter schools," Alonzo said at the time. But "we want to bring change from inside the district, not try to im-prove it on the outside."[44] The rising threat from charter proponents was the institutional elephant in the room. Latina activists had long yearned for diverse and responsive schools for their neighborhoods. Eventually some forty differing nonprofits and neighborhood associations in the low-income district of Pico-Union came together, establishing the Belmont Zone of Choice in 2007. Beyond abolishing attendance zones for kids (as advocated a generation earlier by mag-net school advocates), Cortines agreed to build the first ten pilot schools, offering small and, hopefully, engaging campuses.

Evidence remains scarce on whether pilot schools have contributed to the overall gain in achievement enjoyed by students over the past quarter century. One complication stems from the location of early pilot schools, concentrated in poor and mostly immigrant parts of the city. Pilots in L.A. do not serve a ran-dom distribution of kids. We know more about pilot school effects in Boston. The early growth of 19 pilot schools in Boston has been examined carefully by MIT economist Atila Abdulkadiroğlu and colleagues, tracking 6,228 pilot stu-dents between 2001 and 2009.[45] His team found that organizational features of pilots differed significantly from conventional public schools. Pilot teachers were much younger, on average, than peers laboring in TPS. Pilot staff worked longer hours in order to extend the school day. But these scholars did not detect any value-added advantage of attending a pilot school. After taking into account dif-ferences in family background, pilots failed to buoy kids' learning curves, com-pared with typical growth observed among peers in traditional schools.

2015. Students rally in support of the Equity Is Justice Resolution, which eventually sent hundreds of millions of dollars to high-needs schools in the L.A. Unified School District. Photo by Christina House and reprinted with permission of the *Los Angeles Times*

Moving along this research line, my team assembled data for students entering and moving through pilot high schools from 2007 to 2013. Led by Berkeley economist Caitlin Kearns, we compared the trajectories of 7,390 students entering ninth grade inside a pilot high school, compared with just over 137,000 teens entering TPS. We took into account each pupil's achievement level at the end of eighth grade in order to isolate the discrete benefits of pilot schools during the ninth grade. We also tracked all students into the tenth grade to examine the stickiness of pilots in boosting pupil retention. Our findings proved disappointing on the achievement front—observing no discernible advantage in learning gains among those attending a pilot campus in their first year of high school, relative to the learning curves of TPS peers, after statistically matching the two groups on observed background characteristics and prior achievement.[46]

We did find, as expected, large differences in the family background of pilot students, relative to TPS pupils. Most pilot schools—despite fanning out widely across L.A. Unified—remained in heavily immigrant or second-generation Latino neighborhoods. Young teens entering pilot high schools were more likely to be of Latino heritage, speak Spanish at home, and to be raised by less educated parents, relative to traditional peers. Pilot students lived in census tracts in which the family poverty rate stood at 28 percent, compared with 20 percent in the average tract for L.A. Unified students. Median household incomes equaled $39,500 for pilot students and $47,600 for pupils district-wide (2016 dollars). This is why statistical matching is key when estimating achievement differences between sectors.

One encouraging finding is that students entering pilot schools were more likely to remain in the same school as they progressed, compared with higher transfer and dropout rates exhibited by TPS peers. This is good news for a district that suffers from declining enrollment. We also pinpointed several remarkably effective pilot high schools, where pupil growth exceeded that of traditional counterparts. A second research group found that pilot students enter four-year colleges at significantly higher rates, compared with graduates of TPS high schools.[47] This "stickier" holding power of pilot schools appears to be tied to supportive relationships found inside these small organizations. Analyzing school climate data in 2016, Delia Estrada found that pilots display higher daily attendance rates and achieve nearly identical graduation rates, despite serving much poorer families. Estrada also detailed how pilot students report more robust ties with their teachers, compared with pupils attending conventional schools.[48]

Accumulating Gains from Organizational Diversity?

The civic challengers, by stirring family demand for charter schools, even in L.A.'s poorest parts, enjoyed rising popular legitimacy and political clout. Their steady press for school options led to a new normal—freeing parents from confining attendance zones and diversifying the range of schools to choose from. This radical edge of the pluralist movement also lent newfound influence to loyal insiders, those pushing to expand magnet and pilot schools, as well as dual-language campuses. One may disagree with market ideology or the neoliberal instincts of charter proponents. But they did shift the center of the reform debate, winning credibility for institutional diversity, decentralizing control out to schools, and rethinking the character of social relations inside. Even the teachers' union, following their 2019 strike, won new funding for so-called community schools, speaking to families holistically and offering health services, parent literacy programs, and allied supports. Institutional diversity seemed to beget ever-more-novel social forms.

Pluralists and Power

Which brings us to one final way of gauging the motivations of, and institutional gains accomplished by, the civic challengers. That is, we can step back and take stock of this proliferation of organizational diversity writ large. Rather than evaluating effects for kids or teachers stemming from each separate sector—charters, magnets, pilots, or dual-language programs—we can assess how this diversifying garden of schools touches students and families. Research conducted by fellow scholars helps us tackle this analytical challenge.

Encouraging results stem from work on proliferating zones of school choice (ZOCs) across Los Angeles. Following the popularity of the Belmont Zone of Choice, district leaders begin centering resources on the variegated spectrum of schools, within demarcated areas, most situated in low-income parts of the city. L.A. Unified staff—working with leaders from charter, magnet, and pilot sectors—pitched thicker information for parents and sharpened organizational identities across seventeen such zones by 2021. Many schools within ZOCs enjoy an excess number of applicants. This allows researchers the chance to exploit lottery admissions. Economists Chris Campos and Caitlin Kearns tracked students, 2013–2019, who applied to at least one oversubscribed school, comparing those randomly admitted by lottery against pupils not drawn, returning to their nearby TPS.[49] This approximates a true experiment, at least with regard to achievement effects that can be generalized to oversubscribed schools inside zones of choice.

This research team found that students gaining admission to a high-demand school displayed stronger growth in math and English language arts, about one-fifth *SD* higher, relative to peers who lost school lotteries. These scholars also discovered that scores climbed, on average, for pupils attending schools within ZOCs, compared with schools outside any zone of choice, what they termed a local "market effect." That is, the expansion of ZOCs tends to boost student achievement within them, along with gains tied specifically to high-demand schools. One complication is that a variety of institutional changes were unfolding inside many zones, including new school funding and the spread of pilot schools. This study gets us closer to underlying mechanisms but fails to identify what specific changes elevated pupils inside these zones.

More sobering findings emerge from the Public School Choice (PSC) initiative, pushed through by Yolie Flores and Antonio Villaraigosa, and implemented during a four-year period starting in 2009. This massive alteration of who and how nearly one hundred schools were managed invited careful study. After all, it represented a huge political victory for the radical wing of the new pluralists. Could this broadscale effort to diversify and decentralize the education institution move the dial on student achievement? After all, this reform intended to spur "diverse options for high-quality educational environments, with excellent teaching and learning, for students' academic success," Flores promised at the time.[50] By empowering school design teams inside neighborhoods, parents and educators were to "play a more active role in shaping and expanding the educational options." Decentralized design was to foster ever-rich civic activism inside neighborhoods.

Julie Marsh and Katharine Strunk, professors at the University of Southern California, set out to empirically gauge the effects presumably set in motion by this provocative reform. During the first year of implementation, Superintendent Deasy and the board approved extra funding for 28 newly managed *relief* schools, including pilots and autonomous campuses designed by inventive educators. Another 14 *turnaround* schools were selected with input from various stakeholders. These included reconfigured campuses, staffed by a new roster of teachers. Over the next four years, some 131 schools won "targeted support" under the PSC initiative. But did this bold experiment foster democratic deliberation on the ground or boost student learning?

Marsh and Strunk selected sixteen school cases to observe, including how neighborhood actors—educators, nonprofits, charter firms, and union reps— came together to sketch their brand-new or reconstituted school. Reformers focused on building the capacity of parents and nonprofits to craft new school designs in the initial year of implementation, 2009–2010. The district contracted with several groups, such as United Way, to prepare facilitators of community meetings, even to canvass residents on their preferences for which groups or educators should take over management of PSC schools.

Marsh and Strunk found, perhaps not surprisingly, that most participating parents focused on their child's fate inside traditional campuses, holding little experience in rethinking the wider character of schooling. Disconnects between families and professional reformers, including nonprofit activists, were commonly observed; at times, they were literally speaking different languages. Some parents described these sessions, facilitated by the district or outside firms, as "dog and pony shows" or a "sell job."[51] Deasy complained: "We were still vexed by the low turnout at many of these meetings, [and] it was challenging to go deeper in our conversations." District officials and their nonprofit facilitators tried to learn and regroup. By year three, the research team observed that "eight of 11 Phase II schools demonstrated highly interactive, two-way parent-to-parent conversations during workshops." Organizers were explicitly nudging parents "to consider the interests of all students," Marsh and Strunk reported.

The USC research team reported how established institutions and political alliances tended to dominate planning and implementation steps. Well-intentioned educators, professional nonprofit staffers, and charter operators displayed greater knowledge and social authority when shaping the contours of new schools, compared with often deferential parents. The PSC initiative did succeed in pulling a wider range of players into local civic spaces. But Marsh and Strunk concluded that power differentials were difficult to alter. Gaps in experience, discourse, and material resources proved difficult to bridge, no matter how well meaning the reform technicians.

This resembles political scientist Clarence Stone's argument that "public policy impacts depend upon complementary actions of non-governmental sources," like nonprofits and volunteer groups. But poor and unsophisticated parents, for instance, rarely meet "the substantial threshold tests . . . that [make] even grassroots politics accessible," he wrote, based on fieldwork in Atlanta.[52] The road to school-level innovation required patient deliberation among various neighborhood players in Los Angeles. But district officials tacitly pursued an *engineered strategy* for fostering new forms of schooling. It became a devolution of authority organized from on high, what UCLA scholar Joel Handler skeptically calls "down from bureaucracy."[53]

Marsh and Strunk then asked whether this district-led reform served to lift student achievement over time. They carefully compared 23 schools participating in the PSC program against about 130 schools that came close to being selected under the district's review procedure, offering a credible comparison group. The USC team tracked change in achievement over a three-year period. Whether it's fair to gauge effects on student learning after a short period of implementation, especially when animated by widely varying organizing efforts and observed across scores of neighborhoods, remains a worthy question. Marsh and Strunk did endeavor to identify mediating practices or mechanisms operating between site-level authority and student outcomes.

They found that participating schools discernibly boosted kids' learning curves in reading among the cohort of schools selected to participate in year two, compared with schools that barely missed winning PSC dollars. But by year three, students attending PSC-designated schools did a bit worse than comparison schools. Digging into possible mediators, Marsh and Strunk found that schools selected in year two appeared to benefit from lessons learned from year-one schools. The second-round schools discernibly purged teachers seen as mediocre, the district afforded more time and money to prepare the new staff, and principals reported greater success in fostering a coherent school climate, relative to comparison schools.[54]

The PSC initiative did result in a pair of lasting benefits. It demonstrated how civic challengers could succeed at moderating the legitimacy and regulatory reach of the central bureaucracy. Then, as district leaders allocated dollars to a diversifying range of semiautonomous schools, decentralized control of even conventional campuses became more credible. The logic of site-based governance would blend organizational diversity and liberalized parental choice— no longer a heretical idea advanced only by radical outsiders. Even cautious union leaders agreed to greater flexibility for magnet and pilot schools, early learning centers, and newly formed community schools. Several years later, in 2019, another superintendent, finance banker Austin Beutner, circulated a draft plan for decentering management authority out to "regional directors" across L.A. Unified, chartered to oversee daily operations and, once again, spark innovation in their schools.

Lifting All Boats?

Finally, we might ask whether the *cumulative effects* of liberalized parental choice and organizational diversity contributed to the overall rise in pupil achievement over the past quarter century. Perhaps the district-wide shift toward market dynamics and alternative forms of schooling did motivate educators to innovate and push harder to improve.[55] Yet, pinpointing the causal direction between school diversity and pupil outcomes offers a challenging analytical task. Even in working-class areas of Los Angeles, those who plan where to site a new charter school typically map out safe routes for walking to campus or identify families in nicer apartments, parents with the resources necessary to shop for alternative schools. But if charters are planted in areas populated by more secure or assertive families, then the mere presence of this "treatment" *stems from* household features, and the charter remedy does not necessarily *precede* kids' learning. Estimating causal effects thus becomes a slippery exercise.

One study of charter competition in New York City took into account instances in which a charter opened near a TPS. Temple University economist Sarah Cordes then gauged whether students attending the traditional school benefited from competitive pressure exercised by the new charter school. She found small yet significant gains in reading and math for pupils in proximal TPS. Cordes also discovered stronger effects when the charter was colocated on a single campus with the traditional public school—where competitive dynamics were viscerally felt. She then asked about the mechanisms through which traditional pupils benefited, finding that traditional schools lost enrollment over time to the charters, while TPS resources did not decline under state funding rules, essentially raising per-pupil spending.[56] Examining competitive effects from Florida's statewide voucher program, economists David Figlio and Cassandra Hart also found stronger achievement benefits for TPS students when schools faced nearby competitors, relative to traditional schools located far from charter or private schools.[57]

My team, back in Los Angeles, attempted to detect achievement gains from neighborhood competition among the widening variety of school forms over the period from 2002 to 2013. We discovered that stiffer competition—gauged by the number of charter and private schools surrounding an anchoring traditional school—held modestly *negative* effects on the learning curves of TPS pupils. We mapped the counts of charter and private schools inside a two-mile radius of each traditional elementary school within L.A. Unified's domain, and within three miles of each traditional high school over the eleven-year period. We then associated change in the count of competing schools with change in pupil achievement at each corresponding TPS.

Students attending traditional *elementary schools* achieved at slightly higher levels when their campus was surrounded by *fewer* charter or private schools, compared with peers attending schools that faced higher counts of competing schools. Similarly, the test scores of traditional pupils inched upward at small to modest levels of magnitude in cases where the count of nearby competitors *declined* over the period. Effects were estimated in typical econometric fashion after taking into account a host of pupil characteristics, prior achievement levels, and the fixed effect stemming from each school, capturing unobserved confounders. Declining levels of competition were observed as private schools died off. We observed 803 such organizational deaths over the period. Results for pupils attending traditional L.A. *high schools* that were proximal to dying private schools proved quite similar: their students displayed gains in achievement.[58] More work is required to ensure results are not biased by shifting demographic features of students among these competing sectors.

Still when these findings are weighed alongside the modest, yet upbeat, results from charter schools, it does suggest that gains in one sector may come at the expense of students enrolled in another. More effective teachers may be migrating to charter or private schools. Or, student peer effects may be observed in these nontraditional sectors, given the creaming of stronger pupils or those presenting fewer behavior problems. We arrive again at the pluralist's paradox: Civic challengers succeeded in propagating a variety of school forms, some of which paid off for kids and families. But this widening institutional differentiation may mitigate against making progress in conventional public schools, introducing novel forms of institutional stratification.

Lessons Learned from Civic Challengers

Drawing a sharp circle around the early civic challengers, along with their ideological roots, seemed easy in the 1990s. Civil disruptors like Bill Ouchi and Caprice Young felt burned by labor leaders and education officialdom—conserving actors who lacked the will or capacity to revive public schools in Los Angeles. Once corporate donors, such as Bloomberg, Broad, and Hastings, threw their capital behind charter schools, neoliberal ideals and faith in markets would vividly mark these outside insurgents. But the dynamics of new pluralism, as usual, manifest fluidity, shifting bedfellows and a steady exchange of policy logics among various camps. Those ascending to the L.A. school board a decade later—ultimate insiders such as Yolie Flores and Mónica García—joined with the radical insurgents to hand off scores of campuses to (varyingly) autonomous managers of charter, pilot, and other alternative schools. Then, like in a soccer game, players reposition based on responses by the opposing team. So, inventive educators and district-friendly pluralists pivoted to expand magnet school enrollments, then built scores of pilot schools and dual-language campuses. It's the confluence of organizational competition and plural logics of how to revive staid institutions that hosted ever-greater parental choice and diversifying forms of schooling. And ever-more-novel policy options emerged from both contestation *and* dialogue between loyal insiders and civic challengers.

This kaleidoscopic array of pluralists expressed varying political-economic ideals (how cities and politics should work), along with differing educational philosophies (how schools should work). Yes, champions of capital, like the L.A. Chamber of Commerce, continued to weigh in on educational policy. Members of an evolving labor movement struggled to remain relevant in policy circles. But it was the flourishing social ideals and redistributive passion of the new pluralists that drove much of the reform debate from the 1990s on. Activists like Brenes, Flores, García, Smith, and Villaraigosa led the charge in moving L.A. Unified, this thick-skinned edifice, and crafting new forms of schooling. To this day, family demand for their garden of alternative schools far exceeds supply. The loyal insiders and civic challengers—hesitant interlocuters—opened a third political ground, moving independently of old capital and aging labor to devise a variety of institutional reforms.

Many of the new pluralists—working the inside game or banging on the doors of L.A. Unified from the outside—aimed to create schools that offer students and families membership, a sense of belonging, enveloped within one's cultural milieu. Neither downtown corporatists nor union chiefs were expressing disaffection with uninspired, plain-vanilla public schools. They remained stuck in that nineteenth-century appeal of Protestant schooling, which they tacitly held in common. Instead, the pluralist hunger for coherent and motivating institutions stems from the cultural Left and the quest for ethnic identity, as well as humanistic inklings of educators who press to foster engaging social relations inside schools.

Early advocates of charter schools, such as Steve Barr and Villaraigosa, understood this well, as did inventive teachers in East L.A. who created small high schools and spread dual-language campuses in differing communities. Pedagogical reformers like Judy Burton and Jeanne Fauci pressed for more caring teachers and curricula that spoke to kids' everyday realities, growing up in urban Los Angeles. They pursued smaller-scale campuses in which students and teachers felt warmly respected and efficacious. This was intertwined with the pluralist's respect for human difference, diverse educators who advocated for culturally relevant and justice-focused curricula, teachers who care, and decriminalizing student discipline. In turn, groups like the Community Coalition and Inner City Struggle mounted a decades-long campaign to alter racialized expectations of which kids held the capacity to get ahead, seeking to remake high schools into warmly demanding institutions.

The civic challengers, in short, demonstrated how pluralist politics and inventive policy options can reinvigorate long-stalled institutions. The consequential break from the old public school coalition a generation ago is reminiscent of Albert O. Hirschman's *Exit, Voice, Loyalty*. That is, when civic players demanding change are not heard by an insular authority or institution, the disaffected will break from old loyalties and search out truly responsive organizations, or build anew. This often requires wrestling resources away from withering interest groups. At the same time, the radical challengers opened up political space for moderate comrades—the loyal insiders—to advance their own alternative forms of schooling. And by the early twenty-first century, the two wings of new pluralism had settled on shared principles: decentralizing control of schools to foster cultural relevance and innovation, reducing disparities in how resources are distributed among schools, and crafting schools that offered a sense of belonging and palpable results.

A democratic festival of politics and institutional forms had matured in Los Angeles by 2020—just as Covid-19 and massive street protests arrived in America. Police violence against Black youths, as well as the indiscriminate killing of Black men, sparked the return of racialized outrage, as Angelenos of all backgrounds joined huge demonstrations. Much work obviously remains to be done nationwide. Yet, L.A.'s colorful panoply of pluralists had illustrated over the past quarter century how a new politics could allow diverse groups to organize from their cultural ties and shape institutions that respect differing ways of raising and teaching their children.[59]

Initiating a recent school year, Superintendent Michelle King emphasized how she was advancing "more bilingual education programs, more attention paid to preparing the youngest students in L.A. Unified's system . . . as well as the district's ever-expanding number of magnet programs."[60] Yet, her regime was no longer a coherent school "system" in a Weberian sense. It had become a loose-knit confederation of schools over which a central bureaucracy now exerts diminishing control. Many floors in her downtown skyscraper sit empty, as the center no longer holds. Remnants of the old normal—with capital and labor enforcing a uniform and culturally imperial form of common schooling—are difficult to find in contemporary Los Angeles. Instead, education leaders now bolster their own legitimacy by decentering power out to diverse campuses, talking of richer social relations inside, and spreading the gospel preached by the new pluralists.

Next, I turn to a differing set of civic challengers—those who live and work closer to the ground than top-down decentralists or well-heeled benefactors do. Sarah Manchanda and I examine nonprofit organizations situated in Black and Latino neighborhoods, groups that disrupt politics as usual by organizing parents and students, one by one. They remain largely outside of the education edifice, while allying with loyal insiders, arguing that a thoroughly democratic politics is required to create inclusive and coherent public schools. These grassroots organizers seek a participatory, ever-more-pluralist politics of education.

CHAPTER 4

Organizing Pluralist Politics

WITH SARAH MANCHANDA

Education advocates in Los Angeles spend most days far from city schools. They instead huddle with political allies or eager lawyers, mulling over tactics or reform options. Weeks often go by while they wait to see school officials or private donors, who strategize in comfortable offices. Earnest scholars, too, assume that the velocity of our emails somehow produces gains inside stubborn schools.

Patricia Gonzales held no such illusions. She was already fighting in the trenches at the ripe age of 15, a student at Fremont High School, which still hosts a beehive of Black and Latino students north of Watts. She had joined a club called South Central Youth Empowered Thru Action (SCYEA, *say-yea* for short), organizing with fellow youths to push for change inside Fremont High. The agenda shaped by Gonzales and her coconspirators in 2008 centered on viscerally felt grievances: filthy or locked bathrooms, random searches of backpacks by campus police, a scarcity of rigorous classes. "This was a period when we didn't have the right courses that would set us up to go to college," she recalled.

In this chapter, we report on young civic challengers, like Gonzales, who were mentored and mobilized by a nonprofit group that surfaced in the 1990s. The Community Coalition (Coco in local vernacular) first networked teens inside high schools that dot South L.A.—a vast swath of city blocks marked by wide expressways and empty factories set amid soiled strip malls and doughnut shops, stretching south from downtown. These civic challengers differ dramatically from the corporate moguls advocating for charter schools. But Coco's leaders similarly apply pressure from the outside, which is necessary for moving the education institution, as they see it. Rather than building a competing army of alternative schools, Coco staff labor to build an inclusive, richly democratic politics inside neighborhoods.

To this day, as such issues surface in high schools, Gonzales (who now works at Coco) formulates strategies for nudging campus principals or bureaucrats at L.A. Unified. The challenges are not simple, the fixes not easy: How to improve the capacity of teachers to deracialize their expectations for student learning? When fights or drug dealing emerge out back, who can facilitate a process that restores mutual respect and a shared sense of justice? These human-scale fronts draw from a lesson taught by Saul Alinsky, the Chicago organizer in the 1940s: Rally the disenfranchised around problems touching their daily lives. If the most vivid issue is dirty bathrooms or intrusive police on campus, then pull around the table on that issue. And when you win, everyone involved feels a potent sense of efficacy.

This chapter also details how Coco leaders win on the wider civic stage as well. Community organizers like Coco and Inner City Struggle shy away from charter schools or radical efforts that subvert the legitimacy of L.A. Unified. They do not intend to bring it down. Still, Coco rarely takes the downtown regime as sacred. In 2017, teaming up with the ACLU, for example, they forced the district to allocate $151 million in new funding to South L.A. campuses. They pushed the board to approve another $700 million in 2021, recovering from the pandemic, pegged to a student needs index, distributed to high-needs schools. Coco's leaders do not hesitate to challenge labor leaders, either, even advocating in Gonzales's day for the firing of Fremont High's entire teaching staff. They achieve visible victories, demonstrating to students and parents that organizing together can yield palpable results.

But Patricia Gonzales foresaw little chance of succeeding. She was caught in a cross fire. Fremont High had sunk into a morass of mediocrity and violence just as Gonzales began mobilizing fellow students. Only one-third of Fremont's entering class survived to their senior year. Two in five instructors failed to hold a teaching credential. Test scores had hit rock bottom. Packed to the gills, the campus served more than 4,400 students who attended classes in staggered shifts. Officials at Fremont boasted of how they had cut weapons-related arrests to one per month. Eighteen security staff patrolled the campus, causing students to dub it the "Fremont pen."[1] Youths seemed warehoused by uninspiring teachers who betrayed low expectations, critics argued. These kids weren't going to college anyway, so why challenge them academically?

Fremont High made for eye-opening headlines after a violent melee erupted in the cafeteria, pitting Black students against Latino students. In December 2009,

L.A. schools chief Cortines decided to fire the entire staff, inviting every teacher and administrator to reapply for their job. His decision to turn the school upside down was announced two weeks before the Christmas holiday, poor timing for sure, yet just before Arne Duncan, President Obama's education secretary, was due to visit Los Angeles. Duncan wanted to see schools like Fremont firsthand, places that he slammed as being "dropout factories."

But Gonzales found herself in a difficult position, feeling mixed emotions and conflicting loyalties. She held respect and affection for a few teachers at Fremont who did care about their students, instructors who now faced Cortines's mass firing. "That's when I learned more about the union and the teachers, and how unfair this [staff] reconstitution could be . . . for the students and the families that were part of the community," Gonzales told us. "I couldn't understand—is Coco really on our side?"

Leaders at the Community Coalition did not want to alienate the teachers' union. But nor could they back the status quo. Something radical had to be done to stop Fremont's downward spiral. Coco hosted conversations with parents and neighborhood leaders to formulate an action plan, one that centered on reducing absentee rates, identifying youths before they dropped out, and building a new health clinic for teens and families. Still, this alliance with parents was seen as pitting Black and Latino activists—organized by Coco—against rank-and-file teachers, many of them longtime residents of South L.A. Union leaders were furious with Coco's mobilization of community members, not to mention the Obama administration's local intrusion. Yet, Coco had accented its independence, a grassroots broker dedicated to engaging students and families in democratic conversations and mounting collective political action.

Gonzales stuck with her young mentors at Coco, and ultimately benefited both personally and professionally. She graduated from Fremont High and won admission to Franklin Marshall College, which is situated in an Amish hamlet of Pennsylvania. She went on to achieve a master's degree at Columbia University. Gonzales still returns to Los Angeles each summer to teach at Coco's Freedom School, where kids learn the racialized history of South L.A. families, as well as basic ethics, such as fairness, tolerance, and the pursuit of quality public education. She remains loyal to the organization's method for nurturing leadership skills in young people. "We have 7-year-olds speaking to crowds of over 100, so there's power in that," she said.

Politics Get Personal

Coco was an early settler on L.A.'s third civic terrain, gaining distance from corporate efficiency hawks and labor leaders in the 1980s. British prime minister Tony Blair once called it the *third sector*, with Europe's maturing local activists and nonprofits running health clinics and housing projects, cleaning city

parks, and bringing back farmers markets. What's intriguing about L.A. pluralists, like Coco's leaders, is how they are not satisfied with winning a policy
reform or shifting $700 million in education finance; they also grasp the com-
plexity of sticky organizations and track implementation and foster stronger relationships within institutions. As schools or local organizations improve, the
legitimacy of instigators like Coco grows. They "form a bridge between individual actions . . . and changes in policy, cultures, social hierarchies," as sociologists Irene Bloemraad and Veronica Terriquez put it, allying with a widening
network of nonprofits to foster "a rich infrastructure of formalized civic groups."[2]

Yet, political action is not an abstract process for Coco's leaders—it requires
nurturing and empowering students one by one. Coco advances a double-edged
strategy, pursuing reform in high-level policy circles while mentoring the next
generation of activists down below. This human-scale approach to organizing
came into view one summer morning, the parched concrete outside already
warm to the touch along Vermont Avenue outside Coco headquarters. Inside,
things were heating up, too, as some twenty-five Black and Latino trainees—
all in their twenties and graduates of neighboring high schools—stomped their
feet, clapping and dancing to the varying beats of harambee. It seemed to be an
oasis of joy and solidarity, everyone in motion inside this bright white hall. The
word *harambee* derives from the early days of postcolonial Kenya, meaning *together we can rise*, although in South L.A. it's usually chanted to a hip-hop beat.

Welcome to Coco's three-week training for Freedom School, a political summer camp of sorts for elementary-age and middle school kids. "*Harambee*! Let
me tell you something about me," everyone shouts, inviting a fresh round of
sing-song harmony. The aspiring counselors go around, timidly revealing a bit
about themselves, where they graduated high school and what their prior ties to
Coco are. Then, inspiring quotes from the civil rights era flash on the wall, along
with photos, even lyrics of songs, setting the tone. Shouting in unison, "Touch
it, read it, learn it . . . everybody talk about it!," the exuberance builds for a half
hour, a feeling of synchrony and unity, modeling how these rookie counselors
will open up assemblies and class sessions with their own kids over the summer.
They are trained in how to advance children's reading and writing skills, and
also share photos of the Watts Riot and discuss champions of the civil rights era,
the nature of Chicano identity, assassinations, and setbacks. Coco's seasoned
staff teach new counselors how to boost children's reading skills, to discover
one's ethnic lineage, and to start thinking about going to college. It was the
hopeful and not-so-hidden curriculum of Freedom School, which was set to begin the following month.

We stayed behind in the assembly hall as a dozen people settled into a
horseshoe formation of chairs, many still teens, some wearing colorful caps,
dreads, Nike shoes, be they black or pink. A pair of Coco veterans began to walk

through details of the summer curriculum. Printed pedagogical guides appeared, replete with slide-decks, photos, and classroom exercises—the march on Selma, the rise of Cesar Chavez, the killing of Martin Luther King Jr. "Our Freedom School is such a different kind of school, compared with a traditional LAUSD school," one Coco staffer told us. "It's tough balancing your love [for] the kids with covering the curriculum." Reflecting on the prior summer, she urges trainees to signal: "I care about you, but I need you to read this book."

Detrianna Clark, one demure trainee, sat in the back, rarely speaking up, eclipsed by her more vocal peers. She was a tall and slim young woman, ready with a broad smile yet somehow tentative, her head ducked low throughout the morning session. Clark had graduated from Dorsey High that June. Only her mother attended the campus ceremony. Her brother didn't show, nor did any of her family members, most living nearby. "I knew they weren't gonna come," she told us. "But everybody from Coco was there, the organizers were there, everybody."

Clark had become a SCYEA coordinator the prior year, helping to arrange the noontime meetings of three dozen students, classmates who had united into a compelling force. "In my junior year I came out of my shyness," Clark said. Her work with Coco, including agitating against police on campus and pushing to offer popular elective classes, seemed to advance her own confidence. She helped conduct a pupil survey, revealing that many youths were quitting sports teams to find jobs so they could help their parents cover the rent.

Problems persisted at Dorsey into the spring. "When it gets hot, the fights break out, lots of kids get expelled," Clark explained. She reported that no one held teachers accountable, some sitting at their desk most of the period or showing little sign of challenging students. Yet, Clark perked up when talking about an English teacher who did care, offering honest feedback and praise for her writing. Clark became fascinated with history as well. "My mom hates it when I watch documentaries all the time, [but] these are my bedtime stories." Another teacher hosted a "feminist group" at lunchtime to "talk about the issues going on at Dorsey, court cases, issues that we were facing," Clark said. "She would give us a voice."

At first we couldn't discern why Clark kept her distance as her counseling role at Freedom School quickly approached. She was hesitant to pursue a conversation and quietly awkward among her peers. But as talk turned to her mother, Clark raised her chin a bit and began to open up. Her mother, a bus driver for L.A. Unified, was Clark's sole anchor at home. Turns out that "everybody knows my mom," Clark said. Between bus runs, her mother visited various staff members at Dorsey High, chatting with teachers and administrators. She previously served on the site council at Clark's elementary school. She had planned to enter college after graduating high school, but the mother's boyfriend, a first love who later "went into crack," opposed it. By then, her mother was raising two young children, soon on her own with no financial support. So, Clark's mother buried her own dream of college, finding a job to make ends meet. But mom continued to "push them [Detrianna and her brother] to go farther than she had gone."

Clark would come into her own, nurtured by her ever-present mother, along with young Coco staffers. "I started having my own voice," she said after joining SCYEA in her sophomore year. She played on Dorsey High's softball team, one domain in which she excelled. "I improved my grades after I went to Coco . . . they are like my family. If I need something Tylo [James, a Coco organizer,] is there." Two months after graduating from Dorsey, Clark traveled cross-country to enter Bennett College, a Methodist school in Greensboro, North Carolina. She had attended the Sisterhood Rising conference in L.A., organized by several nonprofits, and the experience "open[ed] my eyes to what women go through," she said. This led her to an expo of Black colleges. The Bennett campus, where "they really hold us accountable to do well," appealed to Clark. She did complain that "people at Dorsey were more politically aware" than her peers at college in North Carolina, which Clark reportedly points out to them in her understated way.

We did not expect to uncover the public emergence of Detrianna Clark during our year inside Coco. This potent nonprofit first became known for combating the crack epidemic, more than a generation ago, then pushing for effective schools in South L.A. But Clark's own blossoming exemplifies the fusion between the personal and the political—a spirit baked into Coco's double-edged strategy for fostering participatory politics. This lends a voice to previously unheard communities, assembling this political cacophony one confident voice at a time. Clark's own personal struggles emerged as Coco organizers brought her into the fold. And these emotional black holes must be explored, as they hamper teens' capacity to gather behind a common cause. "When we talk about how we are gonna change things, they care about what we say," Princess Berry, a junior at Washington High, said. "Everybody is so welcoming, they care about you so deeply." Back at school, teachers "think that you're dumb," she said. "They don't take time to learn what we are interested in."

Pulling Together in South Los Angeles

Karen Bass, a physician's assistant in a South L.A. emergency room, worked at the edge of a war zone in the 1980s. Sirens screamed most nights, patients arriving by ambulance suffering from gunshot wounds or overdosing on crack cocaine. "Loved ones would go missing, helicopters circled the community at all hours, and residents put up bars on their windows," a Coco historical brief reads. "Auto plants, rubber and steel factories—they all closed down—people were so depressed, turning to crack," Bass later recalled. It was difficult to fathom the human toll taken by drugs and deepening poverty.

Stories of loss and resilience abound from this terrifying era in South Los Angeles. Miles Corwin, an *L.A. Times* crime reporter, followed Olivia, a seventh grader who had grown tired of the beatings she received at home, "years of being whipped with an extension cord" by a parent, "smacked in the mouth with a telephone, pounded against the wall." Olivia ran away, found a shelter, and a few months later entered a group home with six other girls. Later a counselor urged her to visit a magnet program at Crenshaw High, the film location for *Boyz n the Hood*. It turned out that Olivia tested in the top 5 percent of students nationwide, then promptly was accepted into the magnet program, eventually winning admission to Babson College in Boston.[3]

Still, the casualties far outnumbered the lucky ones. So, in 1989 Bass pulled together eleven friends in her living room. (The Rodney King riot would occur three years later.) Her caucus did not need to belabor South L.A.'s problems; instead, they agreed to attack them. Winning a small federal grant, they formed a nonprofit dubbed the Community Coalition for Substance Abuse Prevention and Treatment. A quarter century later, now a member of the US Congress, Bass told us how her nonprofit "was born . . . with a goal in mind of organizing the community to turn despair and hopelessness into action." Crack cocaine offered a vivid symptom. But Bass "aimed to build a permanent institution," one that would rally local families and young leaders from inside high schools. From the start, her vision of pluralist politics aimed to bring fresh voices onto the civic stage. She set about creating an organizing powerhouse that exerts lasting change on local institutions and within the hearts and minds of budding activists in South L.A.

Bass had attended Hamilton High on the west side of Los Angeles, and "the Jewish community had all those activists," she recalled. But "white flight was so quick, I never had a chance to meet my neighbors." Bass did learn that "young people can come up with the problems and the solutions that we felt were important." She reported being "a little too young [to] be involved with the Black Panthers," and she wasn't from the American South, so Bass began to craft her own identity, along with an agenda that would attract allies and fellow parents in South L.A. Bass admits to being somewhat of a nerd throughout high school and college. "I grew up watching, studying . . . spending a great deal of time reading about the civil rights movement." After giving birth to her daughter, Bass focused on her career in medicine. But the foundations of her community were crumbling. She realized that only the bloodied symptoms of underlying disparities were being treated in the ER. Bass decided to pull other Black professionals around her dinner table that evening to focus on root causes.

Challenging Old Politics

Bass, from the beginning, aimed to contest established interests "on the outside" when "we needed to protest [and to] work inside" when that made strategic sense. Indeed, the Community Coalition, now with a bite-size name, became bicultural in a political sense: jamming L.A. Unified to redistribute resources toward poor neighborhoods while allying with leading educators on the inside when this tactic accomplished more. Coco's leaders act as civic challengers, helping to fuel a pluralist politics of education while joining with loyal insiders, like school board members and reform-minded educators, to move L.A. Unified. Karen Bass would be elected to the US Congress and rise to chair its Black Caucus. In 2020, she appeared on Joe Biden's short list, vetted as his possible running mate, a post awarded to fellow Californian Kamala Harris.

Beneath high-level politics, Coco nurtures a sense of belonging on the ground, as Black and Latino youths discover how collective action can foster one's own efficacy. "The Community Coalition was a haven for young people like me," Elmer Roldan recalled. "They didn't talk down to young people, they respected us." Roldan, age 13, who was born in Guatemala, "tagged along" one day with his older sister, who was pregnant yet making her way through high school. After meeting a Coco organizer at a noontime gathering, they decided to return. "It was safe, they always had food," Roldan told us. "So, I stuck [with the organization] for 17 years." It spurred remarkable growth in his awareness, politically and interpersonally, that remained with Roldan several years later. "I had never met an African American or a white person," he said. Then, "they instilled in us that we were part of a large movement for social justice, [that] countless people had given their lives . . . [and] that we carry that legacy with us." Coco staff transported Roldan's young cadre to the mountains for retreats and visited California colleges to boost their aspirations.

"There's an incredible power that organizing skills give you—that problems are best solved when you work in partnership with other individuals," Roldan told us. After graduating from Manual Arts High School, he was blocked from entering college, as he was still an undocumented immigrant. So, instead, Roldan became a full-time organizer at Coco, filling that role for twelve years before joining board member Mónica García's staff. From there Roldan would come to direct the education program at United Way downtown. "Coco was such a trailblazer," he said, "to empower young people to organize and to have a voice." And Roldan's full-throated voice grew more influential as a foundation official, aiding similar nonprofits who were active in school reform. Roldan later became a senior advisor to L.A. schools chief Austin Beutner.

Organizing at the Grassroots and Grass Tops

Coco's theory of organizing stems not so much from Saul Alinsky but from Fred Ross, a homegrown L.A. activist who graduated from Roosevelt High, then joined the Methodist church, hoping to become a Protestant minister. But after witnessing the wartime violence inflicted on Latino youths—the Zoot Suit Riots, sweeping through East Los Angeles in the summer of 1943—Ross dedicated himself to secular politics couched in the largely Catholic east side. He went to work for the American Council on Race Relations, then began to organize and mentor Mexican-heritage leaders in Boyle Heights.

Ross would move to Chicago, study with Alinsky for a year, then return to the Los Angeles barrio, mobilizing voter registration drives and creating supports for residents who soon coalesced to form the Community Service Organization. His aim was "to help people speak up and demand their rights . . . to get out front so they could prove to themselves that they could do it."[4] Ross helped launch the political career of Edward Roybal, the first Latino elected to the Los Angeles city council (in 1949) since the nineteenth century, and recruited a young organizer—named Cesar Chavez—up north in the Salinas Valley.

One of Ross's initial campaigns aimed to desegregate schools in Bell Town, a settlement out east in Riverside County. Black and Latino parents were up in arms in 1946 over a proposed school bond that would finance construction of a new school—one solely dedicated to white children and families. Ross consulted with a wealthy L.A. lawyer, David Marcus, who would soon win the nation's first school desegregation suit in federal courts—*Mendez v. Westminster*—on behalf of Latino families. Ross pursued a similar desegregation order in Riverside.[5] He advanced a personalized strategy for organizing—meeting in neighbors' homes, sharing meals together, and scaffolding up from Latino cultural events—as recounted by Aurea Montes-Rodriguez, Coco's vice president and policy strategist. Tough-talking, in-your-face tactics may have worked for Alinsky in Chicago. But in close-knit Latino communities, revealing quieter and cooperative values, culturally situated methods to foster unity are required, Montes-Rodriguez told us. The willingness to act publicly is built from trust and familiar ways of coming together.

How does Coco work alongside allied nonprofits and neighborhood leaders to nurture such grassroots pluralism? This nimble nonprofit certainly stands out, along with compadre nonprofits like Inner City Struggle in East L.A., which was founded by Luis Sanchez with Maria Teixeira in 1995. Other civic groups in Los Angeles, often tied to state or national affiliates, operate closer to what many activists call the *grass tops*. This includes local activists within the California Charter Schools Association and Educators for Excellence, the latter aiming to amplify the voices of Black and Latino teachers outside conventional labor unions. Pilot school principals have formed their own association in L.A. The local Chamber of Commerce stills weighs in on issues facing public schools—defeating in 2019 a tax measure that would have eased L.A. Unified's budget troubles. Overall, these diverse advocates focus on a specific remedy or governance arrangement, from creating small high schools to urging teacher accountability. But their policy remedies very rarely scaffold up from neighborhood deliberations as stirred by Coco. These grass-top organizations may foster close bonds with practitioners (teachers or principals), or strengthen unity within a particular subsector (e.g., charter, magnet, or dual-language educators).

A third set of groups have long fostered pedagogical reforms or richer social relations inside certain networks of schools. These include the Center for Powerful Public Schools (run by Jeanne Fauci, chapter 2) and the Los Angeles Education Partnership, not to be confused with the Partnership for Los Angeles Schools. (We learned about the latter group in chapter 3, the cluster of schools in poor communities that Antonio Villaraigosa, as mayor, first took over.) These groups seek to improve teaching practices or assume independent control of flailing campuses (e.g., under Yolie Flores's handoff of conventional schools examined in chapter 3).

As UCLA's John Rogers has argued: "Public engagement has a community context," one characterized by the cultural habitus, economic clout, and daily aspirations of widely differing families and social classes spread across differing parts of Los Angeles. Still, there is an interdependence among disparate groups as well: "The fate of one's household is tied to the fate of others," Rogers and Marion Orr say.[6] The dynamics of these civic actors resemble action on the soccer field, where each player aims to advance the ball while adjusting to the shifting positions and tactics of others on the field, as the late sociologist Pierre Bourdieu theorized. These diverse civic challengers are both independent and interwoven with one another. So, as groups like Inner City Struggle or Villaraigosa's renegade confederacy press for neighborhood control of schools, this creates space for pedagogical reformers to foster social justice–oriented curricula or more caring ties inside schools.

What's distinct about Coco and fellow organizers is their agility in forming coalitions to address educational disparities. Building a pluralist politics necessitates respect for, and alliances with, other civic players. Rogers details how Inner City Struggle came to lead the multiracial coalition Communities for Educational Equity in 2005 to advance the college-prep ("A-G") curriculum, soon to be pressed by loyal insiders (see chapter 2). Coco executive director Albert Retana complained at the time that "we had been going at it alone for a long time and hadn't been getting anywhere." He was delighted when leading Latinos, including the publisher of *La Opinion*, formed the Alliance for a Better Community, which would later push L.A. Unified on a variety of issues. What began as a Black leadership circle inside Coco would come to ally with Latino activists, mirroring the integrated demographics that swept across South Los Angeles over the past two generations.

The "organizational forms that are developed within movements" have long intrigued students of community action, harking back to how Frances Fox Piven and Richard Cloward explored durable associations within the civil rights movement.[7] Critics like Jane Jacobs and Lewis Mumford had argued in favor of decentralizing the control of civic functions down to neighborhoods, since elite politicians, they assumed, would favor large-scale institutions, not pint-size nonprofits, to foster human-scale engagement. The Kennedy-Johnson White House would fund this localizing revolution in the 1960s, mainly via the Office of Economic Opportunity, which established Head Start, community health clinics, and housing initiatives—run by an unprecedented array of nonprofits inside poor communities and led by predecessors of contemporary activists like Bass, Brenes, and Montes-Rodriguez.[8]

Overall, the rise of young activists and nonprofits in Los Angeles proved remarkable over the past three decades, whether spurred by Left-leaning decentralists or market-oriented neoliberals. The inclination of Angelenos to form community groups certainly varies among sectors. There's been no hesitancy among spiritual organizers, whose religious institutions have spread dramatically since the mid-1980s. The count of churches or religious establishments climbed from 2,126 to 3,258 across L.A. County between 1986 and 2015, rising by 53 percent. (The population grew by 26 percent.)[9] So-called political and advocacy organizations, as defined by the Census Bureau, spread rapidly as well since the 1980s. These tiny-to-large firms range from Coco to the Catholic Archdiocese, from Inner City Struggle to well-heeled business guilds, like the century-old Chamber of Commerce.

Organizing across Generations

"Hiya all, sign in, grab a snack." Tylo James kicks in instantly. Her tone is direct, as if to say, *Time is short, let's get started.* Twenty-five Latino and African American teens ease into a classroom at Washington High School, at first eyes down, filtering James's enthusiasm with caution. But they have shown up for the weekly SC-YEA session. Everyone slides into chairs arranged in a messy arc, the arc shifting into a circle and easing outward as attendance grows, nearly forty fidgeting bodies, a few standing along the perimeter, not sure whether to join the trusting fray.

"So, remember our discussion last week of Black-brown unity?" James picks up from the previous huddle. "Yeah, we self-segregate, have you seen that?" one girl pitches in. "We want to be together [however] because we're all being oppressed here in South L.A.," she says. A Black female channels the riff. "We don't only have friends who are Latino, but I have family, like my uncle, who you have to speak to in Spanish, he's from Honduras." A palpable feeling of candor leavens the conversation among this integrated blend of students. "My family doesn't like Black people," Andrea says. "My parents believe that Black people will steal things." Princess Berry takes over from James, asking, "If the U.S.A. is a place where everyone is supposed to be free, why should we take that freedom away?" James pauses to applaud the frank dialogue. "You guys are leaders, you are moving beyond your comfort zones."

James pivots, pouncing on a second topic as the hour ticks by. "How do you feel unsafe or threatened in your community?" she asks. This month, Coco's organizing team was interjecting a new effort in dialogue with student leaders. They would soon survey peers on the interplay between school climate and neighborhood dangers, brainstorming on ways to dodge risks, stay focused on studying, and become politically aware, all the while urging members to engage teachers, do well in school, and take college-prep courses. Around the room, several teens talk of their daily dance, how they meld into local norms at school, on the street, and while coping with threats from bullies and dope dealers. The likelihood of "gang violence" emerged quickly in the conversation. "I'm walking down [to] the 108th Street store," one Black male volunteers. "The guy asks me, 'Where ya from[?]' [sizing up gang affiliation], but we don't talk back. It makes me feel uncomfortable, even walking in my own community."

Back in Coco's spacious auditorium at the weekly "base meeting" for SCYEA members, Tylo James invites others to speak up on the topic of safety and violence. She stands before a two-story-high whiteboard used for brainstorming ideas, making lists, or mapping organizing strategy. "What's threatening day to day in your neighborhood?" James and fellow organizers press. "Gang violence, rape, liquor store robberies, McDonalds, immigration raids, Nazis, bullying, and fights at school," several animated teens respond. The list becomes eye-opening, articulated by this discerning yet gentle convening of more than sixty teens, each gaining a voice in the civic discourse.

James leans in further: "Okay, so what are the root causes of these problems?" A lively revelry ensued—reminiscent of college sociology classes—over housing, joblessness, fractured families who mark their neighborhoods, compared with (middle-class) Culver City or ritzy Westwood, out by UCLA. It's the genesis of political awakening at Coco, starting with surfacing what youths themselves see day to day, their own conceptions of problems inside schools or neighborhoods. This is followed by a collective analysis of historical forces and contemporary ills that lead to everyday symptoms. Finally, a discussion ensues over how these energized youths might rally together to advance feasible remedies.

"What I lacked the most was a critical consciousness . . . of the overall system," Coco staffer Julia de la Torre told us one afternoon. "I had no critical awareness" of how my Lynwood community fit into the economy and racialized politics of L.A. before entering Williams College. As students learn to listen carefully, to think analytically, they strategize over how to mobilize others to get behind reforms, whether pressing school principals, rallying before the L.A. Unified board, or meeting with local politicians. One dividend, so vividly seen in these animated discussions, is a near-spiritual solidarity—a shared realization of one's place in a broader, often unfair, society while formulating shared pathways for becoming an effective political actor.[10]

Tylo James, Emerging

"Coco taught me how to show up differently in the world," James told us one summer morning during a break at the Freedom School hosted on USC's campus. She had emerged as a compelling Black leader at 24 years of age. James's entry into public spaces still invokes angst for her, as she experiences unsettling flashbacks to a strained childhood. But to watch Tylo James—while discovering what lies beneath her kinetic energy and nonstop candor—one sees a compelling organizer, an upbeat mentor.

Her best friend, fellow sophomore Taylor Griffin, asked James to come along to a SCYEA meeting at Dorsey High in the fall of 2008. "I was like, okay, whatever, let's check it out." Soon after, James was hooked. "It presented an opportunity . . . for me to impact my community." Raised by her grandparents farther south, by the San Pedro harbor, James was rather timid as she entered high school. "There was a lot of dysfunction and chaos in my family," James said. "I didn't necessarily want to be in the spotlight and speaking in public." But she soon discovered "her first mentors" at Coco, including Elmer Roldan, then the director of youth leadership. "I was pushed, as good organizers do, I grew and I evolved." She credits Roldan as "supporting me through my depression." Some of her instructors at Dorsey High were "passionate about their teaching," and James remains in touch with a civics teacher, Don Singleton, who talked of everyday "community conditions, who didn't whitewash it, who agitated us to do something about it." Mentors like Roldan listened carefully, paid attention to her pangs of doubt. "The moments that I remember the most as a youth are when people invested in my personal development, like helping me understand my personal issues," James said.

On the rise by her senior year, James was doing well in classes and becoming more involved in the SCYEA network. When asked to talk at a Coco-hosted session on foster care with Hillary Clinton, she would argue that "relative caregivers are the unsung heroes of the African American community."[11] Articulate and speaking from the heart, James was then selected to speak at a United Way seminar attended by President Obama's education secretary, Arne Duncan. "I met him, we spoke, and we talked about the conditions of schools in South L.A." James talked of Dorsey "not [having] enough resources, folks not having enough textbooks . . . overcrowded classrooms and insufficient teacher support."

But James's close-knit world soon unraveled, just months before graduation. Her best friend, Griffin, the girl who had pulled James into the Coco fold, died in a bizarre car accident. Griffin's mother was behind the wheel, having just dropped Taylor off in front of Dorsey High. As the daughter crossed in front of the car, her mother pulled out quickly, looking back for oncoming traffic. She struck and killed Taylor as fellow students looked on.[12] James would suffer from depression in the coming years but was determined to enter and excel at UCLA. Looking back, she learned from these setbacks. "I think when I have really resistant youth . . . they remind me of me," James said. "But you have to show up as your whole self. When folks are acting up, they just need more attention . . . [seeing] that I can depend on this person for something."

James is not alone among Coco alums. For all of this nonprofit's policy success, building the self-confidence of young Black and Latino youth lies at the heart of their work. "You must feel worthy of applying to college," as one Freedom School teacher said. Or, as SCYEA alum Miguel Dominguez, also admitted to UCLA, told us: "I noticed that my friends in the first semester beg[a]n to disappear," ill-prepared for college. Dominguez graduated with his bachelor's degree, then returned to Coco as the new director of youth organizing.

James revisits how the political quickly becomes personal when organizing youth in poor communities. "I had to unpack my own issues in order to help the youth process what they are going through," she said. "You can't take people beyond where you've developed." Building solidarity among disparate students in such troubled communities requires adult mentors who are steady and consistently there, James emphasized. "The moments that I remember most as a youth, when people . . . helped me understand my personal issues, then bringing that back to the larger political context."

Nurturing Hearts, Minds, and Political Action

By 2017, Coco's leadership had decided to shift its focus to daily safety and school climate, tracking the extent to which youths felt that teachers and counselors were attending to teens in a caring and holistic manner. The priority for lunchtime sessions in high schools, along with rarified policy discussions downtown, flowed from their success in making college-prep courses available to all students, organizing with Inner City Struggle. Others on the social justice wing of the new pluralists, including the ACLU and the Advanced Project, had effectively pushed to reduce suspensions and police surveillance on campuses. But how to enrich the more sublime relationships between students and teachers inside mechanical high schools?

To gauge the worries and perspectives held by students themselves, James and youth leaders at Coco designed a survey administered to more than two thousand students. It covered how teens viewed their comfort levels on the streets, how they made sense of parks, smoke shops, marijuana dispensaries, liquor stores, and vacant lots that dotted their neighborhoods. Students were asked about their feelings of threat, confidence, and "wellness" at school, including the extent to which they experienced sadness or estrangement from teachers and peers. The results proved eye-opening. "The reality is that Crenshaw, Fremont, Hawkins, and Washington [High Schools] all had shootings outside their school in the past four to six months," de la Torre, the Coco organizer, told us. Almost one-third of students reported fear of robbery or gang activity. Focus groups further discovered that youths were eager to find "paid internships and college-prep courses." Many students polled "actually want more opportunities to get paid, and they want more opportunities to go to college," de la Torre said.

Then comes the organizer's pivotal question. How to set reform goals on which students, these fledgling activists, can see discernible progress? "How do we make sure that it's widely felt, that it [the issue] is winnable, that we'll bring a real concrete, tangible change in the living conditions of this community?" de la Torre asked, "With a campaign comes a power analysis. Who are the key players, who are our supporters, who do we need to move?" James began an effort she calls "Wellness Wednesdays," where political education mixes with discussions of personal doubt or problems shared among students. "There are community conditions that we are experiencing on so many different levels," James said. "On an institutional level, on a personal level . . . [for] young people whose parents or community are stuck in survival mode. We don't have time to process or think about the future."

Coco's leaders often succeed by framing fresh dialogue, then ensuring that students and families gain a seat at the table, spotlighting how they define the ills faced by schools and neighborhoods. Policy wonks and professors may be busy tweaking school finances or studying the efficacy of teachers in raising test scores. Meanwhile, Coco and its youth network unearth the disrespect or dashed aspirations that many educators inflict upon students in places like South Los Angeles. The institution of schooling offers no haven in this often heartless world. Yet, the politics of pluralism require this authentic and eye-opening dialogue, according to leaders like Montes-Rodriguez at Coco. And the dialogue that bubbles-up—perhaps shared with the school board, civic leaders, and journalists—tends to legitimate novel policy thrusts.

When L.A. teachers went out on strike in early 2019, for example, UTLA leaders drew from Coco's playbook. Sure, they pushed for salary increases and smaller classes. But the union also demanded funding for additional counselors and social workers, aiming to address the emotional well-being of middle and high school students. It was a priority pulled from Coco's recent campaign for a supportive school climate and human-scale organizations. Once again, this nimble nonprofit had fused personal growth on the ground with policy reforms citywide. UTLA leaders, such as Alex Caputo-Pearl (chapter 2), opted to visit that third civic space, established by Coco and fellow civic challengers over the previous quarter century, then echo the urgency of nurturing caring ties inside schools. For James the political agenda remained focused on the personal. "Just listen, just ask them, let them talk about themselves," she said. "They'll reveal things that probably are hurting or need addressing. When you develop that bond with them, that supportive bond . . . they'll know that I can depend on this person."

Grassroots Pluralism, Discernible Gains?

We have seen how youth activism fosters both personal growth and inventive policy options, inspired by the authentic voices of students and their families. Yet, does this nurturance and mobilization of students yield sustained change inside schools? This question lies on the empirical frontier, a fresh arena for scholars to explore. Much remains to be learned about how differing approaches to youth organizing benefit individuals and communities.

A return to Fremont High does shed some light on the question of results that may stem from Coco-style organizing on the ground. Fremont epitomized dreary "dropout factories," the term earlier used by President Obama's education secretary. Cortines, the L.A. Unified chief, agreed with the diagnosis and purged most teachers in 2009. This humpty-dumpty approach, picking up the pieces after toppling a school, was supported by Coco's leaders in select cases. It's one arena where grassroots organizing yielded rather dramatic institutional change. So, what happened?

We tracked achievement levels at Fremont High in the decade after the teaching staff was reconstituted. The figure on page 142 displays the share of eleventh-grade students who met the state's achievement standard in English language arts beginning with the 2014–15 school year, after California adopted a new testing regime. Fremont students outperformed their peers in neighboring Dorsey and Washington High Schools in the 2015–16 and 2016–17 school years. By the 2016–17 school year, 47 percent had cleared the state's proficiency standard. This, despite the fact that nine in ten students qualified for subsidized meals. In sharp contrast, just 16 percent of Dorsey's eleventh graders achieved this level of proficiency in the same year (eight in ten were eligible for free meals).

Additional indicators further suggest an upbeat turnaround at Fremont High. The fraction of entering ninth graders who graduated four years later climbed from 55 percent in 2010 to 78 percent six years later. Washington High graduated two-thirds of its entering cohorts of students; Dorsey approached Fremont with a 75 percent graduation rate. Analysts have sketched the questionable reliance on web-based "credit recovery" efforts, which may inflate district-reported graduation rates. Still, Fremont vastly expanded access to Advanced Placement courses, raising curricular rigor and preparing more teens for college.

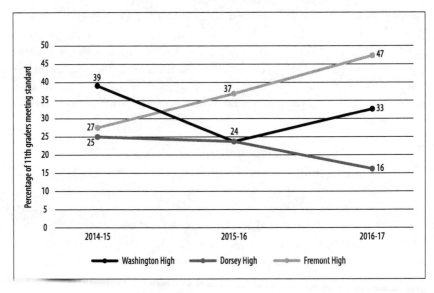

Varying rates of progress at South L.A. high schools, 2014–2016

One-third of its AP enrollees scored 3 or higher, sufficient to gain college-level credit. This level of AP test performance is enjoyed by just 9 and 14 percent of Washington and Dorsey students, respectively.

Something is working in places like Fremont High—fostering student engagement, boosting the rigor of many classes, keeping youth on track for college. This may add up to more buoyant aspirations and stronger academic skills than before. Recall that Coco worked alongside L.A. Unified's effort to recast campus leadership and lift teacher quality at Fremont, all the while ensuring that parents and students held their place at the table.

Still, the causal links remain sketchy. We have much to learn regarding the social mechanisms by which youth organizing comes to alter practices inside schools. Allied groups—such as Inner City Struggle, Educators for Excellence, and the Partnership for L.A. Schools—also foster direct dialogue with students and teachers. These organizers aim to move the dial on a variety of outcomes, from the quality of pedagogy to the motivation and well-being of adolescents. UCLA's Rogers defines "youth organizing as a process . . . within a community [where] a base of young people [are] committed to altering power relationships and creating meaningful institutional change."[13] But how the mentoring of youth activists plays out, and with what sustained effects, varies depending on one's neighborhood and the nonprofit's agility.

These grassroots challengers undoubtedly amplify the voices of those rarely heard on the civic stage. Shared racial experience, along with that search for a commonly grasped identity, help to animate the pursuit of "mobilization and mutuality," as Bloemraad and Terriquez put it. Or, take how Maria Brenes writes of Inner City Struggle's creation in East L.A. a generation ago. It sprouted up from "youth involved in the anti-21 movement, [which] turned into a long-range commitment to build a permanent student organization that would demand the return of public resources, equity and justice to communities of color." California's ballot Proposition 21 would have imposed adult-level penalties on minors convicted of crimes. Anti-immigrant initiatives also fueled youth activism, fostering tighter solidarity among Black and Latino students in East and South Los Angeles, Brenes said. The spread of plural groups—anchored to particular cultural tribes—lent confidence for members to reach out to one another. These new pluralists expressed shared respect, a willingness to learn from the other when it came to institutional change.

By 2010, more than 160 youth-organizing nonprofits operated nationwide, many sharing Coco's doubled-edged strategy of nurturing the confidence and efficacy of youth, as well as advancing policy reform. Membership counts ranged from sixty young people to more than one thousand in a Philadelphia-based nonprofit. One study of youth organizing in Chicago reveals how high schools can foster organizing skills when students partake in real instances of political action, moving well beyond the bland factoids that fill civics classes. Scholars Joe Kahne and Susan Sporte report these positive effects from service learning, blended with explicit training in how to engage with peers, as significant predictors of youths' downstream levels of civic involvement.[14] Rogers similarly argues that the praxis of local organizing imparts "skills and identities that support civic engagement," recasting youths as credible civic players within previously disenfranchised communities. One of the earliest assessments of how youth organizing affects both the participants and civil society stemmed from Freedom Summer campaigns during the civil rights movement, conducted by sociologist Doug McAdam two generations ago.[15]

Backing up theoretically, scholars who study civic action have long dug into how intermediary organizations—human associations that operate between the state and market—strengthen ethnic ties and foster political engagement. The modern state's maturation in the nineteenth century would stigmatize most traditional collectives, then seek to erode the authority of religious leaders, village officials, even the family. But growing disaffection with the bureaucratic state in contemporary times, including the regimentation of common schools, would rekindle loyalty to enveloping associations, from ethnic organizations to evangelical churches. The promise of civic organizing goes back to Alexis de Tocqueville's fascination with volunteer action in nineteenth-century America. This in sharp contrast to centralized regimes in Europe, as well as the social alienation resulting from top-down institutions, certainly including the daily grind of bureaucratic schools. It is these unsatisfying social locations that groups like Coco enter and offer a safe, more engaging harbor.

Sociologists like Claus Offe explore how the state may opt to suppress or thicken the authority of the family or grassroots agencies that aid in the care and nurturing of children. Perhaps it should take a village, as Hillary Clinton wrote, but governments vary widely in how they move resources to local organizations that nurture young children or engage developing adolescents in civil society.[16] Still, theorists no longer see society as solely composed of the state, market, and lone individual (a hangover from the liberal-Protestant regime). Instead, cosmo-politan centers like Los Angeles can be seen as a networked association of civic associations. It's the character of new pluralism—a vast metropolis with a vari-ety of respected (or at least tolerated) social orders, not one regulated by a small and culturally homogenous civic circle, as so vividly seen in L.A. into the late twentieth century.[17] Groups like Coco do not discount the importance of shared, integrating institutions, such as the ideal of public schooling. But the social au-thority of Coco and its fellow organizers is founded upon the authentic voice it lends to cultural variety and pluralist politics.

Veronica Terriquez, the Santa Cruz sociologist who follows this line of think-ing, has assessed how students engaged in political action often experience dif-fering educational trajectories. She tracked 410 high school activists into their 20s, young people, such as Coco alumni, who had participated in organizing efforts in one of several California cities.[18] Her analysis centers on individual-level effects rather than tracing change in the organization of high schools. Yet, she details how youth organizing can remedy the alienation that many teens feel as they wander through faceless institutions. She found that nearly 9 in 10 al-ums of youth-organizing groups came from low-income families. Seventy percent of the engaged youths were of Black or Latino heritage, an additional one-fourth of Asian descent. Terriquez found that youth more often joined non-profits like Coco when their parents were engaged in schools or political issues, similar to Clark's mother, the extroverted bus driver who made a point of know-ing the staff at Dorsey High.

Interviews with youth activists revealed the same nexus between learning organizing skills *and* a spirit of solidarity, acquiring a sense of efficacy as they agitated for reform together. Their comments echo the voices of Coco's youth-ful organizers. "I've always been shy and not much of a public speaker," 18-year-old Emiko told Terriquez. "But I think it gave me a little bit more con-fidence." Or take Daisy, who helped push for college-prep supports in her high school, reporting: "I learned how to organize an event, run things . . . be the leader of something and get it done." Meagan told Terriquez, "I probably wouldn't have thought about politics or social justice and changing my commu-nity" until joining her group. Young veterans of local organizing often found their way into elite universities and historically Black colleges. They remained far more engaged in civic organizations or political causes over time, as gauged by their propensity to volunteer, attend public protests, and vote, relative to a comparison group.

Lessons from Down Under

For Karen Bass—who left Coco in 2010, newly elected to Congress—the long view matters. It has marked the spirit and steady work of her nonprofit for over three decades. The clamor of policy chatter and daily tussles in Los Angeles remains deafening, as in many parts of the nation. School chiefs and board members come and go. L.A. Unified remains under a discerning microscope, criticized by old interests, new pluralists, and ever-eager journalists. It's a vast institution that touches the daily routines of half a million families each day, the region's second largest employer. The global pandemic of 2020–21 closed schools for fifteen months, exacerbating already gross inequities in student learning and the wider vitality of families in Los Angeles.

Bass and her successors at Coco don't hesitate to join in on the issue of the day, especially when the cause fits their long-run strategy: moving adequate dollars to South L.A. schools, stabilizing the teaching force, or thickening relationships inside schools. But for Bass and Coco's contemporary leaders, their north star is to amplify whose voices are heard atop an increasingly noisy civic stage. They labor to nurture a pluralist politics of education. This focus on the long view demands patience and unrelenting momentum. Coco's leaders, including Montes-Rodriguez, have spent the past generation nudging district officials and principals to expand college-prep courses in central-city schools. They have hammered on finance reform since the 1990s. The equity-minded wing of the new pluralists labored for a decade to move the L.A. Unified board and teachers' union to quit dumping mediocre ("must hire") teachers in poor schools.

All the while, Coco has quietly nurtured successive cohorts of young leaders—teenagers often ignored or forgotten amid the anomie of American high schools. Instead of being written off, these apprentices have risen to influential posts in government, foundations, or the L.A. Unified School District. Rather than be distracted by the policy chatter, Coco's leaders stick with their double-edged strategy, advancing on perennial policy fronts while hatching young and potent Black and Latino leaders.

A related lesson stems from the savvy of Coco's leaders in moving with, and adapting to, new pluralism. They helped to define this third political terrain, staking out a civic frontier detached from the old polarity between capital and labor. "The environment has changed," Bass told us. "A number of activists and Coco alums went to work for foundations, some became labor leaders or elected officials." Indeed, Elmer Roldan and Antonio Villaraigosa, coming of age in the early twenty-first century, were certainly not beholden to corporatist reformers, nor were they sympathetic with what they saw as a protectionist labor agenda. Instead, they pressed inventive policies and altered the once hog-tied institution of schooling in unprecedented ways.

Coco and its allies shine a bright light on education and inequality across Los Angeles, gaining influence as they pull reform-minded educators, rising politicians, and even L.A. bureaucrats into their novel civic sphere. The election of close allies to the L.A. school board, such as Yolie Flores and Mónica García, would solidify the influence of contemporary pluralists. Even union leaders rediscovered social justice concerns in 2019, striking for a week, then winning additional counselors to address youths' motivation and emotional well-being, the precise issue pioneered by Coco in the 1990s.

In short, these grassroots organizers do not take for granted the old constitutive rules of urban politics. The civic challengers could no longer tolerate segregated and unequally funded schools, too often staffed by educators who demanded little of students. From their third political vantage point, Coco leaders devised a variety of policy options that have challenged the dominating regime, even created entirely new forms of schooling. The mere variety of policy options and colorful renditions of schooling that took root in Los Angeles over the past quarter century stem from the proliferating nodes of public authority fostered by Coco and similar nonprofits—authors of the new political pluralism. They work mightily to expand who gets to share the civic stage, who shapes the narrative of institutional reform. At every turn, these plural activists lend voice to students and families, inviting the disenfranchised to speak on issues that will shape their own futures. In short, these groups challenge tacit assumptions about the structuring of civil society: who gets a place at the table, which groups define public problems, and how resources are distributed across a colorful variety of institutions and neighborhoods.

Perhaps most vivid, the case of Coco teaches us that many youths respond to simple acts of kindness. To hear the stories of Tylo James or Elmer Roldan, among the poor and otherwise forgotten kids who beat the odds, it's difficult to deny the human-scale success of Coco-style organizing. This cross-generational strategy—where twentysomethings mobilize students to engage the civic discourse and speak out in the streets—appears to yield political efficacy and personal growth for all. Organizing together boosts the confidence of students, along with their knowledge of economic and political history, allowing them to discover a wider context, then rally around a defined common cause. Much research remains in tracing the long-term results of in-the-trenches organizing. Still, we observe in Los Angeles a proliferating array of young political players, authoring novel reform logics that bubble up from down below—brought to the surface by these civic challengers.

CHAPTER 5

Pluralist Politics and Institutional Reform

Pluralists hold that there are many valuable ideals, pursuits, and aspirations for which human beings yearn . . . even those that do not yearn for them can understand that they are worthy of value.

—Victor Muñiz-Fraticelli

What does Los Angeles teach us about the rise of pluralist politics and the capacity of democratic activists to reinvigorate tired institutions? In this chapter, I weigh major lessons learned in two parts, highlighting dynamics and policies that might thicken civil society and then reform public organizations elsewhere in the world.

First, I summarize which policy initiatives, crafted by the new pluralists in L.A., sparked discernible results over the past quarter century and which reform logics fell flat. This plotline begins with how these young activists staked out that fresh civic terrain—gaining distance from corporate lobbies and union leaders—then built new forms of schooling and enriched respect and expectations for learning inside. Much work remains to unearth the political forces and organizational practices that lifted student achievement—buoyed within this sprawling city inhabited by poor and working-class families. Yet, activists and scholars have identified several reforms that somehow elevated the motivation and learning of students.

Second, it's helpful to dissect the rise of pluralist politics in Los Angeles, given its antecedent force in altering thick-skinned institutions like public schools. After all, pluralism as a form of human association has been debated for at least two millennia. In this chapter, I take stock of how contemporary pluralism, as traced in Los Angeles, may differ in its ideological motivations and resulting

challenge of arcane institutions. To grasp the power of local pluralism in altering public organizations, we must theorize its root causes and the social mechanisms through which it operates. To devise inventive urban policy—reforms
that attract sufficient credibility and political clout—let's be clear about what
animates the new pluralists, the organizing methods and models of social organization that they deploy. The democratic renaissance that has flourished in Los
Angeles becomes even more vivid when contrasted with earlier renditions of
pluralism.

I also cast a critical eye on contemporary pluralism, summing up the risks
taken when subverting central authority. The immediate case, as seen in chapter 3, speaks to the widening differentiation of school organizations in L.A.,
yielding early evidence that this may worsen the separation of strong from
weaker students. Threats to the common cause of equity and redistribution also
invite attack from corporate leaders who advocate for greater efficiency and
stronger achievement results, even when they attempt to starve the beast of tax
revenues. Or, take the well-heeled dot-com pluralists who scheme under the old
rules of power: funding the campaigns of local politicians who back charter
schools rather than placing this reform on the table, as one topic for democratic
deliberation. Such risks abound with the decentering drift of pluralism, a paradox that must be squarely faced.

Explaining the Mystery: Which Policy Logics Worked?

We have seen how the activists who emerged in the 1990s pitched a variety of
inventive reforms, aiming to improve teacher quality and detach expectations
for learning from the racial features of students. The new pluralists won more
progressive financing of schools in poor parts of Los Angeles. Civic challengers
and loyal insiders created entirely new forms of schooling, from integrated magnet schools and dual-language programs to controversial charter schools. The
book's middle chapters detailed *who* pressed for reform, *how* they aimed to alter school organizations, and *what* political strategies were employed to get the
job done. Let's first review what's been learned about the effects of each major
reform, especially the subset that discernibly lifted student achievement at some
point between 2002 and 2020.

Both camps of pluralists—whether loyal insiders or civic challengers—shared
a durable set of guiding principles. These core tenets expressed simple logics or
ideologies about how schools could work better: decenter school control away
from L.A. Unified's downtown bureaucracy and out to campus principals, move
new dollars to innovative educators and better resource schools that serve poor
communities, and foster respectful and motivating social relations between students and teachers. Political organizing might center around a discrete reform,
such as widening pupil access to college-prep courses or building human-scale

pilot schools. But ideals underlying advocacy efforts mirrored these core tenets over long stretches of time.

One related lesson is how agile activists often played the inside and outside games simultaneously. The palace revolt led by insurgent board member Yolie Flores, for instance, achieved the transfer of schools to independent site managers and teachers, while normalizing notions of organizational diversity from within the L.A. Unified apparatus. Flores was the consummate insider, successfully elected to the school board. But once installed, she allied with outside agitators, including charter enthusiasts and advocates for small, personalized schools. Similarly, the insurgent teachers who formed New TLA were suspicious of the downtown bureaucracy *and* charter proponents. So, these equity-minded teachers mimicked the independence enjoyed by charter schools while negotiating terms under which they remained union members and retained district-provided health insurance and pensions. Overall, this symbiotic energy between the two camps fostered ever-more-novel policy options and lent wider credibility to both wings of the pluralist movement.

The Inside Game Yields Results

The loyal insiders patiently labored with allies inside L.A. Unified, confident that this far-flung institution could nurture fair and effective schools from within. The table on page 150 offers a summary of which reforms displayed positive or negative effects at some point during the past quarter century. Earlier chapters detailed the policy options that empirically raised achievement or shaped the distribution of learning gains, whether gauged along lines of race or the economic status of students. I offer this overview with some trepidation, given methodological soft spots and the necessity of future research, topics to which I will return.

We saw how the loyal insiders regrouped in the 1990s, after their predecessors failed to racially desegregate, or decentralize control of, schools in Los Angeles. This moderate wing of activists then advanced five specific reforms, overlapping at first with Roy Romer's reign, beginning in 2000. Two of the reform efforts paid off in spades, if we assume that growth in test scores signals important progress in student learning. There was Romer's own push to specify learning objectives—what skills children should acquire grade by grade—then require all teachers to toe his curriculum line. It was a move consonant with tough-love accountability efforts, backed enthusiastically by civil rights organizations and New Democrats, like Bill Clinton and Barack Obama.

Romer's Open Court crusade would micromanage pedagogy and routinize the work of teachers. By intent, it pinned down the cognitive and social aims that came to dominate classroom instruction inside elementary schools. It was demoralizing in many corners and stirred unrelenting opposition from labor.

TABLE 1
Policy actions influencing student achievement or attainment in Los Angeles, 2000–2020

Policy	Benefits for the average student?	Fair distribution of school access or student achievement?
Advocated by loyal insiders		
Specifying curricular aims, regulating teaching methods	+	□
Improving facilities, reduce overcrowding	+	+
Raise teacher expectations, expand college-prep courses	+	□
Progressively distribute dollars to schools in poorest neighborhoods	+	+
Advocated by civic challengers		
Spread of charter schools	+	−
Spread of pilot schools	+	+
Zones of school choice	+	+
Student and community organizing	□	+

Note. Plus and minus signs indicate the direction with which the policy action changed the average student's achievement or educational attainment, or the fair distribution of such benefits. Squares indicate that no significant effect has been observed, as detailed in chapters 2 and 3.

Still, Romer's curricular campaign began to raise children's early literacy and numeracy skills, kick-starting the two-decade-long elevation of student achievement, when skeptics claimed it couldn't be done in a poor and blue-collar metropolis like Los Angeles.

Romer's second contribution seemed rather traditional but long overdue, given how severely overcrowded L.A. Unified's schools had become in the 1990s, especially in poor and immigrant neighborhoods. He successfully rallied voter support for a bevy of revenue bonds, raising more than $19 billion to build some 130 new school facilities across Los Angeles. Romer's policy initiative was aided by enthused new pluralists across the spectrum, from pro-equity nonprofits to Silicon Valley donors worried about the state of public education. We saw in chapter 2 how this massive infusion of construction dollars allowed groups like Inner City Struggle to propose and win a series of small high schools under the "pilot school" banner. A score of early learning centers were erected to dramatically expand slots for preschool-age children, along with expansion of magnet and dual-language programs. The bulk of new facilities went up in lower-income parts of L.A., while the renovation of old facilities unfolded in middle-class communities as well.

Our analysis, along with the extended study by Berkeley economists, revealed strong learning gains for pupils moving from overcrowded campuses to brand-new schools, as detailed earlier. These effect sizes ranged higher for kids who moved out of severely packed schools, those campuses running multiple shifts each day and all year long, often hosting dismal working conditions for teachers. Unlike Romer's curriculum effort, his construction crusade distributed achievement gains mostly to disadvantaged pupils.

The press to ensure college-prep courses for all students was a turning point for the loyal insiders, shifting the reform discourse and winning broad legitimacy for the new pluralists. After winning board approval in 2006, the question became: What does it look like, and how do we alter "entrenched norms" and teacher expectations inside schools? as Maria Brenes put it. The college-prep policy window proved "foundational to the work advanced after that time, like smaller and innovative learning environments," she told me, reflecting on her coalition's progress fifteen years later. The diffuse effects stemming from the A-G campaign are difficult to quantify, but it secured for pro-equity advocates an influential spot on this new civic terrain.

That said, the evidence of discrete benefits felt by students is mixed. The share enrolling in college-prep courses, those approved to count for admission to four-year colleges, has grown dramatically across high schools, as detailed in chapter 2. The same upward trend appears for teens' enrollment in Advanced Placement courses, in which performance is independently assessed. In turn, high school graduation rates have climbed remarkably, which likely aids young Angelenos in the labor market. National assessment scores for eighth graders in L.A. have climbed as well, by more than one grade level in reading and math over the past generation. Performance expectations for Black and Latino students appear to have trickled down into middle schools. These indicators signal a major victory for the social justice wing of the new pluralists, like Brenes and allied leaders at Coco and the ACLU. But the dial remains stuck when it comes to the share of graduates who actually enter and complete four-year colleges. Matriculation into two-year colleges has ticked upward, but just barely, in recent years.

School finance reform offers the final battleground, largely waged by loyal insiders, often in concert with outside agitation by civic challengers. Early successes hark back to the 1970s when the ACLU and Berkeley scholars convinced the California courts to equalize per pupil spending *among school districts*, a reform that survived the subsequent white backlash against desegregation and urban communities. Governor Jerry Brown's similarly ambitious effort nearly four decades later—urged and shaped by pro-equity nonprofits in the state capital—then boosted revenues for L.A. Unified, increasing its budget by about one-sixth relative to prior spending levels. Brown intended to lift the most disadvantaged students and narrow nagging achievement gaps.

My team, along with fellow researchers, found that district officials chose to regressively distribute new dollars out to *elementary schools*, many hosting the district's remaining fraction of middling and affluent families. In contrast, *high schools* in poorer parts of the district benefited most from the fresh infusion, progressively supporting new tutors for English learners, additional counselors, and smaller classes. We uncovered gains in student learning overall, yet no discernible closing of achievement gaps among racial groups could be detected. This finance reform may have sustained the steady climb of student achievement until about 2016, but pupil performance across L.A. Unified soon began to level off.

The high schools that enjoyed the largest funding gains tended to hire young and inexperienced teachers. These new recruits were then often assigned to classes serving English learners. Electives returned to high schools as No Child Left Behind collapsed in Washington. But the rising count of elective courses tended to displace rigorous college-prep courses. These organizational practices help to explain why stubborn disparities in learning have failed to budge, even as average achievement climbed across L.A. Unified. Without mindful planning at the school level, good intentions from governors or local school boards can go badly awry, Loyal insiders attempt to track implementation of their reforms, but how to effectively deploy new financing remains a cloudy organizational challenge.

Outside Agitators Bring Gains and Inequality

Meanwhile, the sharp-edged civic challengers were erecting a parallel network of charter schools. These taxpayer-financed, yet independently run, units formed the most radical incarnation of new institutional forms in Los Angeles. Charter schools steadily attracted a variety of families, eventually slicing the district's budget by about one-fifth in annual revenues. Many Black and Latino educators joined the charter school cause by the late 1990s, odd political bedfellows of corporate Democrats, the former frustrated over failed desegregation efforts and the inability of L.A. Unified and labor leaders to devise effective schools.

Charter schools did prove effective in lifting children's learning curves, relative to conventional schools on average, as detailed in chapter 3. But this alternative sector further separated low- from high-achieving pupils—sifting stronger Black and Latino students out of conventional schools. My team's research shows how traditional schools converting to charter status often seal off their mainly white or Asian-heritage students from kids of color. Meanwhile, new start-up charters attract families who have the wherewithal to shop across this evolving market of schools. This tends to attract parents with higher-achieving youngsters, creating stratified layers of kids even within Black and Latino communities.

Consistent with results observed by Stanford University researchers, we uncovered accelerated rates of learning among pupils attending charter elementary and middle schools, relative to peers remaining in conventional L.A. Unified schools. The largest benefits are accrued by Latino children, most raised in low-income families. What remains troubling is that children already show stronger reading skills and knowledge of math concepts as they *enter* charters at differing grade levels, relative to peers remaining in traditional schools. This "creaming" of higher-performing students may not be ill-intentioned on the part of charter leaders. More likely, it's the time, smarts, and means of particular parents to search out options.

We also reported how conventional schools that face more intense competitive pressure from nearby charters and private schools tend to lose more effective teachers, presumably to the surrounding circle of alternative campuses. Overall, it's difficult to argue that government should forgo ways of lifting working-class parents who struggle to advance better odds for their kids. At the same time, we found no evidence that L.A. Unified leaders are vigorously monitoring or mitigating the stratifying effects of charter schools.

The creation of pilot schools—mostly high schools set in poor neighborhoods—revealed a further contagion of organizational diversity. Institutional variety, matched with liberalized parental choice, offered a complementary strategy for the civic challengers. After taking into account the impoverished families they serve, we could detect no achievement advantage for pilot students, relative to peers remaining in traditional schools. Yet, we did find that pilot high schools retained a greater share of students, enjoying lower dropout rates. Pilot school graduates, despite coming from poorer families than peers in conventional schools, actually enter college at similar rates. Teachers in pilot schools sustain more trusting and collegial relations (as discussed in chapter 2). The tendency of pilot teachers to emphasize social justice themes distinguishes this organizational invention—hosting differing ethical and social convictions, not just distinct curricular themes.

It's the proliferation of zones of choice—building out from the Belmont Zone devised by equity-minded pluralists—that has displayed impressive results, at least for students who enter oversubscribed charters or district-coordinated alternatives, including magnet and pilot schools. My Berkeley colleagues, Chris Campos and Caitlin Kearns, found that students gaining admission to a high-demand school inside these zones displayed stronger growth in reading and math at moderate magnitudes when compared with peers who lost admission lotteries. These scholars also discovered that scores climbed, on average, for pupils attending schools within zones of choice, relative to students remaining in schools outside any zone of choice—what the authors term a local "market effect." Additional research is required to gauge the aggregate long-term effects of the widening array of pro-choice policies that have sprouted up in L.A. Unified. The mere variety of school forms and the legitimation of parental options testify to the rising political clout of the new pluralists.

Into the Weeds

Stepping back from these episodic policy victories, often followed by institutional gains achieved by the new pluralists, a few key lessons emerge. First, these inventive activists were not satisfied with gaining approval of their reforms; they worked in the weeds, inside schools, to implement discernible organizational change. Daily nudging was required to ensure that finance reforms actually moved dollars to the intended schools. ACLU attorneys and their nonprofit allies would return to court or appeal to state authorities when local progress was bogged down. Widening access to college-prep courses required that activists like Maria Brenes and Aurea Montes-Rodriguez and organizations such as the L.A. Partnership attend to the nitty-gritty of implementation inside schools, often working alongside district officials.

That is, these plural activists are rarely satisfied with winning a vote in the state legislature or moving the L.A. school board, then going home. They have labored over the past quarter century to distribute dollars progressively, deracialize teacher expectations regarding student capacities, add college counselors in high schools, and decriminalize discipline practices. At the same time, community organizers, such as Coco and Inner City Struggle, mobilize popular interest in reforms, keeping the pressure on district leaders while apprenticing the next generation of pluralists. The politics of pluralism come to life in erudite policy circles and on the ground with students and parents in a variety of neighborhoods.[1]

Another key lesson stems from how the pluralists have moved institutional change by battling successfully on several fronts at once. The symbiotic political relationship between the loyal insiders and civic challengers—borrowing organizational forms and mobilizing tactics from one another—adds to their shared capacity to mount multiple campaigns. Unlike the old political polarity in Los Angeles, the new pluralists have not pursued a unified or seamless reform agenda. The variety of policy efforts just summarized mirrors the internal diversity and plural character of education activists. They don't always agree on how to frame problems, or on their strategies for altering or competing against the dominating institution. Nurturing civic capacity to alter institutions does not necessarily connote a standard consensus on policy strategy.

Earlier, I raised the point that theorists like Clarence Stone worry about fragmentation of interest groups within the metropolis, presumably constraining civic capacity to advance a common project of institutional reformation. Instead, in Los Angeles we see a diverging spectrum of pluralists who respect one another's strategy, each advancing policy logics within that third political terrain while crafting differing ways to adjust or remake school organizations. It's this diverse range of policy options that helps distinguish contemporary pluralists from their tamer predecessors.

Pluralists act from a "bicameral orientation," as political theorist William Connolly put it. "You love your creed; you seldom leave it entirely in the closet when you enter politics. But you appreciate how it [is] profoundly contestable to many who do not participate in it," Connolly argues.[2] So, Black or Latino activists may mobilize from their particular conception of the institutional problem, then organize in culturally situated ways. The same is true for the ACLU's legalistic logics of reform, or how pedagogical reformers focus on social relations and knowledge inside classrooms. The identity of each group is rooted in their reform creed, *and* they respect and engage the strategies of others.

A Cautionary Note

Before dissecting the underlying anatomy of new pluralism, let's think critically about the quality and limits of evidence to date. Assessing the discrete effects resulting from a given policy reform is always a slippery exercise. Often a baffling array of initiatives unfolds simultaneously, each aimed at the same schools, overlapping in time and institutional space. Romer pushed to clarify learning goals in elementary schools, for instance, then insert his lockstep curriculum just as his massive construction program began. So, how to identify the specific effects of two co-occurring reforms? Earnest researchers prefer to randomly assign students (or units, like schools) to a single "treatment" group to avoid this murkiness (say, kids who enter preschool or a magnet program), then compare effects relative to a control group. But this elegant method often proves impractical or unethical.

Then, there's the old adage that correlation does not imply causality. Just because children attend a charter school and display higher achievement does not imply that the charter campus caused this difference. Scholars have devised quasi-experimental designs that attempt to minimize the threat of unobserved confounders. My team estimated achievement returns from charter and pilot schools using such methods, rendering greater (yet not foolproof) confidence in making causal inferences. It could be that a less visible home practice or attribute of parents explains the charter advantage, and we simply missed it.

Additional empirical results come in the form of suggestive associations—say, between Romer's regulated curriculum and soon-appearing gains in children's literacy scores. The time sequence implies, but does not prove, a causal direction and effect. Here, too, the possibility of omitted factors (for example, the interaction with students moving to a small school *and* experiencing the simpler curriculum) makes correlational findings less convincing. Such confounders may be difficult to observe (the hidden dynamics of why some low-income parents seek out a charter or magnet school while others do not, for instance). Nor do we know much about the cumulative effects of institutional reforms (say, tracing life inside L.A.'s evolving pastiche of schools), including the alleged improvement of social relations inside. We are just beginning to learn how the blossoming diversity of schools may shape teacher migration, perhaps funneling teachers to certain schools in ways that instantiate, rather than narrow, disparities in achievement. Much remains to be learned about what policy options work and for which students and families.

The Future of Pluralism, Old and New

> We always want to see what is hidden by what we are seeing.
> —René Magritte, surrealist painter

It's been easy to spot alternative schools multiplying across Los Angeles, or the proliferating count of charter schools, stirring political angst. Less visible are the original, deep-running forces that gave rise to the spectrum of activists that emerged by the 1990s. We have tracked differing reformers inside the bureaucracy, the likes of school chiefs Romer, Cortines, and Deasy. We learned of the fresh ideals and organizing strategies of new pluralists, such as Aurea Montes-Rodriguez or Ryan Smith, rising out of Latino and Black communities. Then there were the catalytic efforts of well-known nonprofits: the work of Elmer Roldan at United Way or legal tactics of Victor Leung at the ACLU. The raw politics and big money brought to the civic stage by the likes of Reed Hastings, Eli Broad, and Michael R. Bloomberg struck many as, well, in your face.

Less visible are the underlying forces that fostered the rise of this diverse range of new activists—a colorful mélange of players who were neither aligned with (low-tax) corporate interests nor with preservation-oriented union leaders. Why at this moment in social history—in the wake of economic distress and civil unrest—did a diversifying and democratic politics of schooling surface in Los Angeles? How did these young activists gain traction in civil society and steadily nudge the hog-tied institution of public education? In this final section, I unpack the origins and anatomy of new pluralism, then ask what essential lessons can be gleaned from, perhaps even applied to, other cosmopolitan centers around the globe.

Divisive tensions felt by central rulers—stemming from ethnic variety or the spread of plural nodes of authority—go back to Greek and Roman Empires. The perennial struggle of each regime, as influential elites set the social norms of civil society, was to unify and bound a political state in which residents would identify. This challenge persisted as the polity was being pulled apart by diffuse tribes out in the hinterlands (in Latin, literally meaning areas not controlled by the central state). One can read Saint Augustine's vivid descriptions of wild and wooly Carthage in the fourth century, where pagans, Christians, and Roman rulers cavorted together—reminding us how cosmopolitan societies are far from new or tranquil. Medieval scholars used the phrase "pluralism within unity," where tolerance of cultural differences characterized the metropolis, even when a central civil authority was endorsed by most citizens.[3] Amid tribal variety, civic rulers attempted to draw authority from military and religious institutions, or the landed (capitalized) class—gaining the political legitimacy to regulate behavior and beliefs. And circles of civic elites at times must nurture interdependent ties with the rise of novel institutions—witness the eventual alliance of Roman rulers with Christianity, earlier a rival node of popular authority.

The Protestant Reformation and Enlightenment in Europe would foster subversive ideals and political forms as well, challenging royal hierarchies and the Vatican. This required more tolerant accommodation among civic guilds, the nation-state, and cultural hinterlands. One political innovation was the decentralizing notion of *subsidiarity*. The Calvinist jurist Johannes Althusius first articulated this notion in the seventeenth century, pitching the argument that the central state should take on public works or human services only when local agencies failed to muster sufficient resources or managerial capacity. Better for local players to govern within village associations or tribal traditions than attempting to rationalize governance centrally. Common schools in New England—financed and run by town councils—were founded with the spirit of subsidiarity in mind.

The Center Fades

"Political society is governed by norms, not all of which are voluntary," writes philosopher Victor Muñiz-Fraticelli. "But all of which are publicly acknowledged and sustained through institutionally mediated practices."[4] It's local affiliations, civic groups, and ethnic leaders—diffused across decentralized authorities of civil society—that form the bedrock of social action, not centralizing political power, these theorists argue. Questioning the liberal premium placed on the sacred individual under Western political tenets, Alexis de Tocqueville similarly wrote in 1835, after his infamous tour of America: "The right of association is almost as inalienable as the right of personal liberty." Snugly fitting Althusiusan ideals, Tocqueville argued that local groups and their "organic" leaders would reinforce particular norms that provide the glue of democratic societies, not the rationalized policies pressed by a faraway state apparatus.

Flash forward to Governor Jerry Brown, the former Jesuit, who trumpeted the virtues of subsidiarity during his sixteen-year reign over contemporary California. He drew from the Althusiusan notion to justify decentralizing budget decisions—explicitly intended to stir participatory politics locally, moving contention over education down to human-scale levels. Brown's decentering flowed from and further kindled that third political terrain—as L.A.'s colorful agitators gained credibility to rabble-rouse on their *local* civic stage. Whereas state-level politics of education might still swivel around the influence of teachers' unions and corporate lobbies, this old dialect could not hold locally, upset by new pluralism.

One departure from old-world pluralism is that contemporary pluralists rarely abide by old Jeffersonian notions of democratic deliberation. Gone are the decorous days when competing parties came around the table, politely hammering out a compromise, and crafting a single rendition of the common good. This Jeffersonian process of democratic engagement by various interest groups still dominates how we think about local politics, as USC's Julie Marsh explored in her illumination of the new education politics.[5] Yet, a central tendency—an ideological pole anchoring the middle—is typically assumed. It's reminiscent of how Alexander Hamilton, James Madison, and Thomas Jefferson contested differing economic and religious interests, then formulated a compact that all parties could accept. A middle ground that would hold for two centuries.

Yet, the new pluralists of Los Angeles pursued a variety of divergent reforms, even creating a colorful garden of alternative schools. It's this tolerance or respect for differing policies, even diverging ideologies for how schools should work, that marks contemporary pluralism, not the Jeffersonian desire for compromise. So, the integrationist lobby wins resources to expand magnet schools, neoliberal marketeers gain taxpayer dollars for charter schools, and immigrant families prefer equity-minded pilot schools. Even Armenian parents peel off to shape their own dual-language campus. Yes, there's a shared reference point: the insular L.A. Unified bureaucracy and its sluggish ability to respond to cultural and pedagogical varieties. But pluralists then rally around such shared principles to create schools that reflect their particular identity, racial heritage, or pedagogical preference. Rather than opposing your rival's institutional form, the new pluralists pay homage to alternative ideologies and policy logics, even mimic certain organizational forms—when they serve particular ideals, tribes, or material interests.

Convergence toward a unitary resolution tends to blur a group's own racial and cultural identity, or perhaps the advocate's ideology of learning and human development. Therein lies the pluralist's rejection of a hegemonic melting pot, whether applied to cultural assimilation or faith in a single organizational form. At the same time in L.A., we see networks of school organizations—still run under the widening umbrella of public schooling—responding to the multiplicity of families and groups that populate this vast metropolis. It implies accenting the *pluribus* rather than the *unum*. This echoes philosopher Walter Feinberg's definition of the pluralist turn, as when members of "many different cultures should be allowed to pursue their own meanings and traditions in their homes, churches . . . communities."[6] This respect for, and even curiosity about, human difference and novel forms of social cooperation goes well beyond the occidental emphasis on individual rights, or the federalist principle of each province's right to self-determination. Tolerance remains key. So, too, is the task of learning from the ideals and social forms of other tribes—even importing or hybridizing one's own practices. Under this diffuse network of pluralists, it becomes difficult to find the central agency that "allows" this pluralist pastiche of social organizations.

Roots of Contemporary Pluralism

A pair of swift currents further helps to explain the rise of contemporary pluralism in Los Angeles. First, there's the overreach of early developers and their rationalization of massive public works, the uniform kinds of institutions on which L.A. was founded, as examined in chapter 1. This included by the early twentieth century faith held in the city's far-flung and regimented system of common schools. Such modern institutions came with untold uniformity and cultural conformity demanded by the Protestant Angelenos who dominated civil society until the 1990s. The political-economic tenets of Yankee Protestantism offered the underlying bulwark for massive investment in waterways, rail lines, and schools across the Southern California plain. The rationalization of trade and cookie-cutter housing, then industrial factories, became the guiding metaphor for social control inside schools. By the 1960s, the first wave of alienation, revolt against cultural hegemony, and repulsion over inequality would rise in Los Angeles. The profiteering and corruption that helped build modern L.A. served to marginalize and isolate non-Yankee Angelenos as well. The defeat over school desegregation only delayed the new pluralists' press of inclusion, respect, and variegated forms of schooling.

The underlying notions of modern progress imposed hierarchical forms of social organization and cultural hegemony. This included a municipal bureaucracy—beholden to investors, rail magnates, and developers—bent on assigning political rights to property and profit. This did help grow the white middle class and delivered material comforts to twentieth-century Angelenos. But the rationalization of work, learning, and life also conspired to subvert old-world nodes of belonging—social membership expressed inside ethnic or kinship ties, language groups, and places of worship, now stigmatized as backward and tribal. The dominance of impersonal pyramids of control would come to haunt urban elites by the 1960s, giving way to multiple and sustaining nodes of community—further animating the new pluralism.

Georg Hegel had argued a century earlier that modern states must stamp out voluntary organizations, which threatened to subvert the state's rationalizing agenda, the modern idea of progress. After all, the modernists preferred a "bellicose unitarianism," as Connolly calls it.[7] But the new pluralists would tap into the deepening hunger for more fulfilling kinds of social action, in part a return to those intermediate forms of human association. These social networks, arranged along borders of race, class, and religiosity, lend meaning to everyday life and host "intimacy, affection . . . trust and faith," as Robert Dahl writes, along with the "socialization into community norms for the preservation and transmission of culture."[8] The rise of identity politics renewed civic interest in these allegedly backward forms of social membership—ethnic heritage, church, and one's local patois, expressed by communities suddenly proud to speak in many tongues (one practice the modernists hoped to squash).

The cultural Left would rival the economic Left by the 1970s—splintering into identity politics that honored racial, gendered, and social class differences, the pluralist's respect for groups unlike one's own. A contagion of social movements would spread—for example, the Black struggle for liberation from institutionalized forms of racism; the Chicano movement, born in Los Angeles, then spreading across the nation; the feminist cause; and later gay rights. Countless islands of human associations, once draped in privacy and kept down by Protestant conformity, now erupted in pursuit of public recognition. Corporate-style forms of control would come undone, set against L.A.'s postwar enchantment with music, film, and out-there lifestyles. Damning critiques of mindless conformity appeared in books like *Organization Man* and *The Lonely Crowd*, feeding growing disillusion with regimented institutions. Or, take that rotund, martini-slurping businessman who insisted to Dustin Hoffman in *The Graduate* that his future was in plastics.

The rise of new pluralism in the closing fifth of the twentieth century was not just motivated by the attack on centralism and bureaucratic control. It was animated by this robust archipelago of cultural identities and alternative lifestyles as well, which began to reshape political associations and the segmentation of civil society. (Even the phrase "alternative lifestyles" feels dated, yet the ideological shift is lost on modern educators.) Political leaders became hard pressed to define "a substantive common good which the state must be concerned to promote," as political theorist David Nicholls argues. For this inevitably elevates "one conception of culture, politics, and the good life . . . [and] privileges one political agent [to] advance this conception over others."[9] By the 1990s, Californians no longer lived in "a unified world knowable through fixed laws . . . a monistic rationalism or absolutism, which postulates a rational whole in which we are set," as Connolly defines our tortured break from theological certainty and shared faith in (capitalist) progress.[10]

Our gaze in this book has focused on a single metropolis. Yet, these dynamics of difference and disaffection, of course, surface in many human settlements. Kwame Anthony Appiah, the New York University philosopher, reminds us that cosmopolitan networks consist of particular tribes whose members care most about their own. As Cicero said, "Human fellowship will be best served if we treat most kindly those to whom we are most closely connected." Yet, this contradicts the Greek notion that one should become a *cosmopolitan*, literally a citizen of the world, ready to respect and embrace the approaching stranger.[11]

So, when global capitalists or international regulators disregard a society's own economic or cultural interests, they suffer resistance from local tribes, whether voiced by conservatives, gay activists, or critics of the European Union. This postmodern departure advances along two paths. An array of diverging groups and ideologies appears simultaneously on the same civic stage, pressing for alternative forms of social relations, even diverse kinds of institutions. In Los Angeles, we saw this in how loyal insiders and civic challengers battled on several policy fronts at once. In addition, competition among interest groups— vying for popular legitimacy and public resources—may grow intense, stirred by differing ideologies of how institutions should work, toward differing ends. The competitive threat from expanding charter schools offers a vivid case in point. Still, the new pluralists typically respect the work of others, even coalesce around shared ideals, knitting together a common cause (for example, upending ineffective or uninspired educational institutions).

Against this backdrop, the morality of cosmopolitan pluralism strikes many as quite radical, even intolerable, as we have experienced in recent times with the rise of white nativism. To argue that human beings yearn for "many valuable ideals, pursuits, and aspirations," and that one's own group might respect differing pathways though life, as Muñiz-Fraticelli argues, marks the end of monistic beliefs, whether spiritual or cultural in character. We cosmopolitans are being asked to hold our closest affiliations and sacred totems as dear without stigmatizing those of others. All this helps the metropolis cohere. But for surviving nativists or cultural loyalists, cosmopolitan ideals predictably yield disorientation and political resistance.

The Anatomy of Pluralist Politics

It's helpful to clarify these prior cultural and economic streams that gave life to contemporary pluralists in Los Angeles, resembling creeks that fed into a larger confluence. Yet, can we discern persisting features, an observable structure, of this political realignment? I argue that this L.A. story exposes the limits of how we conceive of politics and institutions in the city—long portrayed by political-economy, neoliberal, or naively functionalist models. But I do not abide by chaos theory. Contemporary pluralism manifests certain structural dimensions across geographies and metropolitan communities. In contestation with established interests, we have observed three particular cornerstones of contemporary pluralism: the spread of *diverse forms* of organizations and social networks, *proliferating nodes* of legitimate authority, and the *bricolage character* of policy action. These dynamics animate and reproduce pluralist politics, then exercise the potential to remake institutions.

Like any good story, it's the compelling characters who animate the L.A. plotline. Karen Bass, the ER nurse who crafted a hope-filled and potent community organization. Or, Elmer Roldan, whose Guatemalan mother made sure he attended vibrant magnet schools, and who apprenticed at Coco before running United Way's pro-equity efforts. Still, these inspired activists operated within a fresh structuring of politics. Let's dissect and clarify its anatomy, contrasting basic foundations against older conceptions of what motivates the ideals, economic interests, and politics in metropolitan America.

The new pluralists, as individuals, grew up in particular neighborhoods, sharply bounded by race and class, raised by parents who sought better futures for their children. Ryan Smith was raised in predominantly Black parts of Texas and Los Angeles. Yolie Flores was born into one immigrant enclave between Watts and downtown, and was almost denied access to college by a warm yet traditional mother who insisted her campus would be too far from home (a twenty-five-minute drive). Their own childhoods figured into their favored reforms—laboring to build schools that respect difference, scaffold from kids' daily reality, and taught by teachers who care. Still, an underlying structure of contemporary pluralism stems from, and lends order to, the lived experience of these diverse activists.

Beyond Political Economy

Showered in this light of personal or political pluralism, one realizes that prior accounts of urban politics and institutional change are not wrong. But they do fall short and now appear incomplete. No doubt, wealthy parents will seek to preserve their class position, many enjoying suburban lifestyles on the west side of L.A., where morning fog and sea breezes flow, savoring their Mercedes SUVs and trendy eateries. Selecting a charter or private school may signal greater prestige, a bow toward selectivity. Yet, this is not simply manifest in "white privilege." Visit hip cafés or dress shops in racially integrated parts of Culver City, Echo Park, Asian communities in the Valley, or (mostly Latino) Koreatown, and you will discover ethnic blends of families striving for a better life. These parents make choices that advance their household's interests and, in the aggregate, the cultural identity and status of their tribe.

Still, this political-economy account of metropolitan politics—highlighting competition among social groups for material advantage—fails to capture contemporary dynamics in places like Los Angeles. The explanatory model oversimplifies the variety of policy actors and parental motivations that spur demand for better, more responsive schools. Nor does the dusty polarity between capi-

tal and organized labor suffice in explaining the array of policy innovations that
have bubbled up over the past quarter century. Magnet schools currently receive
more than 73,000 parent applications yearly; more than 165,000 families opt for
a charter school each year in L.A. This occurs in a district where four in five kids
come from a Latino heritage and more than two-thirds qualify for subsidized
meals. Yes, parents are searching for better schools and seeking out livable neighborhoods. But is this dynamic solely animated by the pursuit of class advantage, or might the motivation lie in a deeper yearning for social membership,
where kids feel recognized and respected, along with schools that feel safe and
engaging?

The notion that a dominant cabal manipulates the politics of education has
gained many adherents over the past half century, of late framed as neoliberal
conspiracy. "Every viable agenda for urban school system reform depends on a
coalition of individuals and groups to develop ideas and press for their accep-
tance by government authorities," as Dorothy Shipps says in her analysis of how
elite actors largely drove school reform in Chicago.[12] Or, take Stone's influential account, drawing on how racial interests coalesced to modernize Atlanta.
Yet, he offers a rather dismal forecast for civic players who seek "an open and
penetrable process, yielding to those who become active around particular issues salient to them." Stone's main connotation for pluralist contention equals
"fragmentation," and he argues that civic capacity only arises when dominating
actors form united coalitions.[13]

The plural diffusion of activists and organizations does not preclude unity
around shared aims. Václav Havel, the Czech playwright turned political pris-
oner, advocated scattering the political economy of his Soviet-controlled society "based on the maximum possible plurality of many decentralized, structur-
ally varied, and preferably small enterprises that respect the nature of different
localities . . . and resist the pressures of uniformity."[14] Havel pursued his commitment to thickening civil society and was elected president of the newly democratic Czech Republic following the implosion of the Soviet Empire in 1989.
For Havel, the decentering of institutions was to serve a unifying, nearly spiritual purpose. "The most important thing is not to lose sight of personal relationships," Havel writes, to labor "as beings with a soul and sense of responsi-
bility, not as robots." Contemporary pluralists echo this cultural aspiration,
seeking social organizations that offer a sense of belonging and meaning, and
this requires institutional variety.

The blossoming of differing activists—who advocated ideals and economic
arrangements beyond the interests of concentrated capital and conservative
labor—certainly results in strange bedfellows and fluid alliances. Political scientist Jeffrey Henig emphasizes how racial or ethnic divides can undercut efforts
to rally around shared reforms. Indeed, race played a decisive role, not only in

the biographies and lived experience of L.A. pluralists but also in how they broke from the established polarity between capital and labor by the 1990s. The class and cultural heritage of many Black and Latino leaders displayed little in common with corporate elites or union leaders. Yet, a return to racial or cultural affiliation, set against a plain-vanilla suburban existence, helped fuel new forms of schooling in Los Angeles, along with the pluralist's search for more engaging and responsive social relations inside public education.

The earlier politics of education largely ignored the role of racial divisions, the "importance of politics and coalition building in determining the viability of reform endeavors," as Henig argues.[15] Certainly, a critical mass of players must come together, loosely joined by key principles (for instance, decentralizing governance or nurturing respectful social relations inside schools) to mobilize and ensure that institutional change sticks over time. But we also discover it's the *variability* of reform logics and the *simultaneous* pursuit of differing agendas that invigorate the fresh policy logics advanced by the new pluralists. Shipps similarly highlights the virtues of conflict and contention in Chicago, arguing that Stone views "reform" as a one-dimensional dynamic, when in fact differing kinds of organizational changes are pursued by plural activists amid a fluid swirl of networks and coalitions. Marcus Weaver-Hightower argues that when analysts focus on elite actors, including critics of neoliberalism, within a metropolitan ecology of civic action, they "fail to capture the true complexity of the policy context . . . the various components that influence policy making and implementation across time."[16]

The search for engaging communities with good schools, as the middle class grows more racially diverse, alters the local political economy as well. Take the case of Burbank, adjacent to Hollywood and a once lily-white suburb. The city's schools rest just outside the border of L.A. Unified while serving a diverse rainbow of children, nearly one-half from families living below the poverty line. Yet, Burbank's schools have become remarkably integrated along lines of race and class. To retain middle-class, white, and Asian-heritage families, Burbank educators invest in art and music curricula and in career pathway programs, "which appeal to all parents," as schools chief Matt Hill told me. A pair of elementary schools immerse their students in two languages, English and Spanish. Hill's only problem is that these dual-language programs are so popular that the schools lack enough seats to admit all the white families who apply.[17] It's against this organizational palette that families opt for schools that speak to their cultural or pedagogical preferences. These schools offer kids and parents that feeling of respect and membership, a sense of belonging. In short, cosmopolitan pluralism holds the potential for growing institutions that move beyond the reproduction of class advantage.

Plural Organizations and Social Networks

Neither class domination nor simple functionalist accounts of metro politics fully recognize how cultural variety, along with the pursuit of situated identities, act to diversify the character of human associations and institutions. One huge lesson from L.A. is how plural groups, as they gain political credibility, pursue plural forms of institutions. It's no longer the case that previously disenfranchised groups—the array of non-Protestant "others" once excluded by elite Angelenos—search for assimilative ties in hegemonic organizations. Plural groups begin to build new firms or networks in which they find belonging and everyday efficacy. Sure, economic security and material fairness are key aims in the pluralist quill of policy targets. The central state retains a role in fairly distributing wealth and opening pathways for getting ahead. But markets and government rarely substitute for the coherence provided by close ties—ethnic networks, family, church, and local schools. These tribal affiliations invoke cultural particulars, whether a family experiences status and belonging in a lily-white suburb or the bustling barrio of East Los Angeles.

Recall the late nineteenth century, when L.A.'s downtown elites and cautious Progressives agreed on a single animating force: modern economic progress required incorporating foreign groups into the Yankee melting pot. This cultural (Protestant) gruel assured political stability and the promise of material opportunity for all. Rationalizing institutions, like common schooling, were designed to socialize these strangers to the dominant racial and religious frame. Cosmopolitan pluralism, in bright contrast, recognizes particular locations for social affiliation, no longer hosted in vast, Weberian-like hierarchies. Under cosmopolitan pluralism, the city is not a place that demands seamless acculturation. It's a sprawling location that hosts countless associations and networks, human-scale circles that envelope tribal members. After all, the etymology of the word *civility* implies a place where strangers can forge a relationship. The city has long been viewed as the place "where strangers are most likely to meet," as sociologist Richard Sennett once wrote.[18] Pushing further, the pluralist turn fosters a wider checkerboard of civic spaces as pluralists press for greater economic parity within a world of cultural difference. This tandem policy agenda has come to be viewed as politically legitimate and fair, a shared aspiration across the demographic archipelago.

The pluralist turn also implies the demise of monistic institutions, such as centrally regimented forms of schooling. Instead, a diverse collection of associations—from devotees of indie music to quilting clubs, diverse schools or health care providers—now rival the graying institutions that insist on universal forms of language, knowledge, and everyday behavior. But as pluralist politics become embodied in diverse organizations, serving a variety of "public" aims, these institutions further legitimate and distinguish human difference. We saw in chapter 3, for instance, how the spread of charter schools spurred the creation of their own lobby in the state capital, which obtains greater funding for their preferred organizational form. Pilot school principals in L.A. have organized their own association to advance their rendition of education. Differentiated forms of schooling advance segmented constituencies that demand their own slice of public resources. This, in turn, challenges what is defined as a public organization and which forms of social cooperation are particular, even private, in character.

Proliferating Nodes of Authority

We also observed how contemporary pluralists pursue two novel strategies. They labor to *diffuse social authority* and political action across multiple locations, democratizing the organizational locations of influence. Plural activists also piece together *novel policy logics*, aiming to alter social relations inside institutions or devise entirely new ones. They essentially tinker toward alternative utopias, cobbling together a variety of ideals and organizational models, an exercise in *policy bricolage*.[19] The blend of decentering control of schools then progressively funding sites that serve low-income families offers one inventive policy logic. Collateral efforts—say, expanding dual-language programs or social justice–oriented pilot schools—are pursued by loyal insiders who legitimate multiple cultural or pedagogical positions, reflecting differing notions of teaching and learning. The net effect is to establish multiple locations of social authority from which inventive policies or institutional reforms can then be attempted.

Yes, conservative chieftains of capital will still work to limit public investment. Labor leaders may harp on preserving their own members' interests. In contrast, pluralists open a wider political terrain, advancing a variety of ideologies and economic strategies, from how kids are socialized in school to how taxpayer dollars are distributed among differing forms of schooling. The common enemy across the internally diverse movement of pluralists remains bland and monistic institutions. It's "only through participation in the civil structures of political activity that man's autonomy, and with it that of reason, [are] guaranteed," as Immanuel Kant argued.[20] Building out a participatory politics, democratizing who's at the table defining problems and posing remedies, is key to the everyday work of pluralists. From a widely democratized discourse stems a wider variety of social arrangements and public institutions.

This is not to say that power and money are evenly spread across political actors. It remains a lumpy playing field in Los Angeles. Earlier, I reported on how pro-charter advocates—like Hastings, Broad, and Bloomberg—continue to donate millions of dollars to local politicians who pledge allegiance to this cause. Yet, the pluralists have moved to level the playing field. The pro-equity wing has succeeded in legitimating small high schools, pilot campuses, and magnet programs—each winning credibility and material resources. Or, consider the ability of Coco and Inner City Struggle to deliver hundreds of parents and students to school board meetings downtown when a pressing issue requires their advocacy. This same coalition moved the L.A. Unified board in 2021 to allocate $700 million to the most hard-pressed schools as they recover from the deadly pandemic.

The dispersed political landscape that's evolved resembles "a plurality of relatively autonomous organizations within the domain of the state," as Dahl puts it.[21] Muñiz-Fraticelli calls this a "plurality of normative phenomena within [a] domain of practical reason," where even the state must now foster "several sources . . . of legitimate authority," from funding charters to pitching the virtues of bilingual learning.[22] This tacitly legitimates varying logics for how schools are financed and managed each day, and the social relations to be fostered across campuses. More broadly, the constitutive rules of civic engagement must now include the new pluralists, their various logics of reform, and alternative ways of organizing schools.

Fleshing out an episode from chapter 2 helps illustrate how pluralists have dispersed social authority more widely on the civic stage. Helping to settle the L.A. teachers strike in 2019, union leader Alex Caputo-Pearl proposed new funding and job posts for schools located in poor neighborhoods, along with shrinking class sizes. It was a rare instance of the teachers' union supporting progressive targeting of resources to lift the most disadvantaged students. Caputo-Pearl had echoed one plank of the pluralist platform—behavior never predicted by old-school functionalist or political-economy conceptions of metropolitan politics.

Or take the case of charter school activists who highlight their shiny new campuses in poor parts of Los Angeles, dodging any debate over charters that operate in gated communities. To be credible, even pro-market advocates must mimic the discourse of social justice, deploying what sociologist Pierre Bourdieu called *symbolic capital*—accumulated stocks of signs and ideals now prized by the new pluralists. The currency of these symbols—equity, decentralized governance, mission-driven curricula, rigorous and caring relations inside schools— was first established, and remains bolstered, by the new pluralists. (A year later, board member Jackie Goldberg, a tight UTLA ally, tried to abolish the Student Equity Needs Index [SENI], which has sent nearly $1 billion to high-needs schools, a move soundly defeated after central-city parents and students testified in opposition.)

Bricolage: Cobbling Together Novel Policy

The formulation of inventive policy makes for the final element of new plural-ism's underlying anatomy. We have seen how these activists typically begin with a lean causal logic for how the institution can work better, what some call *pol-icy logics*. Chapter 2, for instance, explored the half-century-old debate in L.A. over decentralizing school control, whether this devolution of authority moves out to charter schools in white gated communities or to schools competing with one another in the Belmont Zone of Choice, serving immigrant Latino fami-lies. Decentering control, causally speaking, is tied to the authority of principals or neighborhood advocates over budgets and teacher hiring. This, the logic argues, then leads to the recruitment of stronger teachers and greater cohesion among staff and students.

Such causal sequences are rarely tested in advance. Instead, they are fungi-ble images, the coin of the realm, for how activists theorize about fixing recal-citrant institutions. The simplicity and portability of each policy logic help mo-bilize key actors behind the alleged fix. Expanding access to college-prep classes will boost teacher expectations, advocates claim. Or, magnet schools with a particular curricular mission will rally pupils and teachers around a shared enterprise and reap the benefits of racial integration. Pluralist soil gives root to a variety of policy logics. These easily grasped causal models then travel across interest groups eager to find more effective, caring, or culturally situated mech-anisms through which institutions just might work better.

Much of this book weighed the empirical validity of key policy logics that stuck in the education sector, many authored by the new pluralists. That is, the causal fixes that did empirically lift students or better motivate teachers. But this key structural feature of pluralism is not positivist in nature. The dynamic cen-ters on the fact that a plural range of actors, when gaining a toehold on the civic stage, proliferate diversifying policies. We have explored how the new pluralists—whether loyal insiders or civic challengers—successfully devised and expanded a diverse population of schools, as well as altered social relations and pedagogical rigor found inside campuses. Each reform sprouted up from seed-ing and legitimating an inventive logic.

Not all logics gain sufficient political support. Some do, yet fall short when implemented inside sticky, often routinized public institutions. But these causal models—centered on better organizing life inside institutions—reflect differing "norms of rationality," as Patricia Thornton and her colleagues argue. Thorn-ton emphasizes macro logics, such as whether organizations operate under a "family" metaphor or perhaps staff are nurtured as "professionals." Alternatively, the organizing logic may mirror a credible "corporate" logic of efficiency.[23] We can extend Thornton's broad notion of logics to the social or material mechanisms that operate within policy spheres—easily grasped causal models for altering the behavior of organizations or individuals inside private firms or public institutions.

What's useful for pluralists is that policy logics travel through space and time, gaining currency far beyond their original authors or adherents. Recall how enthusiasm for school-site management first surfaced in the 1980s, as the corporate-led LEARN coalition hoped to decentralize school control and professionalize teaching (chapter 2). Their initiative failed, but the core logic of granting power to principals lived on, rekindled by charter school advocates, along with teachers who created social justice–focused pilot schools. Likewise, diffuse or regimented logics for specifying learning aims and improving pedagogical rigor resurfaced frequently over the past quarter century. We saw this compact causal model in Superintendent Romer's hard-edged version, then again as pro-equity groups worked to implement rigorous college-prep courses for high school students.

As reform logics become credible, a variety of civic activists begin to play in parallel fashion with one another, altering the constitutive rules of the game. These logics come to move about civic spaces independently of any particular civic actor. When shifting resources to high-needs schools served the interests of both the ACLU *and* the L.A. schools chief, the logic's appeal helped to unite otherwise contentious groups. And the resilient life of certain policy logics helps to explain how disparate groups come together in the third civic realm. The tandem logics of decentralizing who runs schools, when married with parental choice, attracted unexpected allies—from dot-com donors to neighborhood-control advocates in Black and Latino communities. It's the mending together of such logics that can attract a powerful coalition. It becomes an exercise in bricolage, a cobbling together of preexisting logics into a fresh causal argument for how to better organize schools.

Dominating logics of social control or economic distribution can operate at multiple institutional levels simultaneously. The pro-equity wing of pluralists continues to assume that a centralized L.A. Unified structure is required to redistribute funding to schools in the poorest neighborhoods. On another front, it's the dismantling of central controls that's the priority. Overall, the demise of the old order and hegemonic institutions does not mean that central nodes of social authority disappear. And multiple policy logics may operate in contradiction with one another.

At the same time, policy logics offer attractive devices around which diverse pluralists can discover common cause: liberalizing parental choice of schools, devising small high schools, or fostering warm and demanding expectations for all students. Adhering to a certain logic helps foster a "thick network of pluralism," as Connolly argues.[24] Various civic groups reach consensus on a shared logic that signals how to improve the social organization of schools. In this way, pluralists may subvert tired forms of centralization while rallying around a shared reform agenda.

In sum, the underlying forces that animate the L.A. story come into plain sight as the anatomy of contemporary pluralism is revealed. This city's political economy involves more than the pursuit of class or racial advantage. It also entails the pursuit of identity and social membership, and these aspirations implicate civic spaces and contested institutions. Finding schools in which children feel safe and meaningfully engaged reflects the pursuit of finding one's place, a haven in a sometimes heartless world. In turn, as cultural communities gain pride and civic respect, a wider range of activists labors to create responsive institutions—striving to match the cosmopolitan array of ideals, languages, and practices for how best to raise children. The power of pluralism then stems from the capacity of advocates to disperse social authority across multiple groups, innovative educators, students, and parents—that colorful array of players climbing atop the civic stage over the past quarter century. These new civic players then borrow or devise policy logics, gaining support for their portable models that portend to enliven institutions.

This X-ray of pluralism's anatomy offers more than an academic portrait. These deep-running dynamics also challenge how policy analysts and tacticians conceive of collective action in cosmopolitan regions of the world. A politics that blends economic fairness, cultural cohesion, and belonging invites a novel policy agenda, one that new pluralists in Los Angeles have well honed over the past generation. It's one reason that public schools remain so pivotal to the new urban politics: this human-scale institution promises to foster closer social ties, a sense of common cause inside neighborhoods. Consider how the new pluralists win politically by uniting fluid and transient coalitions of actors, depending on the ideology and economic interests in play. Or, the traveling of policy logics and bricolage required to gain legitimacy for fresh and persuasive models of institutional reform.

Looking Back, Moving Forward

A final check-in with key players seemed prudent as I completed this book. Schools had been shuttered for over a year by the pandemic. But vaccination rates soon inched upward, and schools reopened with a sense of trepidation. Educators and commentators even dreamed of resetting the institution of schooling, perhaps enlivening classrooms with the digital and social innovations that teachers had forged out of necessity. The unevenly felt health crisis and police killings of Black citizens had, once again, heightened public concern with inequality. "We are a hot-spot for the pandemic," Maria Brenes underlined. "The east side and South L.A., showing the worst infection rates, lack of ICU beds, deaths, and unemployment." Yet, Brenes remained forward-looking. "It's an opportunity to reimagine schools, because now we know how vital they are," she said.

Asked about her proudest accomplishments over the past quarter century, Brenes returned to her victory in 2005 to extend college-prep courses to all high school students. The discrete policy change was monumental in her mind. Yet, the coalition building with Inner City Struggle, Coco, and their equity-minded allies proved equally consequential in the long term. It forced L.A. Unified officials to explain dismal graduation rates and gross disparities in achievement among racial groups. Winning the debate over whether only certain students deserved quality schools, and how teacher expectations had become racially arranged, put these new pluralists on the political map. "We envisioned schools [that] humanize students, support them holistically . . . acknowledge who they are and where they come from," Brenes told me in 2021. But instead, teens and parents faced "institutional racism," overcrowded campuses, and differing assumptions about kids' capacities to achieve, based on their racial or social-class backgrounds, she recalled.

Convincing the L.A. school board that educators must work to ensure that all kids hold the option of entering college "really shifted the narrative about the root causes of poor academic outcomes," Brenes said. "It was the system that was deficient, not the families." This seismic jolt in expectations led to the question, What facilitates school environments that meet the rigor expected under A-G (college-prep) courses? Here the district's school construction effort greased the wheels to build small high schools, Brenes told me, along with advancing the zones of choice in which a variety of magnet, pilot, and dual-language campuses began to proliferate. "These were to be college preparatory academies," creating the "opportunity to become more creative and bold." And with the east side zone of choice, "now there's competition in a good way for the benefit of families and students." Brenes also celebrated the SENI distribution formula, reporting that the "equity alliance" will push to apply to larger shares of the L.A. Unified. "The $283 million is not enough," especially as L.A. schools recover from nearly a year of running online.

Victor Leung, the ACLU litigator, also emphasized how winning on progressive finance interacts with efforts to cultivate an engaging school climate for students and teachers. He touted two finance reforms as "the big game changers." Leung first emphasized the *Williams* victory in 2004, in which California settled with the ACLU to guarantee a minimum count of textbooks and sufficient instructional materials, as well as safe and clean facilities for all students. "It wasn't just us [who worked on the case]," Leung said. "We were joined by Public Advocates and the Mexican American Legal Defense and Education Fund."

For Leung, the "big victory legislatively" was Governor Brown's Local Control Funding initiative in 2013. Allied advocates successfully lobbied in the state legislature "to move toward an equity-based system . . . [under which] districts serving higher-needs students do receive more money," he said. "Now they just have to spend it properly . . . making sure the money goes to the right places." Recall that in 2017, the ACLU and Coco reached a settlement requiring that L.A. Unified allocate another $151 million to schools in low-income parts of the district.

But allocating money to "the right places" is difficult to achieve through litigation alone, even assuming we knew empirically what staffing patterns, forms of schooling, and pedagogy are most effective in lifting student motivation and achievement. "The hard part here is culture change," Leung admitted. "These are [legal] tools to change the narrative, but it's up to hyperlocal actors, good principals, and administrators, who actually believe in these things." Leung, echoing a pluralist refrain, talks of "holistically supporting students," attending to their social-emotional learning, especially in the moment, as schools reopen following the Covid-19 pandemic. Leung commends "labor's big push for community schools" under Alex Caputo-Pearl, "campuses that support students more than in just an academic way."

Aurea Montes-Rodriguez, the forceful strategist at Coco, spoke of the uneven capacity of school principals to think boldly and enrich relations between teachers and students, the pluralist draw on humanist logics, not simply reallocating material resources. Even when the pluralist alliance wins progressive funding, principals and teacher leaders may simply apply Band-Aids to the most glaring organizational wounds. "Schools with intermediaries, like the Partnership [for L.A. Schools], receive supports that enable principals to better understand the overall budget," Montes-Rodriguez told me. "This is why we are focusing on the district's capacity to support these [central-city] schools. It is a question of leadership, but also [of] how . . . we keep resources stable in these schools for three to five years." After principals succeed in turning around pallid campuses, they often seek promotions into the district bureaucracy, she emphasized, rather than being rewarded for inspiring management inside schools.

According to Montes-Rodriguez, a fresh generation of union leaders bodes well for progressively financing schools, even nurturing teachers who respect and build instruction from the daily struggles and questions asked by urban students. With regard to the UTLA, "it's early to know how much they will be able to move," she said. "We do see more points of agreement—standing up at the LAUSD board meeting [in 2020], saying, 'Yes, we must defund the [L.A. Unified] school police'—where they are with us." Montes-Rodriguez reports curiosity among new labor leaders over the SENI budget index, directing dollars to high-needs schools. "UTLA is receptive, she said. "As they say, 'Okay, let's look at your list, let's understand the SENI [budget formula], let's have the conversation.' We are seeing more spaces where they [union leaders] are support-

2020. Hundreds of students and community members gather at the Miguel Contreras Learning Complex in East Los Angeles, urging the L.A. Unified School District to defund its police force. Photo by Al Seib and reprinted with permission of the *Los Angeles Times*

ing the demands of students and parents, which emerges from the organizing." Here, too, we see how older, still powerful interests begin to dance with the new pluralists, advancing novel policy together, a richer political romance.

Ryan Smith keeps the long view in mind. Recall that he's the inventive organizer who filled the avenue with classroom desks outside L.A. Unified headquarters. He became a student organizer in L.A. at the age of 15, "when I came of age politically," and "Aurea [Montes-Rodriguez] was my boss at YUCA . . . when she was in college."[25] Smith would rise to oversee United Way's education portfolio, prior to Elmer Roldan's arrival. Of late, he accents the importance of "implementation advocacy," such as the SENI allocation formula, "how advocates have become a lot more sophisticated . . . going back to refine the index . . . for how the district can invest more money to support the highest-needs schools. You can't just pass a policy, applaud, and go onto the next big fight," Smith said. "The proof is really in the implementation."

"L.A. has dealt with the major issues that other cities face," Smith told me: "how to support opportunity and achievement gaps, xenophobic policies, the conversation around the emergence of charter schools." Yet, the success of fellow pluralists in L.A. stems from the fact that it's a "coalition city," as Smith puts it. "A lot of progressive education policies have come on the heels of successful coalition building." He calls Coco and Inner City Struggle "sister organizations," which successfully pushed the "student- and teacher-led A-G equity campaign, a cause that I grew up with." He noted the success of decentralized networks, such as pilot schools and the Partnership for Los Angeles Schools, "moving hundreds of millions of dollars into high-needs schools . . . and [then] showing [them how to accomplish] the highest rates of achievement growth."

"For a long time we focused on the larger education reform efforts, like standards and accountability. But in Los Angeles that era has moved on to an educational and racial justice effort," Smith told me. "There's a history of institutional and economic racism that's played itself out. So, there's a conversation . . . that puts the focus on the institutional and the historical context." He stressed the importance of "finding . . . evidence-based practices to best support Black students." Overall, Smith bows toward strengthening pluralist coalitions and stays centered on implementation, as the array of policy wins multiplies. It's staying focused on how to alter human-scale dynamics inside schools that Smith emphasizes, pinpointing the social practices that still deflate the futures of Black and Latino students.

Pluralist Scaffolds and the Common Good

Despite the promise of contemporary pluralism, we must avoid viewing these dynamics through rose-colored glasses. First, dominant groups rarely yield their economic or political might without a prolonged fight. When the center fails to hold, eroded by divisive cultural or racial difference, the strongest tribe often resists. In addition, our analysis detailed how embracing human variety—be it ordered by plural cultural or class-based forms—can operate to preserve and tacitly legitimate inequality. "E pluribus unum" makes for a nifty motto, but it's difficult to sustain the political tolerance and institutional diversity that the Latin ideal implies. It makes for the pluralist's paradox.[26]

A related challenge is how to solidify the pillars of pluralism. The flourishing of civic activists who advance a respectful and tolerant civic discourse remains a fragile development, even in Western-like democracies. The revival of white nationalists in America and Europe—one group that literally attacks fellow citizens who express differing languages, identities, and lifestyles—makes for an obvious case in point. More broadly, dominant or threatened groups have lashed out at those who threaten their own economic security or social status. Back in Los Angeles, this includes the descendants of California elites like Henry Huntington and Leland Stanford, many of today's corporate leaders, and white voters who question public investment in schools that serve other people's children. Yet, the intolerance and disinterest in the Other is not limited to conservatives. We see the absence of pluralist respect when wealthy liberals look down their noses at working-class families or try to "fix" poor parents. Recall when Hillary Clinton infamously painted supporters of her campaign opponent, Donald Trump, as "deplorables." This works against the long-term viability of cosmopolitan pluralism.

The ideology of modernity still relies on the sacred individual as market actor, one who seeks material advantage, a better job, gaining the freedom to secure that patch of home in a tree-lined suburb. The ongoing sprawl of housing and freeways that marks the cliché of L.A. began rolling nearly a century and a half ago, when early investors aimed to build that Arcadian nirvana, shaped by Protestant verve and faith in capitalist expansion. Instead, contemporary pluralists urge us to rethink this dominant frame for how we organize civil society—to respect and be curious about alternative ways to work and learn, how to put fairness above self-interest. But respect for, and perhaps curiosity about, strangers outside one's tribe remains a brittle endeavor. This is why the politics of education remain pivotal. Until we arrange shared institutions to respect and respond to differing cultural frames, teaching cooperation in the context of difference, metropolitan democracy remains in doubt.

The pluralist's paradox remains equally slippery. We have seen how cultural and political variety becomes embodied in alternative forms of schooling. The book's middle chapters detailed how the spread of various forms of schooling in Los Angeles have led, in some cases, to motivating workplaces for teachers and steeper learning curves for students. But the widening differentiation among schools also worked to reinforce inequality. We discovered two worrisome examples. As charter schools expanded across L.A., they admitted students (early in grade cycles) who already outperformed their peers who remained behind in traditional public schools. Magnet schools offer a second case, where selective admissions of students, coming from a variety of racial and class backgrounds, act to separate high- from low-achieving youngsters.

This bittersweet result of the pluralist revolution is that student achievement steadily climbed over the past quarter century, on average, while disparities in learning curves failed to narrow among Asian-heritage, Latino, and white pupils. Black students actually drifted further behind all of these groups. College-going rates are improving for a wide variety of L.A. Unified graduates, albeit at a glacial pace. Still, for all the success of equity-minded pluralists, students of color remain at the back of the line when it comes to school success.

Overall, the politics of education in this vast metropolis have witnessed a radical restructuring. Contemporary pluralists in Los Angeles—carving out that third political terrain—have advanced fairness and placed cultural and educational variety front and center. In turn, the once lifeless institution of public schooling now shows a vital pulse, adapting from within and being stiffly challenged on the outside, and somehow lifting student learning for nearly a generation. This institutional renewal was driven largely by the young activists who arose in the 1990s, those who departed from conservative elites and labor leaders clinging to the status quo. Critics said it could not be done. But the new pluralists animated a political realignment and novel institutional reforms, remaking many public schools in Los Angeles.

The cosmopolitan fabric of L.A. no longer resembles its old Spanish plaza, once bounded materially and culturally by military barracks and the Catholic church that still stands. Instead, a more inclusive civic stage hosts a breathless array of activists—those who foster inventive ways of reshaping schools that now appeal to differing communities across this dispersed metropolis. In a sense, the players and arenas of political engagement have come to mirror the worlds of indie music, social media, or tattoo parlors. The desired ends vary, and the social means employed are loosely harmonized by a variety of collective actors. Still, each field of human activity unfolds in a recognized and coherent genre, a theater that unfolds with a variety of scripts and players, each ensuring visceral feelings of membership and belonging for many. "To be an agent means to be capable of exerting some degree of control over the social relations in which one is enmeshed," writes sociologist William Sewell Jr. "Agency is implied by the existence of structure."[27] In Los Angeles, we observe the dawning of fresh and nimble institutional arrangements.

As identity politics and racial conflict intensified across the nation in the 1990s, sociologist Todd Gitlin warned of a "twilight of common dreams," fearing the loss of shared public projects and the dismantling of a unified civil society in America.[28] But perhaps the tale of pluralist politics in Los Angeles offers a hopeful dawning of interwoven dreams. The politics of education that has emerged is founded on ethnic and cultural building blocks. Each offers a coherent identity, replete with shared customs and idioms, a familiarity that fosters membership. From this cultural archipelago, we have seen different groups finding common cause in lifting the institution of schooling. It's the constant negotiation between the celebration of difference and the formulation of shared reforms that marks new pluralism, arbitrating between institutions that elevate all children while ensuring efficacy and meaning.

This feisty network of contemporary pluralists has energized a new metropolitan politics. They have moved an institution once given up for dead in Los Angeles. It's their unrelenting flurry of protests downtown, engagement of civic leaders, even mentoring the rising generation of activists, that has diversified forms of schooling and enlivened social relations inside. The new pluralists seem to weave an eye-catching quilt of sorts, composed of colorful and varied patches, but one that comforts all. And this stems from a local politics of education that has become more democratic, more inventive, and more promising.

ACKNOWLEDGMENTS

In 2007, I tagged along to a meeting with Guy Mehula, chief of facilities for the Los Angeles Unified School District. A muscular tactician who operates with military efficiency, Mehula asked a provocatively candid question while overseeing the district's $19.5 billion effort to erect more than one hundred new schools: Was this enormous investment—spurring a construction boom across L.A. for two decades—working to lift student achievement? Jeff Vincent, a wonderful colleague at Berkeley, and DC facilities expert Mary Filardo invited me along. Never missing a chance to visit my hometown, I headed south from Berkeley.

It proved to be a fruitful engagement. We soon created a sizable data set that allowed us to track hundreds of thousands of kids throughout their educational careers. We followed many from overcrowded campuses, where they were packed like restless sardines, into brand-new schools. Young children entered sparkling early learning centers. Other pupils sorted into charter schools, magnet schools, or dual-language programs, alternative schools of various shapes and sizes. We visited this diversifying array of innovative schools, talking with pupils and teachers, from aging and dismal facilities in the central city to campuses in tony West L.A. that resembled Ivy League preparatory academies.

The plot thickened as we discovered that the learning curves of most students were climbing upward. So, with equally vigorous colleagues—Luke Dauter, Caitlin Kearns, Doug Lauen, Joonho Lee, and Anisah Waite—our questions grew wider. Did charter schools make a difference in boosting achievement across Los Angeles? What about the benefits of retaining young teachers in central-city high schools? How were new dollars, politically won by a young generation of activists, being distributed among schools and neighborhoods? Perhaps the blossoming of civic commitment to public education, expressed from colorful corners of Los Angeles, was bringing this sluggish institution back to life.

Nearly a decade later, deeper questions seeped into my mind. I began to feel that an underlying puzzle was escaping my grasp. Who were these diverse activists that animated such inventive reforms? Why, over the past quarter century, had they surfaced with such political vitality and creativity? I had been missing the wider institutional forest while focusing on all the technical trees. A larger story about the evolving character of civic activism and institutional change was waiting to be told.

Dear and trusted locals guided me as I adjusted my journey. I cannot thank them sufficiently for all they shared with me. These steady and demanding counselors included Howard Blume, Maria Brenes, Miguel Dominguez, Jeanne Fauci, Yolie Flores, Karin Klein, Victor Leung, Sara Mooney, Aurea Montes-Rodriguez, John Rogers, Elmer Roldan, Ryan Smith, and Marc Wilson. Key staffers inside L.A. Unified generously shared data, endless hours of conversation, and critical reviews of our work, especially Tony Atienza, Rachel Bonkovsky, Derrick Chau, José Cole-Gutiérrez, Samuel Gonzalez, Kathy Hayes, Matt Hill, Cynthia Lim, Donna Muncy, Babatunde Ogunwole, Lorena Padilla-Melendez, Rena Perez, Megan Reilly, Pedro Salcido, and Cheryl Simpson. John Deasy, the former schools chief, was always available for thoughtful dialogue. Current or former school board members—Flores, Mónica García, Kelly Gonez, and Caprice Young—have been equally open and insightful along the way.

Working alongside young scholars added joy and camaraderie to this intellectual sojourn as well. These graduate students, contributing to the years of fieldwork, appear on the title page. Sarah Manchanda and I worked closely together during our inspiring year at the Community Coalition, a story we tell in chapter 4. She also delved into the cultural and institutional history of Los Angeles, which clarified the percolating conditions that gave rise to contemporary activists and civic debate over schooling. Caitlin Kearns and Malena Arcidiacono studied where new forms of schooling were sprouting in various parts of the city, and how this created competitive pressure on conventional schools to innovate. Joonho Lee, an endearing colleague and quantitative wizard, codirected our study of where all the new funding went across disparate campuses, and how this affected pupils and school organizations. Melissa Ancheta labored the longest on this volume, tracking down facts and figures, adding to prior frameworks and literatures in order to situate our own analysis. In addition, Iza Benedicto and Celina Lee Chao tirelessly recorded life inside a bevy of charter schools, helping us understand why many did prove effective in lifting children from low-income families (while also threatening a new form of stratification).

My own intellectual ancestry harks back to Émile Durkheim, who accented the primacy of belonging and social cohesion for all human actors—often found in small-scale institutions that sustain human vitality, a sense of efficacy, and purpose to everyday life. But the perennial challenge is how to build institutions that deliver on this promise. Looking back, one antecedent question soon surfaces: How to devise a local politics that advances such fulfilling social organizations? That is, the interplay between civic activism and institutional change holds consequences for each generation, especially in how fairly we distribute opportunity among plural groups and their children.

This framing of the problem and how we study it have been informed by the work of Anthony Bryk, William E. Connolly, Joan Didion, Neil Fligstein, Václav Havel, Jeffrey Henig, John W. Meyer, Victor Muñiz-Fraticelli, Claus Offe, Richard Rodriguez, and Fred Ross. Pages inside my copy of *Learning from L.A.* by Charles Kerchner are dog-eared and weathered. The same goes for Judith Raftery's *Land of Fair Promise*, an early history of schooling and Progressive reform in Los Angeles. To grasp the inventive cultural spirit of California—and the resulting challenge to staid institutions—Jessica Grogan's book *Encountering America* is a must read.

You would not be holding this volume without generous funding from the California Community Foundation, California Endowment, the Stuart and Spencer Foundations, and United Way of Greater Los Angeles. A heartfelt thanks to Elise Buik, Susan Dauber, Sophie Fanelli, Mary Lou Fulton, Antonia Hernández, and Peter Rivera. Each funder patiently supported the accumulation of evidence and my team's own civic engagement, all within a prickly and politicized context. Friends and colleagues offered candid suggestions for how to clarify and substantiate core arguments. They include Chris Ansell, Chris Campos, Elise Castillo, Julie Marsh, Deb McCoy, Marcela Maxfield, Terry Moe, Bill Ouchi, John Rogers, Elizabeth Robataille, María Rojas Concha, and William Welsh. I am forever indebted to Yolie Flores.

Special thanks are due Kyle Gipson, my premiere editor at Johns Hopkins University Press, for seizing on the argument that I endeavored to advance. Kyle artfully moved the manuscript through the review process. Several anonymous reviewers nudged me this way and that, making for a finer, better-written book. Greg Britton and Kim Johnson skillfully moved this book to publication with agility and timely humor. Nicole Wayland copyedited the entire manuscript with care and precision. Julia Day took her sharp pencil to earlier pieces of the manuscript, which helped to clarify my arguments.

I was born to a nurturing mother from Oklahoma; my father hailed from the Protestant Upper Midwest. I arrived in Los Angeles in the middle period, between the city's prewar modernization and the diversified sprawl that marks L.A. today. I grew up outside Pasadena, sneaking under the fence to explore lush gardens, where horses ran and grown-ups placed bets at the Santa Anita racetrack. I would enter, then drop out of, UCLA, couch surf in Torrance and muse over how to find my place in this rangy metropolis. Vietnam was winding down as my own quandary was winding tighter. I decamped to Mexico's central highlands.

But I remained curious over how Angelenos weave together a sense of belonging amid the alienating vastness of traffic and graying strip malls, struggling through a harsh and segregated economy. Like many others, I remain intrigued with how the school institution might better distribute opportunity for the next generation, along with fostering a richer sense of human connection. I admit to yearning for those Arcadian days, walking the beach in Santa Monica or watching Sandy Koufax pitch at Chavez Ravine, catching a concert at the Hollywood Bowl on a warm summer evening. Yet Los Angeles has never stood still. Its uncertain promise, energized by tribal bonds and civic projects, set amid imagination and illusion, will keep shaping the American experience.

Most of all, thanks to my toughest critic and warmest mate, Mary Berg, who reveals the incisive mind and big heart of a caring physician. I'm so lucky to walk and talk with her most mornings. And to Caitlin and Dylan, who teach me daily about how to enrich these human ties. Thank you all.

Notes on the Vernacular

1. Google's Ngram Viewer offers a tool for tracing the historical prevalence of the acronym *L.A.* since the 1880s.

2. Waldie, "Angelino, Angeleno, Angeleño."

3. Luis Noe-Bustamonte, Lauren Mora, and Mark Hugo Lopez, *About One in Four Hispanics Have Heard of Latinx.* Washington, DC: Pew Research Center, 2020.

4. From the online portal of the Oxford English Dictionary: en.oxforddictionaries.com/definition/tribe.

5. Kotkin, *Tribes,* 3.

Prologue

1. Moe, *Politics of Institutional Reform.*

2. Reviews of the neo-institutional account appear in DiMaggio and Powell, *New Institutionalism.* Scott, *Institutions and Organizations.*

3. Lukes, *Power.*

4. The shift away from the integrationist ideal in some circles after the 1980s is detailed in a chapter titled "*E Pluribus Plures*" in Schulman, *The Seventies.*

5. Feinberg, *Common Schools, Uncommon Identities.*

6. This case is examined by the *New York Times* editorial board in "Did de Blasio Put Politics Ahead of Yeshiva Students?"

7. Touraine, "Method for Studying Social Action," 909.

8. Most recently, see Henig, *End of Exceptionalism.* Quote appears in Henig, "Reading the Future of Education Policy," 2013.

9. Clark, Hero, Sidney, Fraga, and Erlichson, *Multiethnic Moments.* Informative case studies from several cities appear in Warren and Mapp, *Match on Dry Grass,* which discusses an ethic of caring that permeates the work of many nongovernmental organizations, motivating their efforts to build stronger social relationships among students, families, and educators—that spirit of common cause.

10. Lemann, *Transaction Man,* 263.

11. Havel, *Power of the Powerless.*

12. Dahl, *Dilemmas of Pluralist Democracy.*

13. Fuller, *Organizing Locally.*

14. Muñiz-Fraticelli, *Structure of Pluralism.*

15. On Stone's conception of civic capacity and fostering unity among metropolitan stakeholders, see Stone, "Looking Back to Look Forward."

16. Connolly, *Pluralism*, 79.

17. Oakeshott, *On Human Conduct*.

Chapter 1 · Civilizing Los Angeles

Epigraph. Appearing in Stegner, *Angle of Repose*, 377, drawing on the letters and nonfiction life of California settler Mary Hallock Foote.

1. Krist, *Mirage Factory*, 7.

2. Letters appear in Kipen, *Dear Los Angeles*, 280–281, 400.

3. Kipen, *Dear Los Angeles*, 375, 404.

4. Krist, *Mirage Factory*, 59.

5. Starr, *Inventing the Dream*, 13–14.

6. See Judith Rosenberg Raftery's critical history (*Land of Fair Promise*, 7–8) of Los Angeles public schools.

7. Bancroft, "Some Chinese Episodes," 562.

8. "At first the fire truck was pulled by laborers, until the city raised enough money to buy two horses, who trudged through dusty, ungraded streets toward the trouble." The hand-drawn truck would bog down in the sand, one volunteer reported, as the building in flames burned to the ground. This first-person account of the town's ragtag civic officials, their mishaps, mischief, and small steps forward, appears in Kuhrts, "Tenth Annual Report," 67–68.

9. Quotations appear in Winther, "Rise of Metropolitan Los Angeles," 392.

10. Starr, *Inventing the Dream*, 12–13.

11. Reported from D. Johnson, "Serpent in the Garden," 244.

12. Citing California statutes from 1855, Griswold del Castillo, *Los Angeles Barrio*, 115.

13. Broad-shouldered Americanos were not entirely new to Los Angeles. The Mexican census of 1836 reported twenty-nine whites among the fifty "foreigners," which included "Spainards" as well. The entire census of 1836, just five years after Mexico's independent rule of Alta California, is detailed in Layne, "First Census," 83.

14. The early history of Los Angeles's geographic expansion is detailed by Guinn, "Area of Los Angeles City."

15. Graham, *Dream Cities*, 31.

16. The rise of good-government advocates in L.A., positioned between the corrupt cabal of developers and the rising socialist party, is detailed in Mowry, *California Progressives*.

17. Native Americans in California held no known conception that human creatures *owned* water; it was, instead, a gift of nature to be shared. The old colonial authority pressed its own notion of a collective good—riparian rights to water—from the mid-sixteenth century forward. Farmers and villagers could simply draw from the Los Angeles River when it ran adjacent to one's land. The pueblo's original charter amended this tradition by appointing a zanjero who issued permits to a primitive cobweb of canals that extended off the river. Much has been written about the early provision of water in Spanish and post-statehood Los Angeles, including Hundley, *Great Thirst*. For a detailed history of the water wars in Los Angeles, see Nadeau, *Water Seekers*.

18. This episode of water politics is detailed in Gumprecht, *Los Angeles River*, 63–67, along with illuminating photographs.

19. Starr, *Inventing the Dream*, 200–208, details the Southern Pacific's political dealings during the latter third of the nineteenth century.

20. Guinn, "Los Angeles in the Later Sixties," 67.

21. The Common Council was renamed the City Council in 1889 after voter approval of the first municipal charter for Los Angeles. C. N. Bliss and W. P. Bliss were codirectors of the Southern Pacific Company, along with H. E. Huntington at least through 1913.

22. Quoted by Fogelson, *Fragmented Metropolis*, 85.

23. Fogelson, *Fragmented Metropolis*, 85.

24. Electric coaches by 1909 ran eighteen miles south of downtown to Huntington Beach, east to Whittier, and even into the mountains north of Pasadena to a quaint town called Alpine Tavern. In 1880, interurban rails sported just eleven miles of track. When Huntington bailed out of the business—soon undercut by the automobile—more than one thousand miles of rail crisscrossed Los Angeles County.

25. Fenwick, "Modern City's High-School System," 117–118.

26. Fogelson, *Fragmented Metropolis*, 84.

27. Alexander, *Civil Sphere*, 7.

28. Calvin's treatise aimed at King Francis I in 1537, quoted by Eire, *Reformations*, 292.

29. Kerr-Peterson, *Protestant Lord*, details how the Protestant Reformation gave birth to the notion that secular authorities could ensure tolerance of differing spiritual commitments and religious sects—while favoring Protestant values with "public" schools. On Unitarian ideology, see Matteson, *Lives of Margaret Fuller*, 67.

30. The "white spot" descriptor stemmed from multiple sources. It did not always imply the racial purities of Los Angeles. *The New York Tribune* ran a US map in 1921 showing the hottest business regions in the nation, including a large white area covering Southern California. The May Company department store in 1925 ran a full-page ad for white cotton garments, calling Los Angeles "the great white spot of America." But it was Chandler, the *L.A. Times* publisher, who repeatedly referred to his city as "the white spot of America" when celebrating the infrequency of labor unrest, purportedly honest government, and sunny aesthetics. When Japanese families attempted to integrate select white neighborhoods in the 1920s, "keep the white spot white" became a rallying cry. For review of this white-spot discourse, see Wild, *Street Meeting*.

31. Nordhoff, *California*, 178.

32. Discussed by Laslett, *Sunshine Was Never Enough*, 16–20.

33. Weingarten, *Thirsty*, 18–20, reviews Nordhoff's book and its long-term influence on the rose-colored views of Los Angeles held by many easterners who came West during the latter third of the nineteenth century.

34. Schipske, *Early Long Beach*, 27.

35. Schipske, *Early Long Beach*, 62–63.

36. Summarized by Winther, "Rise of Metropolitan Los Angeles," 400.

37. Martin Luther's close ally, Ulrich Zwingli, urged his Swiss countrymen to recast piety as living one's faith by building a transcendent society that celebrated individual rights, freedom from central powers, and returning authority to the laity. Schools should

prepare the young to "serve the Christian community, the common good, the state and individuals," he wrote. Zwingli's starting point was "that theology, piety, and social and political concerns were inseparable," wrote Carlos Eire (*Reformations*, 234). And "one's religious duty involved a reliable, punctual, and efficient performance of task and obligations required by the vocation itself." See Kalberg, *Protestant Ethic*, 25.

38. Heyrman, "Puritanism and Predestination."

39. Abraham and Kirby, *Oxford Handbook of Methodist Studies*.

40. Meyer, Tyack, Nagel, and Gordon, "Public Education as Nation-Building in America," 599.

41. Luther's sermon titled "On Keeping Children in School" is quoted by Eire, *Reformations*, 594.

42. Rodriguez, *Days of Obligation*, xvi.

43. A ideological dynamic analyzed by Tyack and Tobin, "The 'Grammar' of Schooling," 369–372.

44. Guinn, "Los Angeles in the Later Sixties," 65.

45. US Census Bureau figures, compiled by Fogelson, *Fragmented Metropolis*, 76, table 3.

46. Fenwick, "Modern City's High-School System," 119.

47. Early report of the Los Angeles Civic Association cited by Williamson, "Civic Association," 181, 184.

48. Williamson, "Civic Association," 181.

49. Henry Demarest Lloyd, quoted by Graham, *Dream Cities*, 53.

50. Krist, *Mirage Factory*, 43.

51. Krist, *Mirage Factory*, 59–60.

52. Cited by Raftery, *Land of Fair Promise*, 41.

53. Griswold del Castillo, *La Familia*, 101.

54. Reported by Laslett, *Sunshine Was Never Enough*, 42.

55. Layne, "First Census," 83.

56. Small-scale manufacturers began to thrive by the 1880s, altering the character of labor and social class. The big-ticket item was the distilling of liquor and producing wine: these firms reported almost $400,000 in capital investment by 1880. Distilleries would grow to $4.1 million in capital investment by 1910. These firms were followed by wagon- and carriage-makers, flour mills, and saddleries in terms of reported capital worth. Technological advances contributed to gains in value-added manufacturing, boosting productivity and pay as well. The city's small-scale manufacturers, such as makers of cigars, dresses, and wagons, employed 706 individuals by 1880, including 41 children younger than 15 years of age. The value of manufactured items exceeded the cost of raw materials, wages, and debt by 29 percent, yielding a significant profit for owners. By 1890, tin, copper, and sheet iron manufacturers came online, growing almost twentyfold by 1910 citywide. Flour milling operations climbed tenfold during this same period. Yet, while jobs in these manufacturing sectors continued to grow, commercial and agricultural employment would come to dominate in this largely white, often white-collar, city. Data appear in US Bureau of the Census, "Manufactures," 93–94. Original analysis by Sarah Manchanda.

57. US Bureau of the Census, "Manufactures."

58. Discussed by Splitter, "Education in Los Angeles," 104, 113.

59. Martin, "Unauthorized Workers," 146.

60. Los Angeles merchant Joseph Newmark complained of having to offer $100 a month to attract skilled Chinese servants from San Francisco in the 1870s, while paying a Native American and his wife $15 a month for their combined services. If not arriving in San Francisco, these groups of "coolies" would disembark at a Latin American port, be sold for about $350 each, then shipped north to California. Chinese farmworkers earned $20 a month with room and board in the early 1880s, while rail workers earned $31 monthly without housing in the prior decade. All told, more than a quarter million Chinese immigrated to California during the nineteenth century, including well-educated merchants. See Glass, *From Mission to Microchip.*

61. Literacy rates—the respondent's reported ability to read and write as recorded by census enumerators—are calculated for residents of the City of Los Angeles. See US Bureau of the Census, "School Enrollment," 134, table 9; 386, table 49.

62. Griswold del Castillo, *Los Angeles Barrio*, 85–87.

63. Bond, "Negro in Los Angeles." The son of J. Max Bond became a renowned Manhattan architect. One nephew, Julian Bond, was the civil rights activist and Georgia legislator. A remarkable obituary of Bond Sr., who became the first president of the University of Liberia, appeared in Pace, "J. Max Bond Sr., 89."

64. De Graaf, "City of Black Angels," 328, table 1.

65. Laslett, *Sunshine Was Never Enough*, 180.

66. Ayres reporting on early schooling in Los Angeles is discussed by Splitter, "Education in Los Angeles."

67. Enrollment data compiled by Splitter, "Education in Los Angeles." The wider rationalization of childhood, shifting the daily lives of children and youths into classrooms, raised questions as well. Take poet Ina Donna Coolbrith's (*Road to School*) skepticism over the modern organizing of childhood by 1881, reminiscing over how she took her own good time with a childhood friend, walking along a wooded path, celebrating "yet once more thy brave voice raise . . . in thy truant's cause, for tasks unlearned, for wasted days, for His broken laws."

68. Bettinger, "Twenty-Five Years in the Schools of Los Angeles."

69. Kerchner, Menefee-Libby, Mulfinger, and Clayton, *Learning from L.A.*, 27.

70. The city (elementary) and high school districts would further centralize operations in 1961, merging to become the L.A. Unified School District.

71. Harris is quoted by Kerchner, Menefee-Libby, Mulfinger, and Clayton in *Learning from L.A.*

72. Mention of Hearst's steady benevolence toward kindergartens appears in Jones, "First Benefactors." For details on how San Francisco's developing literary community crafted the ideals and portrayal of postbellum California, including in the eyes of East Coast observers and boosters, see Tarnoff, *Bohemians.*

73. Detailed in letters written by Severance and reported by Raftery, *Land of Fair Promise*, 22–23.

74. Raftery, *Land of Fair Promise*, 153.

75. Deverell, *Whitewashed Adobe*, 153–154.

76. Commission of Immigration and Housing of California, *Home Teacher.*

77. Quoted from the Commission of Immigration and Housing of California by Romo, *East Los Angeles*, 62–63.

78. Gibson, "Immigrant Woman," 5–9.

79. Student enrollment detailed by Raftery, *Land of Fair Promise*, 11–12.

80. Bates, "A Study of Development of Elementary Education," 111. Average daily attendance was reported at just 56 percent of all children who had enrolled in school.

81. Griswold de Castillo, *La Familia*, 95–96.

82. Quoted by Spaulding, "Development of Organization and Disorganization," 281.

83. See De Graaf, "City of Black Angels," 328, table 1.

84. Gould, "Intermediate Schools of Los Angeles," 419, 427.

85. Bartlett, *Better City*, 72.

86. Graham, *Dream Cities*, 31–32.

87. This commentary appeared in the *Southgate Gardener*, a local newspaper, in 1919. Cited by Nicolaides, *My Blue Heaven*, 18.

88. Nicolaides, "'Where the Working Man is Welcomed,'" 523.

89. Nicolaides, *My Blue Heaven*, 17.

90. Nicolaides, *My Blue Heaven*, 22.

91. Bond ("Negro in Los Angeles") interviewed a shrewd African American real estate dealer who schemed with "one of my white friends" who tipped him off when construction began in an all-white development. The Black real estate agent would give his friend money to buy a lot or new home, then not so subtly show up, threatening to move in. "I would buy the property sometimes for $200 and sell it for $800 . . . the white people would pay any price to keep the colored folks out of their communities."

92. Raftery, *Land of Fair Promise*, 102–105. During the interwar period, the racist ordering of work and housing would harden the geographic and psychological distancing of ethnic tribes that continues to mark contemporary Los Angeles. Earlier in the late nineteenth century, Henry Huntington often purchased a right-of-way for his regional rail lines from citrus growers, cattle ranchers, or land speculators. At the end of each pathway, getting ready to lay shiny new tracks, Huntington erected modest hotels and shops to serve a gaggle of engineers and hourly wage earners: the Blacks, Eastern Europeans, and Mexicans who graded the soil, cut wooden ties, and laid hundreds of miles of track across the L.A. basin. Huntington's famed Red Cars would soon roll, boosting land prices and inducing home building. The labor camps—such as those founded in Watts, South Pasadena, and West Hollywood—became toughened enclaves of poor-to-blue-collar families that persist to this day.

93. Griswold del Castillo, *La Familia*, 43–44.

94. Tightly aligned with Black churches was the Young Women's Christian Association (YWCA), the agency "which provides a program of character building for the womanhood of Los Angeles." The Twelfth Street branch had organized more than five hundred teens into Girl Reserve Clubs in the 1930s, who provided volunteer aid to needy Black families. Bond stressed how such early nonprofits "[give] opportunities to Negro women to assume positions of leadership . . . whose chances to participate in the cultural aspects of urban life are limited."

95. McWilliams and Meier, *North from Mexico*.

96. Details appear in Thompson, *America's Social Arsonist*.

97. Reported by Schrag, *Paradise Lost*.

98. Leonard would soon go native, fostering growth of the "encounter culture," as journalist Peter Schrag called it (*Paradise Lost*). Leonard founded the Esalen Institute at Big Sur, "home of far-out apostles of human potential."

99. Interviewed by Jakob Dylan in the 2018 film *Echo in the Canyon*, referring to Laurel Canyon, sitting along the Pacific Coast on the West Side of Los Angeles. Slater, *Echo in the Canyon*.

100. Didion, *Slouching Towards Bethlehem*.

101. Rustin, "Watts."

102. Quoted by Laslett, *Sunshine Was Never Enough*, 269.

103. Mann, *Taking on General Motors*, 40.

104. Friedhoff, Wial, and Wolman, *Consequences of Metropolitan Manufacturing Decline*.

105. Johnson, "Remarks at the Signing of the Immigration Bill."

106. Historical demographic trends are detailed by Ethington, Frey, and Myers, *Racial Resegregation*.

107. Gitlin, *Twilight of Common Dreams*, 88.

108. Lemann, *Transaction Man*, 225.

Chapter 2 · Palace Revolt

1. Quoted by Watanabe and Cesar, "LAUSD Outlines Plan,"AA4.

2. Quoted by Watanabe, "L.A. Unified Budget," AA4.

3. I prefer *new pluralists* to encircle this new generation of activists and civic players, rather than the label *third sector*, which is at times used in similar contexts. Related civic movements animated by ethnic-rooted leaders and nonprofit organizations have agitated apart from the state and market, sometimes including labor allies, as did early Progressives and socialists in Los Angeles or, more broadly, labor-aligned uprisings in eastern Europe, such as Solidarity in Poland or Václav Havel's revolt in the Czech Republic. Yet, in contemporary L.A. the new pluralists established a third political terrain, staked out separately from capital *and* labor.

4. Marsh, "Political Dynamics of District Reform," 1.

5. Layton, "Democratic Mayors Challenge Teachers Unions." See also Marsh and Wohlstetter, "Recent Trends in Intergovernmental Relations," for how the Obama administration's alliance with civil rights groups, along with some distancing from union leaders, served to strengthen the hand of reform groups and nonprofit organizations locally.

6. For one historical review, see Romero, "Militarization of Police."

7. Quotations appear in Schneider's study of white flight in the 1970s, "Escape from Los Angeles," 1002.

8. Pastor, Benner, and Matsuoka, *This Could Be the Start of Something Big*.

9. Immigration statistics compiled by the History Channel, "U.S. Immigration since 1965." Migratory waves from the south were not new. Racialized prejudice and social distancing had widened across Southern California in the early twentieth century as Mexicans flocked north for plentiful jobs in agriculture, laying rails, and building suburban homes for others. The count of foreign-born Mexicans living in California climbed from just over 8,000 in 1900 to 368,000 in 1930. By 1929, S. J. Holmes, a UCLA professor, felt compelled to publish a paper, titled "Perils of the Mexican Invasion," warning of high rates of "virulent smallpox . . . typhus brought in by the Mexicans, a people living under unwholesome conditions."

10. Data from the US Census Bureau, "QuickFacts: Los Angeles County."

11. Reported by Sampson, Schachner, and Mare, "Urban Income Inequality," 104.

12. Storper, *Keys to the City.*

13. Oakes, "Testimony on *Williams* School Finance Case."

14. A fifty-year retrospective of the walkout mounted by Chicano high school students in Los Angeles appears in Sahagun, "Architects of a Movement," B1.

15. Schneider, "Escape from Los Angeles."

16. Card, Mas, and Rothstein, "Tipping and the Dynamics of Segregation."

17. Clark and Maas, "Schools, Neighborhoods and Selection."

18. This information is based on my research team's analysis, led by Cristián Ugarte, drawing from state Department of Education data.

19. "Straight Out of Compton."

20. Sampson, Schachner, and Mare, "Urban Income Inequality," 110.

21. These data come from 2013 American Community Survey estimates, as reported by Ray, Ong, and Jimenez, "Impacts of the Widening Divide."

22. Details and illustrative maps appear in Fuller, Castillo, Lee, and Ugarte, "Will $4 Billion in New Spending Make a Difference?"

23. Data from county public health demographer Rollin-Alamillo, *Recent Birth Trends in Los Angeles County.*

24. Blume, "Romer Gives Last Annual Address," B4.

25. Colvin, "First-Graders' Scores Surge," B3.

26. Helfand, "Reading Taught the Scripted Way," B2.

27. About one grade level in learning performance in reading can be associated with a ten-to-twelve-point difference in scale scores. Statisticians at the National Assessment of Educational Progress ("Interpreting NAEP Results") do warn that this is a rough benchmark, given that differing kinds of knowledge are being assessed at the fourth, eighth, and twelfth grades.

28. Data elements were compiled by the California Department of Education, then analyzed by Malena Arcidiacono.

29. This pivotal episode—for students and community organizing groups—is detailed by Rogers and Morrell, "A Force to Be Reckoned With," 228–245.

30. Rogers and Morrell, "A Force to Be Reckoned With," 236–238.

31. Details appear in United Way, "Progress in Los Angeles Schools."

32. One longitudinal analysis finds that less than one-third achieved an A or B grade point average during their high school years. Only one-fourth who sat for the SAT college admissions exam scored above the national average. Back in 2008, just 25 percent of L.A. Unified graduates entered a four-year college within one year, and another 41 percent entered a community college. For the class of 2014, college-going rates remained essentially the same: 27 percent entered a four-year college and 42 percent entered a community college. Phillips, Yamashiro, and Jacobson, "College Going in LAUSD."

33. McDermott, "*Serrano*: What Does It Mean?"

34. Oakes and Rogers, *Learning Power.*

35. Well-off districts like Laguna and Newport-Mesa—districts with affluent residents and a weak commercial tax base—complained that Democrats in the state capital were providing equalization aid to urban districts, even as Proposition 13 limited total revenue for all districts (essentially true empirically). See Reyes, "Newport Teachers Close to Strike."

36. This episode of overcrowded schools and the local organizing it sparked is detailed in Fuller, Recinos, and Scholl, "Voter Support"; Fuller, Vincent, Bierbaum, Kirschenbaum,

McCoy, and Rigby, "Smart Schools, Smart Growth"; Colmenar, Estrada, Lo, and Raya, "Ending School Overcrowding in California"; and Oakes and Rogers, *Learning Power.*

37. National Assessment of Educational Progress, "Trial Urban District Assessment."

38. This shift in local political support for school construction in Los Angeles is detailed in Fuller, Recinos, and Scholl, "Voter Support."

39. Welsh, Coughlan, Fuller, and Dauter, "New Schools, Overcrowding Relief."

40. Lafortune and Shônholzer, "Measuring the Efficacy and Efficiency of School Facility Expenditures."

41. Fuller, Vincent, Bierbaum, Kirschenbaum, McCoy, and Rigby, "Smart Schools, Smart Growth."

42. Historical spending figures come from annual reports filed by the state controller on school district spending by budget category for 1976. California State Controller, "School Districts and Community College Districts." These data can be compared with contemporary reporting on the same accounting categories.

43. Brown, "Governor Brown Signs Historic School Funding Legislation." Michael Kirst, Brown's long-term education advisor, details how they moved this monumental legislation through the political process in Kirst, "Understanding Successful Politics."

44. Perhaps fitting for Jerry Brown, the former Jesuit seminarian, the decentralizing thrust of subsidiarity was articulated most recently by Pope Pious XI in 1931 ("Encyclical," section 79). "Just as it is gravely wrong to take from individuals what they can accomplish by their own initiative and industry and give it to the community, so also it is an injustice and at the same time a grave evil and disturbance of right order to assign to a greater and higher association what lesser and subordinate organizations can do."

45. California State Controller, "School Districts and Community College Districts."

46. Price and Sawyer, *Health and Welfare Board Retreat 8-29-2017.*

47. For review of these descriptive findings and downstream organizational effects, see Lee and Fuller, "Does Progressive Finance Alter School Organizations?"

48. The settlement between the Community Coalition of South Los Angeles and L.A. Unified is carefully worded, allowing the district to deny any inappropriate action, despite the state education department's ruling that it had not expanded or improved services for disadvantaged students in proportion to the dollars they generate. The compromise also highlights distinct remedies that purportedly would lift these youngsters, including academic and social-emotional support of students, greater access to college-prep courses, improved parent engagement, and "credit recovery" programs to raise high school graduation rates. The formal agreement appears in "Community Coalition and Reyna Frias Settle."

49. Interview conducted August 31, 2009.

50. Disclosure: John Rogers and I provided analytic support for LA-FE over its eighteen-month life span, identifying change in school-by-school budget allocations as Governor Brown's new funding arrived to L.A. Unified.

51. Empirical findings for Los Angeles and among California schools appear in Lee and Fuller, "Does Progressive Finance Alter School Organizations?"

52. Findings on how new dollars were distributed among L.A. Unified schools—along with resulting effects on teacher staffing, curricular and social organization, and student achievement—are reported in United Way, "Progress in Los Angeles Schools," and Lee and Fuller, "Does Progressive Finance Alter School Organizations?"

53. Looking back, we know little about the discrete effect of the Open Court era on student achievement. True experimental studies of this curricular package show discernible bumps in reading proficiency, compared with control groups, but not with the sustained magnitude that accumulated during the subsequent generation. A careful review of Open Court's effects—estimated through true experiments and less rigorous designs—appears in Slavin, Lake, Chambers, Cheung, and Davis, "Effective Reading Programs."

54. The editorial board of the *Los Angeles Times* ("John Deasy's Future") expressed concern over Superintendent Deasy's possible firing by the school board, which soon followed.

55. Felch, Song, and Smith, "Seniority over Quality."

56. In 2018, the Gates Foundation issued an empirical epitaph of sorts, quietly burying their earlier enthusiasm and half-a-billion-dollar investment in teacher evaluation and merit pay. For almost a decade this hefty funder supported district and charter school efforts to observe and assess teacher performance, pedagogical skills weighed by their impact on student growth, tools at times linked to teacher promotion decisions. But, "in the end, there were no big payoffs in terms of improved graduation [rates] or achievement of students in general," said lead researcher Brian Stecher (*Improving Teaching Effectiveness*), "and low income and minority students in particular."

57. In New York City, Black students were being suspended at a rate barely exceeding their enrollment percentage.

58. Blume, "Suspension Figures."

59. Quoted by Rott, "L.A. Schools Throw Out Suspensions."

60. Hashim, Strunk, and Dhaliwal, "Justice for All?"

61. Urevich, "Referrals of Students to Police."

62. Leung, Mendoza, and Cobb, "Here to Learn."

63. Kohli, "L.A. Unified Board Votes."

64. This reallocation strategy, consistent with the pluralist agenda, would rile others on the political Left. One analysis published by the *L.A. Progressive* claimed that García was "engineering the distribution of education funds through a weighted formula [shaped by] the ideological interests of a . . . 'privatizing sector' furthered at the expense of the public" (Roos, "Outflanking the CTA from the Left"). But this neoliberal allusion ironically referred to the pluralist victories to distribute more funding to poor schools, along with efforts to better engage and motivate students.

65. Quotes and reporting by Blume and Kohli, "L.A. Unified Police Chief Resigns."

66. Oakes and Rogers, *Learning Power*, 13.

67. A variety of viewpoints on the broadly defined issue of "privatization," including differing opinions among members of the teachers' union, appear at Voices Against Privatizing Public Education, an online forum: https://www.facebook.com/CitizensFor EducationRestoration/?hc_ ref=ARQzcs7newQwRu6eKBNRPYTdjsDs E2XUqy1Er7FFjbU 7nJ2sncNeVjYuk9q8swZ9drw&fref=nf.

68. Caputo-Pearl, "Schools L.A. Students Deserve," 2.

69. Quote appears in Goldstein, *Teacher Wars*, 257.

70. A history of Caputo-Pearl's rise in union politics appears in Goldstein, *Teacher Wars*. Also see Blume, "UTLA Elects a New Leader."

71. Aron, "Who is Alex Caputo-Pearl?"

72. One review of the so-called education spring, and the limited role initially played by union leaders, appears in Fuller, "Teachers are Organizing."

73. Caputo-Pearl, "Why Los Angeles Teachers May Have to Strike."

74. Dingerson, "Building the Power," 3.

75. Movimiento Estudiantil Chicano de Aztlán (MECHA) was founded by Latino activists in "rejection of the assimilationist and accommodationist melting pot ideology that had guided earlier generations of activists." The Chicano movement, born in Los Angeles and the American Southwest, aimed to establish "self-determination" in cultural and political spheres, another pluralist impulse that would shape the tenor of community organizing in parts of Los Angeles. MECHA, "Movimiento Estudiantil."

76. Milkman, *L.A. Story.*

77. One organizer, George Hardy, came south to L.A. from San Francisco in 1946, complaining of driving two hours in "this overgrown village" to visit bowling alleys, hotels, and office centers, where he met with low-paid workers. This booming postwar city still suffered from "open-shopitis," as Hardy called it. Yet, by the late 1950s, Hardy's robust union had organized one-third of all custodians who cleaned offices downtown. They were moving to unionize service workers in the public sector, including L.A. Unified. See Selvin, *Champions of Labor.*

78. Fligstein and McAdam, *Theory of Fields.*

Chapter 3 · *Outside Agitators*

1. A young William Ouchi wrote his doctoral dissertation, titled "A Novel Approach to Organizational Control," at the University of Chicago in 1972. It is focused on how to decentralize and foster norms inside firms that strengthen social cohesion among workers. This provided the basis for Ouchi, *Theory Z.*

2. Gaebler and Osborne, *Reinventing Government.*

3. Arenstam, "Netflix CEO Pushes Charter Schools."

4. A historical review of this line of thinking appears in Fuller, *Organizing Locally.*

5. Banks, "Door Opens to Revamp L.A. Schools," B1, B10.

6. Kerchner, Menefee-Libby, Mulfinger, and Clayton, *Learning from L.A.,* 122, 166.

7. Quoted by Kerchner, Menefee-Libby, Mulfinger, and Clayton, *Learning from L.A.,* 169.

8. Lukes, *Power.*

9. Chubb and Moe, *Politics, Markets, and America's Schools.*

10. I reviewed the interplay between charter schools and voucher proposals for *The Atlantic* in Fuller, "Verdict on Charter Schools."

11. Additional details regarding these data appear in United Way, "Progress in Los Angeles Schools," based on analysis by Malena Arcidiacono at the University of California, Berkeley.

12. Sociologist James Coleman wrote extensively on mechanisms and student-level effects of school desegregation. See, for example, Coleman, Kelly, and Moore, "Recent Trends in School Integration."

13. Data reported by the Los Angeles Unified School District, "Recommendations for Increasing Equity."

14. Kohli, "Parents Who Want Their Kids in L.A.'s Most Competitive Magnet Schools."

15. Community Magnet Charter School, "About CMCS." http://www.community magnet.org/about-cmcs (accessed April 14, 2021).

16. Orfield, "Lessons of the Los Angeles Desegregation Case," 338–339.

17. Sangeorge, "California Ballot Initiative."

18. Woo, "All L.A. Schools to Be Year-Long," A15.

19. Woo, "Magnet Schools in L.A.," A36.

20. Daley, Le, and Ganon, "Magnet Smarter Balanced Assessment Results."

21. Engberg, Epple, Imbrogno, Sieg, and Zimmer. "Evaluating Education Programs."

22. Bifulco, Cobb, and Bell, "Can Interdistrict Choice Boost Student Achievement?"

23. Dauter and Fuller, "Student Movement in Social Context."

24. The book (Medved and Wallechinsky, *What Really Happened to the Class of '65?*) follows various graduates covered in the original *Time* magazine piece, which then led to the miniseries featuring actors Tony Bill, Jane Curtin, Larry Hagman, and Leslie Nielsen.

25. Chastang and Seo, "Driven to Learn."

26. Byrnes, "School is Succeeding," A8.

27. Details on the school's performance, along with first-person accounts from enthused students, have been reported in Merl, "No Frills School," B6.

28. Rubin. "Broad Gives to Charter School Group," B6.

29. Russo, *Stray Dogs, Saints, and Saviors*, 89.

30. Blume, "Surprise Big Spender."

31. This single category of corporate reformers and pro-market conservatives is reviewed by Scott, DeBray, Lubienski, Hanley, Castillo, and Hedges, "Politics of Charter School Evidence," 209–210.

32. Material from these interviews and details of the Villaraigosa era appear in Fuller, "Palace Revolt in Los Angeles?"

33. From an interview conducted by phone with A. J. Duffy on October 20, 2009.

34. Email communication with Yolie Aguilar Flores, September 2009. Partially reported in Fuller, "Palace Revolt in Los Angeles?"

35. Quote and details of empirical findings appear in Hayasaki, "Charters' Test Gains Higher," B6.

36. This analysis appeared in an unpublished paper circulated from the Graduate School of Education at Stanford University by David Rogosa in 2003.

37. Raymond, "Charter School Performance in Los Angeles."

38. Findings detailed in Lauen, Fuller, and Dauter, "Positioning Charter Schools in Los Angeles."

39. These findings appear in Shin, Fuller, and Dauter, "Heterogeneous Effects of Charter Schools."

40. Bulkley, Marsh, Strunk, Harris, and Hashim. *Challenging the One Best System.*

41. For one recent review, see Winters, Clayton, and Carpenter, "Are Low-Performing Students More Likely to Exit Charter Schools?"

42. Civic debate over these charter school findings appeared in a *Los Angeles Times* report: Blume, "For Charter Students, a Learning Gap."

43. Quote and additional analysis appear in Nesoff, "Belmont Zone of Choice," 1. A detailed chronicle of these complex organizational efforts leading to the Belmont Zone of Choice appears in Martínez and Hunter Quartz, "Zoned for Change."

44. Nesoff, "Belmont Zone of Choice," 2.

45. Abdulkadiroğlu, Angrist, Dynarski, Kane, and Pathak, "Accountability and Flexibility in Public Schools."

46. Kearns, Lauen, and Fuller, "Competing with Charter Schools."

47. Fauci and Hunter Quartz, "Decade of Innovation," report college attendance rates of pilot school graduates six years out. Data originally compiled by Meredith Phillips and Kyo Yamashiro at UCLA.

48. Estrada, "Utilizing the Lens of Cultural Proficiency." Pupils were asked, for instance, "Do teachers go out of their way to help students?" Seven in ten pilot students responded "agree" or "strongly agree," compared with just six of ten in conventional district schools. These statistically significant differences appeared in answers to several questions regarding the social climate of schools (sampling about 74,000 students).

49. Campos and Kearns, "Options and Opportunities."

50. Yolie Flores's reform logic is discussed by Marsh, Strunk, Bush-Mecenas, and Huguet, "Democratic Engagement in District Reform," 57.

51. Marsh, Strunk, Bush-Mecenas and Huguet, "Democratic Engagement in District Reform."

52. Stone, "Looking Back to Look Forward," 310–311. For local cases of how groups struggle to unite around education issues, see Stone, Henig, Jones, and Pierannunzi, *Building Civic Capacity.*

53. Handler (*Down from Bureaucracy*) builds from policy cases to contrast how actors may push to decentralize control from within centralized bureaucracies, similar to the "palace revolt" initiated by Flores and Villaraigosa, in contrast to when community-level actors or nongovernmental organizations lobby from below for greater school-site or neighborhood control.

54. Summative effects on student achievement, along with discussion of likely mechanisms that affected the ups and downs of schools participating in Public School Choice, are detailed by Strunk, Marsh, Hashim, Bush-Mecenas, and Weinstein, "Impact of Turnaround Reform on Student Outcomes."

55. Thanks go to Elizabeth Robitaille, who gently needled me years ago to tackle this worthy empirical question. We have only scratched the empirical surface.

56. Cordes, "In Pursuit of the Common Good."

57. Figlio and Hart, "Competitive Effects of Means-Tested School Vouchers."

58. Digging deeper, this trade-off is partially explained by the migration of more effective teachers. We calculated the so-called value-added score of each L.A. Unified teacher, which captures learning gains displayed by each teacher's students by year. We found that TPS *elementary* teachers displayed *lower* value-added scores (especially for children's reading scores) when surrounded by a growing count of competing schools within a three-mile radius, compared with TPS peers in schools with stable or declining competition.

Teacher value-added scores also ranged lower in schools situated in poor neighborhoods, compared with middle-class areas. Even after taking neighborhood wealth and family social class into account, teacher effectiveness still appeared weaker in traditional schools that faced rising competition. We observed a similar pattern among *high school* teachers working in TPS that faced varying levels of competition nearby. These patterns are consistent with my team's earlier finding that teachers working in pilot and charter schools report higher levels of trust, efficacy, and overall job satisfaction than peers laboring in traditional schools (Fuller, Waite, Chao, and Benedicto, "Rich Communities in Small High Schools?"). This may hold positive spillover effects for student achievement, although more work is required to substantiate this link. On variation in teacher motivation among differing types of L.A. high schools, see Fuller, Waite, and Torres Irribarra, "Explaining Teacher Turnover."

59. Public broadcasting reporter Kyle Stokes has covered this issue in Los Angeles. Stokes, "Kids in LAUSD Who Most Need Dual Language Instruction."

60. Reported by Phillips, "L.A. School Superintendent Michelle King."

Chapter 4 · *Organizing Pluralist Politics*

1. For details on acrimony and violence at Fremont High School, see Smith, "Campus Oasis Amidst the Violence." Arne Duncan, President Barack Obama's education secretary, argued why teaching staff must be replaced in schools like Fremont High in Macray, "Instigator."

2. Bloemraad and Terriquez, "Cultures of Engagement," 214.

3. Miles Corwin, a *Los Angeles Times* crime reporter, spent the 1996–97 academic year inside L.A. Unified high schools and their surrounding communities. Corwin, *And Still We Rise.*

4. This quote appears on a website maintained by Fred Ross's son, himself active in California politics. See https://www.fredrosssr.com/about/. A detailed biography of Fred Ross Sr. is available by Thompson, *America's Social Arsonist.*

5. This episode is recounted by Thompson in *America's Social Arsonist*, 67–71. Marcus seemed like an unlikely champion, living in a Pasadena mansion replete with tennis court and swimming pool. But Marcus was known to revisit the humiliation of violin recitals as a young boy in the Midwest, playing behind a curtain. His family was Jewish, and he still experienced the sting of anti-Semitic comments after coming West to attend USC.

6. Orr and Rogers, *Public Engagement for Public Education*, 10.

7. Piven and Cloward, *Poor People's Movements*, xv.

8. For a careful review of the "community control" debate in the wake of the Kennedy and Johnson administrations, see Adam Walinsky's review essay of Daniel P. Moynihan's *Community Action in the War on Poverty* (Walinsky, "Maximum Feasible Misunderstanding").

9. The Census Bureau compiles Internal Revenue Service counts of nonprofit organizations and paid staff members. Yet, the bureau shifted how they sort various kinds of civic or business nonprofits between 1996 and 2006, resulting in noisy time trends. US Census Bureau, "County Business Patterns Datasets."

10. These strategies for mobilizing youth or families are taught within programs that train advocates and community organizers, like the curriculum found at the Portland Underground Graduate School, "Direct Action Organizing."

11. This session occurred during Hillary Clinton's presidential campaign in May 2016. Lewis, "Hillary Clinton Visits Community Coalition."

12. Local news outlets reported on this tragedy, including Leimert Park Beat, "Taylor Griffin Galloway, Family Mourn Loss."

13. Paraphrasing reports appearing in Rogers, Mediratta, and Shah, "Building Power, Learning Democracy." See also Sullivan, Edwards, Johnson, and McGillicuddy, *Emerging Model for Working with Youth.*

14. Kahne and Sporte, "Developing Citizens."

15. McAdam, McCarthy, and Zald, "Social Movements."

16. See, for example, Offe, *Reflections on America*.

17. A comprehensive theoretical review appears in Muñiz-Fraticelli, *Structure of Pluralism*.

18. Terriquez, "Training Young Activists." For a recent review of the youth organizing field, see Baldridge, "Youthwork Paradox."

Chapter 5 · Pluralist Politics and Institutional Reform

Epigraph. Muñiz-Fraticelli, *Structure of Pluralism*, 15.

1. One nonprofit manager of local campuses, the Partnership for Los Angeles Schools (created by former mayor Antonio Villaraigosa), has codified their implementation guide for how to accomplish lasting organizational change inside schools. See *Partnership Playbook*.

2. Connolly, *Pluralism*, 4.

3. For a discussion of how both ancient and modern societies have struggled with centrifugal pluralist dynamics, see Seligman, *Idea of Civil Society*, 156–183.

4. Muñiz-Fraticelli, *Structure of Pluralism*, 56–60.

5. A thoughtful examination of the earlier democratic-deliberation model of pluralism appears in Marsh and Hall, "Challenges and Choices."

6. Feinberg, *Common Schools, Uncommon Identities*, 6.

7. Connolly, *Pluralism*, 3. I earlier reviewed shifting sentiments expressed toward intermediary groups and organizations going back to the Protestant Reformation in Fuller, *Organizing Locally*.

8. Dahl, *Dilemmas of Pluralist Democracy*, 31.

9. Nicholls is quoted and his theoretical position discussed by Muñiz-Fraticelli, *Structure of Pluralism*, 37.

10. Connolly, *Pluralism*, 69.

11. Cicero quoted by Kwame Anthony Appiah in *Cosmopolitanism*, xviii. Appiah writes further on the history and implications of cosmopolitan thought in the West in *Lies That Bind*.

12. Shipps, *School Reform Corporate Style*, 180.

13. See Clarence Stone's review paper on urban political regimes and the key role of unity, or coherent coalitions, to advance institutional change. Stone, "Civic Capacity."

14. Havel, *Disturbing the Peace*, 15–17.

15. See Henig, Hula, Orr, and Pedescleaux, "The Color of School Reform." In addition, my conversations with Diana Casanova regarding her thesis research contributes to my thinking.

16. Weaver-Hightower, "Ecology Metaphor for Education Policy Analysis," 153. See also Janelle Scott's review of how the array of activists, nonprofits, and intermediary organizations are often missed in conventional politics of education. Scott et al., "Politics of Charter School Evidence."

17. I interviewed Matt Hill for an essay on successful efforts at integrating schools in Fuller, "Joe Biden Seems to Think School Segregation Is Nearly Unsolvable."

18. Sennett, *Fall of Public Man*, 264.

19. Appreciation goes out to the late David Tyack, a wonderfully supportive mentor in American history. His phrase "tinkering toward utopia" refers to successive generations of

reformers who have incrementally adjusted, but rarely transformed, the institution of schooling (see Tyack and Cuban, *Tinkering toward Utopia*). The anthropologist Claude Lévi-Strauss used the word *bricolage* in the context of how storytellers devise mythological or moral tales, the practice of recombining existing elements to create something new. Lévi-Strauss, *Savage Mind*.

20. Kant's thinking is paraphrased and detailed by Seligman, *Idea of Civil Society*, 43.

21. Dahl, *Dilemmas of Pluralist Democracy*, 21.

22. Muñiz-Fraticelli, *Structure of Pluralism*, 1.

23. On the topic of how organizational logics become encapsulated within policy strategies, I'd like to offer special thanks to Laura Tobben for a wonderful conversation. See also Thornton, Ocasio, and Lounsbury, *Institutional Logics Perspective*. Julie Marsh and colleagues offer a provocative analysis of whether varying "institutional logics" among schools in Los Angeles actually yield differing pedagogies and social relations inside. Marsh, Allbright, Bulkley, Kennedy, and Dhaliwal, "Institutional Logics in Los Angeles Schools."

24. Connolly, *Pluralism*, 8.

25. YUCA, Youth United for Community Action, another civic group created in the 1990s, as discussed briefly Rogers and Terriquez, *Learning to Lead*.

26. Cicero coined an early version of the phrase, emphasizing how the character of families and local village ties offer the essential foundations of human society. Cicero, *Ethical Writings of Cicero*.

27. Sewell, "Theory of Structure," 20.

28. Gitlin, *Twilight of Common Dreams*.

Abdulkadiroğlu, Atila, Joshua Angrist, Susan Dynarski, Thomas Kane, and Parag Pathak. "Accountability and Flexibility in Public Schools: Evidence from Boston's Charters and Pilots." *Quarterly Journal of Economics* 126, no. 2 (2011): 699–748.

Abraham, William, and James Kirby. *Oxford Handbook of Methodist Studies.* Oxford: Oxford University Press, 2009.

Alexander, Jeffrey. *The Civil Sphere.* New York: Oxford University Press, 2006.

Appiah, Kwame Anthony. *Cosmopolitanism: Ethics in a World of Strangers.* New York: W. W. Norton, 2006.

———. *The Lies That Bind: Rethinking Identity.* New York: Liveright, 2018.

Arenstam, Julia. "Netflix CEO Pushes Charter Schools, Flexibility at CABL Lunch." *Greater Baton Rouge Business Report*, December 12, 2019. https://www.businessreport.com/newsletters/netflix-ceo-pushes-charter-schools-flexibility-at-cabl-lunch.

Aron, Hillel. "Who Is Alex Caputo-Pearl: Meet the Maverick Union Leader Behind the Teachers Strike." *Los Angeles Magazine*, January 14, 2019. https://www.lamag.com/citythinkblog/alex-caputo-pearl/.

Baldridge, Bianca. "The Youthwork Paradox: A Case for Studying the Complexity of Community-Based Youth Work in Education Research." *Educational Researcher* 49 (2020): 618–625.

Bancroft, Hubert. "Some Chinese Episodes." In *The Works of Hubert Howe Bancroft: California Inter Pocula Vol. 35.* San Francisco: History Company, 1888.

Banks, Sandy. "Door Opens to Revamp L.A. Schools." *Los Angeles Times*, January 17, 1992.

Bartlett, Dana Webster. *The Better City: A Sociological Study of a Modern City.* Los Angeles: Neuner Company Press, 1907.

Bates, Elizabeth. "A Study of the Development of Elementary Education in Los Angeles City." Master's thesis, University of Southern California, 1928.

Besecker, Megan, and Andrew Thomas. "Student Engagement Online during School Facilities Closures." Los Angeles: Independent Analysis Unit, L.A. Unified School District, 2020.

Bettinger, M. C. "Twenty-Five Years in the Schools of Los Angeles." *Annual Publication of the Historical Society of Southern California* 8, no. 1/2 (1909–1910): 67–75.

Bifulco, Robert, Casey Cobb, and Courtney Bell. "Can Interdistrict Choice Boost Student Achievement? The Case of Connecticut's Interdistrict Magnet School Program." *Educational Evaluation and Policy Analysis* 31, no. 4 (2009): 323–345.

Bloemraad, Irene, and Veronica Terriquez. "Cultures of Engagement: The Organizational Foundations of Advancing Health in Immigrant and Low-Income Communities of Color." *Social Science and Medicine* 165 (2016): 214–222.

Blume, Howard. "Romer Gives Last Annual Address to Administrators." *Los Angeles Times*, August 24, 2006.

———. "UTLA Elects a New Leader." *Los Angeles Times*, April 30, 2014.

———. "For Charter Students, a Learning Gap." *Los Angeles Times*, December 22, 2015.

———. "Suspension Figures Called 'Alarming.'" *Los Angeles Times*, March 6, 2016.

———. "A Surprise Big Spender Funds Attack Campaign Mailers in Key L.A. School Board Races." *Los Angeles Times*, February 18, 2020.

Blume, Howard, and Sonali Kohli. "L.A. Unified Police Chief Resigns after District Slashes Budget." *Los Angeles Times*, June 30, 2020. https://www.latimes.com /california/story/2020-06-30/lausd-unified-budget-school-police-reopening.

Bond, J. Max, Sr. "The Negro in Los Angeles." PhD diss., University of Southern California, 1936.

Brown, Jerry. "Governor Brown Signs Historic School Funding Legislation." Sacramento: Office of the Governor, 2013. https://www.ca.gov/archive/gov39/2013/07/01/news18123 /index.html

Bulkley, Katrina, Julie Marsh, Katharine Strunk, Douglas Harris, and Ayesha Hashim. *Challenging the One Best System: The Portfolio Management Model and Urban School Governance.* Cambridge, MA: Harvard Education Press, 2020.

Byrnes, Susan. "School is Succeeding Far Beyond Projections." *Los Angeles Times*, April 2, 1994.

California State Controller. "School Districts and Community College Districts Payments and Offsets." https://www.sco.ca.gov/ard_mancost_payments_offsets.html.

Campos, Christopher, and Caitlin Kearns. "Options and Opportunity: Evidence from Zones of Choice." Unpublished manuscript. Berkeley: Department of Economics, 2021.

Caputo-Pearl, Alex. "Schools L.A. Students Deserve Campaign." *United Teacher*, September 1, 2017. https://www.utla.net/news/schools-la-students-deserve-campaign -unapologetic-about-what-students-educators-need.

———. "Why Los Angeles Teachers May Have to Strike." *Los Angeles Times*, January 6, 2019. https://www.latimes.com/opinion/op-ed/la-oe-caputo-pearl-teachers-strike -20190106-story.html.

Card, David, Alexandre Mas, and Jesse Rothstein. "Tipping and the Dynamics of Segregation." *Quarterly Journal of Economics* 123, no. 1 (2008): 177–218.

Chastang, Carol, and Diane Seo. "Driven to Learn: Minority Students Endure Long Days to Be Bussed to Westside Schools." *Los Angeles Times*, June 19, 1994.

Chubb, John, and Terry Moe. *Politics, Markets, and America's Schools.* Washington, DC: Brookings Institution, 1990.

Cicero, Marcus Tullius. *Ethical Writings of Cicero* (De officiis, Book 1, Section 56). Translated by Andrew P. Peabody. Boston: Little, Brown, 1887.

Clark, Susan E., Rodney E. Hero, Mara S. Sidney, Luis R. Fraga, and Bari A. Erlichson. *Multiethnic Moments: The Politics of Urban Education Reform.* Philadelphia: Temple University Press, 2006.

Clark, William, and Regan Maas. "Schools, Neighborhoods and Selection: Outcomes across Metropolitan Los Angeles." *Population Research and Policy Review* 31, no. 3 (2012): 339–360.

Coleman, James, Sara Kelly, and John Moore. "Recent Trends in School Integration, 1968–1973." Washington, DC: Urban Institute, Paper No. 7224341 (1975).

Colmenar, Raymond, Francisco Estrada, Theresa Lo, and Richard Raya. "Ending School Overcrowding in California: Building Quality Schools for All Children." Oakland, CA: Policy Link and the Mexican American Legal Defense and Education Fund, 2005.

Colvin, Richard Lee. "First-Graders' Scores Surge in Reading Test." *Los Angeles Times*, October 10, 2001.

Commission of Immigration and Housing of California. *The Home Teacher: The Act, with a Working Plan and Forty Lessons in English.* Sacramento, 1916. https://archive.org /stream/hometeacheractoocali/hometeacheractoocali_djvu.txt.

"Community Coalition and Reyna Frias Settle with Los Angeles Unified School District." *Los Angeles Times*, September 14, 2017. http://documents.latimes.com /community-coalition-LAUSD-settlement/.

Community Magnet Charter School. "About CMCS." http://www.communitymagnet .org/about-cmcs. Accessed April 14, 2021.

Connolly, William. *Pluralism.* Durham, NC: Duke University Press, 2005.

Coolbrith, Ina. *A Perfect Day and Other Poems.* London: Wentworth Press, 2019.

Cordes, Sarah A. "In Pursuit of the Common Good: The Spillover Effects of Charter Schools on Public School Students in New York City." *Education Finance and Policy* 13, no. 4 (2018): 484–512.

Corwin, Miles. *And Still We Rise: The Trials and Triumphs of 12 Gifted Inner-City Students.* New York: Harper Perennial, 2000.

Dahl, Robert. *Dilemmas of Pluralist Democracy: Autonomy versus Control.* New Haven, CT: Yale University Press, 1982.

Daley, Glenn, Tien Le, and Sydney Ganon. "Magnet Smarter Balanced Assessment Results, Spring 2018." Los Angeles: Los Angeles Unified School District.

Dauter, Luke, and Bruce Fuller. "Student Movement in Social Context: The Influence of Time, Peers, and Place." *American Educational Research Journal* 53, no. 1 (2016): 33–70.

De Graaf, Lawrence. "The City of Black Angels: Emergence of the Los Angeles Ghetto, 1890–1930." *Pacific Historical Review* 39, no. 3 (1970): 323–352.

Deverell, William. *Whitewashed Adobe: The Rise of Los Angeles and the Remaking of Its Mexican Past.* Berkeley: University of California Press, 2005.

Didion, Joan. *Slouching Towards Bethlehem: Essays.* New York: Farrar, Straus and Giroux, 1968.

DiMaggio, Paul, and Walter Powell, eds. *The New Institutionalism in Organizational Analysis.* Chicago: University of Chicago Press, 1991.

Dingerson, Leigh. "Building the Power to Reclaim Our Schools." Los Angeles: Los Angeles Alliance for a New Economy, 2019.

Editorial Board. "Did de Blasio Put Politics Ahead of Yeshiva Students?" *New York Times*, December 25, 2019. https://www.nytimes.com/2019/12/25/opinion/yeshivas-investigation -de-blasio.html.

Eire, Carlos. *Reformations: The Early Modern World, 1450–1650*. New Haven, CT: Yale University Press, 2016.

Engberg, John, Dennis Epple, Jason Imbrogno, Holger Sieg, and Ron Zimmer. "Evaluating Education Programs That Have Lotteried Admission and Selective Attrition." *Journal of Labor Economics* 32, no. 1 (2014): 27–63.

Estrada, Delia. "Utilizing the Lens of Cultural Proficiency to Judge the Impact of Autonomous Schools from the Student Perspective." PhD diss., Claremont Graduate University, 2017.

Ethington, Philip, William H. Frey, and Dowell Myers. *The Racial Resegregation of Los Angeles County, 1940–2000*. Los Angeles: University of Southern California (Public Research Report No. 2001-2004), 2004.

Fauci, Jeanne, and Karen Hunter Quartz. "A Decade of Innovation: How the LAUSD Pilot School Movement is Advancing Equitable and Personalized Education." Policy brief. Los Angeles: Center for Powerful Schools.

Feinberg, Walter. *Common Schools, Uncommon Identities: National Unity and Cultural Difference*. New Haven, CT: Yale University Press, 1998.

Felch, Jason, Jason Song, and Doug Smith. "Seniority over Quality: When Budget Cuts Hit, Many of L.A.'s Most Promising Teachers Were Laid Off." *Los Angeles Times*, December 5, 2010.

Fenwick, Arthur. "A Modern City's High-School System: Los Angeles." *School Review* 24, no. 2 (1916): 116–129.

Figlio, David, and Cassandra Hart. "Competitive Effects of Means-Tested School Vouchers." *American Economic Journal: Applied Economics* 6, no. 1 (2014): 133–156.

Fligstein, Neil, and Doug McAdam. *A Theory of Fields*. New York: Oxford University Press, 2015.

Fogelson, Robert. *The Fragmented Metropolis: Los Angeles, 1850–1930*. Berkeley: University of California Press, 1967.

Friedhoff, Alec, Howard Wial, and Harold Wolman. *The Consequences of Metropolitan Manufacturing Decline: Testing Conventional Wisdom*. Metro Economy Series for the Metropolitan Policy Program. Washington, DC: Brookings Institution. https://www.brookings.edu/research/the-consequences-of-metropolitan-manufacturing-decline-testing-conventional-wisdom/.

Fuller, Bruce. *Organizing Locally: How the New Decentralists Improve Education, Health Care, and Trade*. Chicago: University of Chicago Press, 2015.

———. "The Verdict on Charter Schools?" *The Atlantic*, July 8, 2015. https://www.theatlantic.com/education/archive/2015/07/the-verdict-on-charter-schools/397820/.

———. "Palace Revolt in Los Angeles? Charter School and Latino Leaders Push Unions to Innovate." *Education Next*, April 10, 2010. https://www.educationnext.org/palace-revolt-in-los-angeles/.

———. "Teachers are Organizing, but What about Teachers' Unions?" *Education Week*, May 21, 2018. https://www.edweek.org/teaching-learning/opinion-teachers-are-organizing-but-what-about-teachers-unions/2018/05.

———. "Joe Biden Seems to Think School Segregation Is Nearly Unsolvable: These Efforts Prove Him Wrong." *Los Angeles Times*, August 27, 2019. https://www.latimes.com/opinion/story/2019-08-26/joe-biden-kamala-harris-school-desegregation-burbank-lausd.

Fuller, Bruce, Elise Castillo, Joonho Lee, and Cristián Ugarte. *Will $4 Billion in New Spending Make a Difference? Narrowing Achievement Gaps in Los Angeles.* Research report. Berkeley: Graduate School of Education, 2016.

Fuller, Bruce, Amanda Recinos, and Barbara Scholl. *Voter Support for Los Angeles School Facility Bonds, 2002–2006.* Research report. Berkeley: Graduate School of Education.

Fuller, Bruce, Jeff Vincent, Ariel Bierbaum, Greta Kirschenbaum, Deborah McCoy, and Jessica Rigby. *Smart Schools, Smart Growth: Investing in Education Facilities and Stronger Communities.* Research report. Berkeley: Policy Analysis for California Education, 2009.

Fuller, Bruce, Anisah Waite, Celina Lee Chao, and Iza Mari Benedicto. "Rich Communities in Small High Schools? Teacher Collaboration and Cohesion Inside 25 Los Angeles High Schools." Research brief. Berkeley: University of California, 2014.

Fuller, Bruce, Anisah Waite, and David Torres Irribarra. "Explaining Teacher Turnover: School Cohesion and Intrinsic Motivation in Los Angeles." *American Journal of Education* 122, no. 4 (2016): 537–567.

Gaebler, David, and Ted Osborne. *Reinventing Government: How the Entrepreneurial Spirit is Transforming the Public Sector.* New York: Basic Books, 1992.

Gibson, Mary. "The Immigrant Woman." *California Outlook,* XVI (1914): 5–9.

Gitlin, Todd. *The Twilight of Common Dreams: Why America is Wracked by Culture Wars.* New York: Metropolitan Books, 1995.

Glass, Fred. *From Mission to Microchip: A History of the California Labor Movement.* Berkeley: University of California Press, 2016.

Goldstein, Dana. *The Teacher Wars: A History of America's Most Embattled Profession.* New York: Anchor Press, 2015.

Gould, Arthur. "The Intermediate Schools of Los Angeles." *School Review* 28, no. 6 (1920): 419–443.

Graham, Wade. *Dream Cities: Seven Urban Ideas That Shape the World.* Gloucestershire, England: Amberley Publishing, 2016.

Griswold del Castillo, Richard. *La Familia: Chicano Families in the Urban Southwest, 1848 to the Present.* Notre Dame, IN: University of Notre Dame Press, 1984.

———. *The Los Angeles Barrio, 1850–1890: A Social History.* Berkeley: University of California Press, 1979.

Guinn, James. "Los Angeles in the Later Sixties and Early Seventies." *Annual Publication of the Historical Society of Southern California* 3, no. 1 (1893): 63–68.

———. "The Area of Los Angeles City Was Enlarged." *Annual Publication of the Historical Society of Southern California* 9, no. 3 (1914): 173–180.

Gumprecht, Blake. *The Los Angeles River: Its Life, Death, and Possible Rebirth.* Baltimore: Johns Hopkins University Press, 1999.

Handler, Joel. *Down from Bureaucracy: The Ambiguity of Privatization and Empowerment.* Princeton, NJ: Princeton University Press, 1996.

Hashim, Ayesha, Katharine O. Strunk, and Tasminda K. Dhaliwal. "Justice for All? Suspension Bans and Restorative Justice Programs in the Los Angeles Unified School District." *Peabody Journal of Education* 93, no. 2 (2018): 174–189.

Havel, Václav. *The Power of the Powerless: Citizens against the State in Central Eastern Europe.* London: Routledge, 1985.

———. *Disturbing the Peace.* New York: Vintage Books, 1991.

Hayasaki, Erika. "Charters' Test Gains Higher, Study Shows." *Los Angeles Times*, June 18, 2003.

Helfand, Duke. "Reading Taught the Scripted Way." *Los Angeles Times*, July 30, 2000.

Henig, Jeffrey. *The End of Exceptionalism in American Education: The Changing Politics of School Reform*. Cambridge, MA: Harvard Education Press, 2013.

———. "Reading the Future of Education Policy." *Education Week*, January 7, 2013. https://www.edweek.org/policy-politics/opinion-reading-the-future-of-education-policy/2013/01.

Henig, Jeffrey, Richard Hula, Marion Orr, and Desiree Pedescleaux. *The Color of School Reform: Race, Politics, and the Challenge of Urban Education*. Princeton, NJ: Princeton University Press, 1999.

Heyrman, Christine. "Puritanism and Predestination." Divining America, TeacherServe. National Humanities Center. Accessed April 15, 2021. http://nationalhumanitiescenter.org/tserve/eighteen/ekeyinfo/puritan.htm.

History Channel. "U.S. Immigration since 1965." Updated June 7, 2019. http://www.history.com/topics/us-immigration-since-1965.

Holmes, Samuel. "Perils of the Mexican Invasion." *North American Review* 227, no. 5 (1929): 615–623.

Hundley, Norris, Jr. *The Great Thirst: Californians and Water, 1770s–1990s*. Berkeley: University of California Press, 1992.

"John Deasy's Future." *Los Angeles Times*, October 3, 2014. https://www.latimes.com/opinion/editorials/la-ed-deasy-lausd-20141003-story.html.

Johnson, Daniel. "A Serpent in the Garden: Institutions, Ideology, and Class in Los Angeles Politics, 1901–1911." PhD diss., University of Southern California, 1996.

Johnson, Lyndon B. "Remarks at the Signing of the Immigration Bill." Liberty Island, New York, 1965. https://m.arquivo.pt/wayback/20160516063650/http:/www.lbjlib.utexas.edu/Johnson/archives.hom/speeches.hom/651003.asp.

Jones, William. "The First Benefactors." *University of California Magazine* 5, no. 3 (1899): 101–117.

Junger, Sebastian. *Tribe: On Homecoming and Belonging*. New York: Hachette, 2016.

Kahne, Joseph E., and Susan E. Sporte. "Developing Citizens: The Impact of Civic Learning Opportunities on Students' Commitment to Civic Participation." *American Educational Research Journal* 45, no. 3 (2008): 738–766.

Kalberg, Stephen, trans. Introduction to *The Protestant Ethic and the Spirit of Capitalism: The Revised 1920 Edition* by Max Weber and Stephen Kalberg, 8–66. New York: Oxford University Press, 2011.

Kearns, Caitlin, Douglas Lee Lauen, and Bruce Fuller. "Competing with Charter Schools: Selection, Retention, and Achievement in Los Angeles Pilot Schools." *Evaluation Review* 44, no. 2 (2020): 111–144.

Kerchner, Charles, David Menefee-Libby, Laura Steen Mulfinger, and Stephanie Clayton. *Learning from L.A.: The Institutional Change in American Public Education*. Cambridge, MA: Harvard Education Press, 2008.

Kerr-Peterson, Miles. *A Protestant Lord in James VI's Scotland: George Keith, Fifth Earl Marischal (1554–1623)*. Vol. 8. Suffolk, UK: Boydell Press, 2019.

Kipen, David. *Dear Los Angeles: The City in Diaries and Letters, 1542 to 2018*. New York: Modern Library, 2018.

Kirst, Michael. "Understanding Successful Politics for California School Finance Reform." Paper presented at the Annual (Online) Meeting of the American Educational Research Association, April 2020.

Kohli, Sonali. "Parents Who Want Their Kids in L.A.'s Most Competitive Magnet Schools Face Daunting Odds." *Los Angeles Times*, October 13, 2016. https://www.latimes.com/local/education/la-me-edu-most-selective-magnets-20161010-snap-story.html.

———. "L.A. Unified Board Votes to End Random Student Searches." *Los Angeles Times*, June 18, 2019. https://www.latimes.com/local/education/la-me-edu-random-searches-lausd-20190618-story.html.

Kotkin, Joel. *Tribes: How Race, Religion and Identity Determine Success in the New Global Economy*. New York: Random House, 1994.

Krist, Gary. *The Mirage Factory: Illusion, Imagination, and the Invention of Los Angeles*. New York: Broadway Books, 2019.

Kuhrts, Jacob. "Tenth Annual Report of the Pioneers of Los Angeles County and the Annual Publication of the Historical Society of Southern California." *Historical Society of Southern California* 7, no. 1 (1906): 67–68.

Lafortune, Julien, and David Shônholzer. "Measuring the Efficacy and Efficiency of School Facility Expenditures." Working paper. Berkeley: Department of Economics, 2019. http://www.cirje.e.u-tokyo.ac.jp/research/workshops/emf/paper2019/emp1223.pdf.

Lauen, Douglas Lee, Bruce Fuller, and Luke Dauter. "Positioning Charter Schools in Los Angeles: Diversity of Form and Homogeneity of Effects." *American Journal of Education* 121, no. 2 (2015): 213–239.

Layne, Gregg. "The First Census of the Los Angeles District: Padron de la Ciudad de Los Angeles y Su Jurisdiction Año 1836." *Quarterly: Historical Society of Southern California* 18, no. 3 (1936): 81–99.

Layton, Lyndsey. "Democratic Mayors Challenge Teachers Unions in Urban Political Shift." *Washington Post*, March 30, 2012. https://www.washingtonpost.com/nat/education/democratic-mayors-challenge-teachers-unions-in-urban-political-shift/2012/03/30/gIQAoxoJmS_story.html.

Lee, Joonho, and Bruce Fuller. "Does Progressive Finance Alter School Organizations and Raise Achievement? The Case of Los Angeles." *Educational Policy* 34 (2020): 1–37.

Leimert Park Beat. "Taylor Griffin Galloway, Family Mourn Loss of Young Girl Killed in Tragic Accident in Front of Dorsey High School." February 13, 2011. https://www.leimertparkbeat.com/profiles/blogs/taylor-griffin-galloway-family.

Lemann, Nicholas. *Transaction Man: The Rise of the Deal and the Decline of the American Dream*. New York: Macmillan, 2019.

Leung, Victor, Ana Mendoza, and Jessica Cobb. "Here to Learn: Creating Safe and Supportive Schools in Los Angeles Unified School District." Los Angeles: American Civil Liberties Association, 2018.

Lévi-Strauss, Claude. *The Savage Mind*. Paris: Librairie Plon, 1962.

Lewis, Jason. "Hillary Clinton Visits Community Coalition." *Our Weekly Los Angeles*, May 26, 2016. http://ourweekly.com/news/2016/may/26/hillary-clinton-vists-community-coalition/.

Los Angeles Unified School District. "Recommendations for Increasing Equity in Enrollment Practices." Los Angeles, 2021.

Lukes, Steven. *Power: A Radical View*. London: Palgrave Macmillan, 2005.

Macray, Douglas. "The Instigator: A Crusader's Plan to Remake Failing Schools." *New Yorker*, May 4, 2009. https://www.newyorker.com/magazine/2009/05/11/the-instigator.

Mann, Eric. *Taking on General Motors: A Case Study of the Campaign to Keep GM Van Nuys Open*. Los Angeles: UCLA Center for Labor Research and Education, 1987.

Marsh, Julie. "The Political Dynamics of District Reform: The Form and Fate of the Los Angeles Public School Choice Initiative." *Teachers College Record* 118, no. 9 (2016) 1–54.

Marsh, Julie, Taylor Allbright, Katrina Bulkley, Kate Kennedy, and Tasminda Dhaliwal. "Institutional Logics in Los Angeles Schools: Do Multiple Models Disrupt the Grammar of Schooling?" *American Journal of Education* 126, no. 4 (2020): 603–651.

Marsh, Julie, and Michelle Hall. "Challenges and Choices: A Multidistrict Analysis of Statewide Mandated Democratic Engagement." *American Educational Research Journal* 55, no. 2 (2018): 243–286.

Marsh, Julie, Katharine Strunk, Susan Bush-Mecenas, and Alice Huguet. "Democratic Engagement in District Reform: The Evolving Role of Parents in the Los Angeles Public School Choice Initiative." *Educational Policy* 29, no. 1 (2015): 51–84.

Marsh, Julie A., and Priscilla Wohlstetter. "Recent Trends in Intergovernmental Relations: The Resurgence of Local Actors in Education Policy." *Educational Researcher* 42, no. 5 (2013): 276–283.

Martin, Philip. "Unauthorized Workers in US Agriculture: Old Versus New Migrations." In *Illegal Immigration in America: A Reference Handbook*, edited by David W. Hanes and Karen E. Rosenblum. Westport, CT: Greenwood Press, 1999.

Martínez, Ramón Antonio, and Karen Hunter Quartz. "Zoned for Change: A Historical Case Study of the Belmont Zone of Choice." *Teachers College Record* 114, no. 10 (2012): 1–40.

Matteson, John. *The Lives of Margaret Fuller*. New York: W. W. Norton, 2012.

McAdam, Doug, John McCarthy, and Mayer Zald. "Social Movements." In *Handbook of Sociology*, edited by N. J. Smelser, 695–737. Beverly Hills, CA: Sage, 1988.

McDermott, John. "*Serrano*: What Does It Mean?" *California School Boards* 34, no. 2 (1975): 4–9.

McWilliams, Carey, and Matt S. Meier. *North from Mexico: The Spanish-Speaking People of the United States*. New York: Greenwood Press, 1990.

Medved, Michael, and David Wallechinsky. *What Really Happened to the Class of '65?* New York: Random House, 1977.

Merl, Jean. "No Frills School Makes Its Mark." *Los Angeles Times*, June 25, 2001.

Meyer, John W., David Tyack, Joanne Nagel, and Audrey Gordon. "Public Education as Nation-Building in America: Enrollments and Bureaucratization in the American States, 1870–1930." *American Journal of Sociology* 85, no. 3 (1979): 591–613.

Milkman, Ruth. *L.A Story: Immigrant Workers and the Future of the US Labor Movement*. New York: Russell Sage Foundation, 2006.

Moe, Terry. *The Politics of Institutional Reform: Katrina, Education, and the Second Face of Power.* New York: Cambridge University Press, 2019.

Movimiento Estudiantil Chicano de Aztlán (MEChA). "Movimiento Estudiantil." Accessed April 15, 2021. http://www.chicanxdeaztlan.org/p/history.html.

Mowry, George. *The California Progressives.* Chicago: Quadrangle Books, 1951.

Muñiz-Fraticelli, Victor. *The Structure of Pluralism.* New York: Oxford University Press, 2014.

Nadeau, Remi. *The Water Seekers.* New York: Doubleday, 1950.

National Assessment of Educational Progress. "Trial Urban District Assessment: Reading Highlights, 2003." Accessed April 16, 2021. https://nces.ed.gov/nationsreportcard/pdf /dst2003/2004459.pdf.

———. "Interpreting NAEP Results." Accessed April 16, 2021. https://nces.ed.gov /nationsreportcard/reading/interpret_results.aspx.

Nesoff, Jeremy. "The Belmont Zone of Choice: Community-Driven Action for School Change." *Horace* 23, no. 4 (Winter 2007): http://files.eric.ed.gov/fulltext/EJ853147.pdf.

Nicholls, David. *The Pluralist State: The Political Ideas of J. N. Figgis and His Contemporaries,* 2nd ed. London: Palgrave Macmillan, 1994.

Nicolaides, Becky. *My Blue Heaven: Life and Politics in the Working-Class Suburbs of Los Angeles, 1920–1965.* Chicago: University of Chicago Press, 2002.

———. "'Where the Working Man is Welcomed': Working-Class Suburbs in Los Angeles, 1900–1940." *Pacific Historical Review* 68, no. 4 (1999): 517–559.

Noe-Bustamonte, Luis, Lauren Mora, and Mark Hugo Lopez. *About One in Four Hispanics Have Heard of Latinx.* Washington, DC: Pew Research Center, 2020.

Nordhoff, Charles. *California: For Health, Pleasure and Residence. A Book for Travelers and Settlers.* New York: Harper and Brothers, 1873.

Oakes, Jeannie. "Testimony on the *Williams* School Finance Case." 2002. http:// decentschools.org/expert_reports/oakes_report_3.pdf.

Oakes, Jeannie, and John Rogers. *Learning Power: Organizing for Education and Justice.* New York: Teachers College Press, 2006.

Oakeshott, Michael. *On Human Conduct.* Oxford: Oxford University Press, 1975.

Offe, Claus. *Reflections on America: Tocqueville, Weber and Adorno in the United States.* Cambridge: Polity Press, 2005.

Orfield, Gary. "Lessons of the Los Angeles Desegregation Case." *Education and Urban Society* 16, no. 3 (1984): 338–353.

Orr, Marion, and John Rogers, eds. *Public Engagement for Public Education: Joining Forces to Revitalize Democracy and Equalize Schools.* Palo Alto: Stanford University Press, 2011.

Ouchi, William. "A Novel Approach to Organizational Control." PhD diss., University of Chicago, 1972.

———. *Theory Z: How American Business Can Meet the Japanese Challenge.* New York: Avon, 1982.

Pace, Eric. "J. Max Bond Sr., 89, an American Who Headed Liberian University." *New York Times,* December 18, 1991. https://www.nytimes.com/1991/12/18/nyregion/j-max -bond-sr-89-an-american-who-headed-liberian-university.html.

Partnership for Los Angeles Schools. *Partnership Playbook.* 2020. https://playbook .partnershipla.org/.

Pastor, Manuel, Jr., Chris Benner, and Martha Matsuoka. *This Could Be the Start of Something Big: How Social Movements for Regional Equity Are Reshaping Metropolitan America*. Ithaca, NY: Cornell University Press, 2015.

Phillips, Anna. "L.A. School Superintendent Michelle King Pushes for 100% Graduation." *Los Angeles Times*, August 8, 2017. https://www.latimes.com/local/education/la-me-edu-state-of-lausd-20170808-story.html.

Phillips, Meredith, Kyo Yamashiro, and Thomas Jacobson. "College Going in LAUSD: An Analysis of College Enrollment, Persistence, and Completion Patterns." Los Angeles: UCLA School of Public Policy, 2017.

Piven, Frances, and Richard Cloward. *Poor People's Movements: Why They Succeed, How They Fail*. New York: Vintage Press, 1979.

Pope Pius XI. "Encyclical of Pope Pius XI on Reconstruction of the Social Order to Our Venerable Brethren." 1931. http://www.vatican.va/content/pius-xi/en/encyclicals/documents/hf_p-xi_enc_19310515_quadragesimo-anno.html.

Portland Underground Graduate School. "Direct Action Organizing." 2020. https://www.pugspdx.com/direct-action-organizing.

Price, Scott, and Janice Sawyer. *Health and Welfare Board Retreat 8.29.17*. Los Angeles: Los Angeles Unified School District, 2017. https://boe.lausd.net/sites/default/files/08-29-17HealthWelfareRetreatPresentationWithAppendices.pdf.

Raftery, Judith. *Land of Fair Promise: Politics and Reform in Los Angeles Schools, 1885–1991*. Stanford, CA: Stanford University Press, 1992.

Ray, Rosalie, Paul Ong, and Silvia Jimenez. "Impacts of the Widening Divide: Los Angeles at the Forefront of the Rent Burden Crisis." UCLA Luskin School of Public Affairs, Center for the Study of Inequality, 2014. https://knowledge.luskin.ucla.edu/wp-content/uploads/2018/01/Impacts-of-the-Widening-Divide-Los-Angeles-Renters-Ziman_2014-08W.pdf.

Raymond, Margaret. "Charter School Performance in Los Angeles." Stanford, CA: Center for Research on Education Outcomes, Stanford University, 2014.

Reyes, David. "Newport Teachers Close to Strike." *Los Angeles Times*, February 13, 1982.

Rodriguez, Richard. *Days of Obligation: An Argument with My Mexican Father*. New York: Viking Penguin, 1992.

Rogers, John, Kavitha Mediratta, and Seema Shah. "Building Power, Learning Democracy: Youth Organizing as a Site of Civic Development." *Review of Research in Education* 36, no. 1 (2012): 43–66.

Rogers, John, and Ernest Morrell. "A Force to Be Reckoned With: The Campaign for College Access in Los Angeles." In *Public Engagement for Public Education*, edited by Marion Orr and John Rogers, 227–249. Palo Alto: Stanford University Press, 2011.

Rogers, John, and Veronica Terriquez. *Learning to Lead: The Impact of Youth Organizing on the Educational and Civic Trajectories of Low-Income Youth*. Los Angeles: UCLA Institute for Democracy, Education, and Access, 2013. https://files.eric.ed.gov/fulltext/ED574627.pdf.

Rollin-Alamillo, Louise. *Recent Birth Trends in Los Angeles County*. Los Angeles: Office of Health Assessment and Epidemiology, 2015. http://www.publichealth.lacounty.gov/epi/docs/Birth_Trends_Health_Brief_Final.pdf.

Romero, Dennis. "The Militarization of Police Started in Los Angeles." *L.A. Weekly*, August 15, 2014. http://www.laweekly.com/news/the-militarization-of-police-started-in-los-angeles-5010287.

Romo, Ricardo. *East Los Angeles: History of a Barrio.* Austin: University of Texas Press, 1983.

Roos, Sara. "Outflanking the CTA from the Left: How Anti-Racist Demands Are Captured by Privateers." *Los Angeles Education Examiner*, July 21, 2020. https://la-edex.org/outflanking-cta-from-the-left-how-anti-racist-demands-are-captured-by-privateers/.

Rott, Nathan. "L.A. Schools Throw Out Suspensions for 'Willful Defiance.'" *National Public Radio*, May 15, 2013. https://www.npr.org/2013/05/15/184195877/l-a-schools-throw-out-suspensions-for-willful-defiance.

Rubin, Joel. "Broad Gives to Charter School Group." *Los Angeles Times*, November 30, 2006. https://www.latimes.com/archives/la-xpm-2006-nov-30-me-broad30-story.html.

Russo, Alexander. *Stray Dogs, Saints, and Saviors: Fighting for the Soul of America's Toughest High School.* San Francisco: Jossey-Bass, 2011.

Rustin, Bayard. "The Watts." *Commentary Magazine*, March 1966. https://www.commentarymagazine.com/articles/bayard-rustin-2/the-watts/.

Sahagun, Louis. "The Architects of a Movement." *Los Angeles Times*, March 10, 2018. https://www.pressreader.com/usa/los-angeles-times/20180310/281736974967477.

Sampson, Robert, Jared Schachner, and Robert Mare. "Urban Income Inequality and the Great Recession in Sunbelt Form: Disentangling Individual and Neighborhood-Level Change in Los Angeles." *Russell Sage Foundation Journal of the Social Sciences* 3, no. 2 (2017): 102–128.

Sangeorge, Robert. "A California Ballot Initiative Restricting Busing to Achieve Desegregation." United Press International, March 22, 1982. https://www.upi.com/Archives/1982/03/22/A-California-ballot-initiative-restricting-busing-to-achieve-desegregation/1199385621200/.

Schipske, Gerrie. *Early Long Beach.* San Francisco: Arcadia Publishing, 2011.

Schneider, Jack. "Escape from Los Angeles: White Flight from Los Angeles and Its Schools, 1960–1980." *Journal of Urban History* 34, no. 6 (2008): 995–1012.

Schrag, Peter. *Paradise Lost: California's Experience, America's Future.* Berkeley: University of California Press, 1998.

Schulman, Bruce. *The Seventies: The Great Shift in American Culture, Society, and Politics.* New York: Free Press, 2001.

Scott, Janelle, Elizabeth DeBray, Christopher Lubienski, Johanna Hanley, Elise Castillo, and Samantha Hedges. "The Politics of Charter School Evidence in Local Context." In *School Choice at the Crossroads*, edited by Mark Berends, R. Joseph Waddington, and John Schoenig, 205–234. New York: Routledge, 2019.

Scott, W. Richard. *Institutions and Organizations: Ideas, Interests, and Identities.* 4th ed. Beverly Hills: Sage, 2013.

Seligman, Adam. *The Idea of Civil Society.* Princeton, NJ: Princeton University Press, 1995.

Selvin, David. *Champions of Labor.* London: Abelard-Schuman, 1967.

Sennett, Richard. *The Fall of Public Man.* New York: W. W. Norton, 1977.

Sewell, William, Jr. "A Theory of Structure: Duality, Agency, and Transformation." *American Journal of Sociology* 98, no. 1 (1992): 1–29.

Shin, Hyo Jeong, Bruce Fuller, and Luke Dauter. "Heterogeneous Effects of Charter Schools: Unpacking Family Selection and Achievement Growth in Los Angeles." *Journal of School Choice* 11, no. 1 (2017): 60–94.

Shipps, Dorothy. *School Reform Corporate Style: Chicago, 1880–2000.* Lawrence: University of Kansas Press, 2006.

Slavin, Robert, Cynthia Lake, Bette Chambers, Alan Cheung, and Susan Davis. "Effective Reading Programs for the Elementary Grades: A Best-Evidence Synthesis." *Review of Educational Research* 79, no. 4 (2009): 1391–1466.

Slater, Andrew, dir. *Echo in the Canyon.* New York: Greenwich Entertainment, 2018.

Smith, Lynn. "A Campus Oasis Amidst the Violence." *Los Angeles Times*, April 11, 2001. https://www.latimes.com/archives/la-xpm-2001-apr-11-cl-49697-story.html.

Spaulding, Charles. "The Development of Organization and Disorganization in the Social Life of a Rapidly Growing Working-Class Suburb." PhD diss., University of Southern California, 1939.

Splitter, Henry. "Education in Los Angeles: 1850–1900." *Historical Society of Southern California Quarterly* 33, no. 2 (1951): 101–188.

Starr, Kevin. *Inventing the Dream: California through the Progressive Era.* New York: Oxford University Press, 1985.

Stecher, Brian, Deborah Holtzman, Michael Garet, Laura Hamilton, John Engberg, et al. *Improving Teaching Effectiveness: The Intensive Partnerships for Effective Teaching through 2015–2016.* Santa Monica: RAND, 2018. https://www.rand.org/pubs/research_reports/RR2242.html.

Stegner, Wallace. *The Angle of Repose.* New York: Doubleday, 1971.

Stokes, Kyle. "The Kids in LAUSD Who Most Need Dual Language Instruction Aren't Enrolling Yet." *KPCC Radio*, January 18, 2018. https://www.scpr.org/news/2018/01/18/79893/the-kids-in-lausd-who-most-need-dual-language-inst/.

Stone, Clarence. "Civic Capacity: What, Why, and from Whence." In *Institutions of American Democracy: The Public Schools*, edited by Susan Fuhrman and Marvin Lazerson, 209–234. New York: Oxford University Press, 2005.

———. "Looking Back to Look Forward: Reflections on Urban Regime Analysis." *Urban Affairs Review* 40, no. 3 (2005): 309–341.

Stone, Clarence, Jeffrey Henig, Bryan Jones, and Carol Pierannunzi. *Building Civic Capacity: The Politics of Reforming Urban Schools.* Lawrence: University of Kansas Press, 2001.

Storper, Michael. *Keys to the City: How Economics, Institutions, Social Interaction, and Politics Shape Development.* Princeton, NJ: Princeton University Press, 2013.

"Straight Out of Compton: You Have Heard of White Flight, Now Consider Black Flight." *The Economist*, February 16, 2008. http://www.economist.com/node/10697106.

Strunk, Katharine, Julie Marsh, Ayesha Hashim, Susan Bush-Mecenas, and Tracey Weinstein. "The Impact of Turnaround Reform on Student Outcomes: Evidence and Insights from the Los Angeles Unified School District." *Education Finance and Policy* 11, no. 3 (2016): 251–282.

Sullivan, L., D. Edwards, N. A. Johnson, and K. McGillicuddy. *An Emerging Model for Working with Youth.* New York: Funders' Collaborative on Youth Organizing, 2003.

Tarnoff, Ben. *The Bohemians: Mark Twain and the San Francisco Writers.* New York: Penguin Press, 2014.

Terriquez, Veronica. "Training Young Activists: Grassroots Organizing and Youths' Civic and Political Trajectories." *Sociological Perspectives* 58, no. 2 (2015): 223–242.

Thompson, Gabriel. *America's Social Arsonist: Fred Ross and Grassroots Organizing in the Twentieth Century.* Berkeley: University of California Press, 2016.

Thornton, Patricia, William Ocasio, and Michael Lounsbury. *The Institutional Logics Perspective: A New Approach to Culture, Structure, and Process.* New York: Oxford University Press, 2012.

Touraine, Alain. "A Method for Studying Social Action." *Journal of World Systems Research 6*, no. 3 (2000): 900–918.

Tyack, David, and Larry Cuban. *Tinkering toward Utopia: A Century of Public School Reform.* Cambridge, MA: Harvard University Press, 1995.

Tyack, David, and William Tobin. "The 'Grammar' of Schooling: Why Has It Been So Hard to Change?" *American Educational Research Journal* 31, no. 3 (1994): 453–479.

United Way. *Progress in Los Angeles Schools: Rigor, Fairness and Engaging Families.* Los Angeles, 2018.

Urevich, Robin. "Referrals of Students to Police Are Still a Problem at L.A. Schools." *Capital and Main*, June 12, 2019. https://capitalandmain.com/referrals-of-students-to-police-are-still-a-problem-at-los-angeles-schools-0612.

US Census Bureau. "County Business Patterns Datasets." Washington, DC, 2018. https://www.census.gov/programs-surveys/cbp/data/datasets.html.

———. "QuickFacts: Los Angeles County, California." Accessed April 16, 2021. https://www.census.gov/quickfacts/fact/table/losangelescountycalifornia/SEX 255216#viewtop.

U.S. Bureau of the Census. "Manufactures in Each State and Territory: 1880, Table 4." Washington, DC, 1881.

———. "School Enrollment." Tables 9 and Table 49. Washington, DC, 1901.

Waldie, D. J. "Angelino, Angeleno, Angeleño." KCET History and Society, January 10, 2011. https://www.kcet.org/shows/lost-la/angelino-angeleno-and-angeleno.

Walinsky, Adam. "Maximum Feasible Misunderstanding." *New York Times*, February 2, 1969. https://movies2.nytimes.com/books/98/10/04/specials/moynihan -community.html.

Warren, Mark, and Karen Mapp. *A Match on Dry Grass: Community Organizing as a Catalyst for School Reform.* New York: Oxford University Press, 2011.

Watanabe, Teresa. "LAUSD Okays Budget: Spending on Teachers, Needy Students to Grow." *Los Angeles Times*, June 24, 2014. https://www.latimes.com/local/education/la -me-lausd-budget-20140625-story.html.

Watanabe, Teresa, and Stephen Cesar. "LAUSD Outlines Plan to Spend $837 Million on Disadvantaged Students." *Los Angeles Times*, April 8, 2014. https://www.latimes .com/local/la-me-lausd-students-20140409-story.html.

Weaver-Hightower, Marcus. "An Ecology Metaphor for Educational Policy Analysis: A Call to Complexity." *Educational Researcher* 37, no. 3 (2008): 153–167.

Weingarten, Marc. *Thirsty: William Mulholland, California Water and the Real Chinatown.* Los Angeles: Rare Bird Books, 2015.

Welsh, William, Erin Coughlan, Bruce Fuller, and Luke Dauter. "New Schools, Overcrowding Relief, and Achievement Gains in Los Angeles." Policy brief. Berkeley: Policy Analysis for California Education. http://edpolicyinca.org/sites/default/files/pace_pb_08.pdf.

Wild, Mark. *Street Meeting: Multiethnic Neighborhoods in Early Twentieth-Century Los Angeles.* Berkeley: University of California Press, 2005.

Williamson, Burton. "The Civic Association as a Factor of Greater Los Angeles." *Annual Publication of the Historical Society of Southern California* 8, no. 3 (1911): 180–187.

Winters, Marcus, Grant Clayton, and Dick Carpenter II. "Are Low-Performing Students More Likely to Exit Charter Schools? Evidence from New York City and Denver." *Economics of Education Review* 56 (2017): 110–117.

Winther, Oscar. "The Rise of Metropolitan Los Angeles 1870–1940." *Huntington Library Quarterly* 10, no. 4 (1947): 391–405.

Woo, Elaine. "Magnet Schools in L.A.—Elitism or Top Education?" *Los Angeles Times*, January 10, 1988.

———. "All L.A. Schools to Be Year-Long: Decision by Board, Effective in 1989, Promises Radical Changes.." *Los Angeles Times*, October 13, 1987. https://www.latimes.com/archives/la-xpm-1987-10-13-mn-13744-story.html.

INDEX

Page numbers in *italics* refer to illustrations.

Abdulkadiroğlu, Atila, 116
Abdullah, Melina, 83
ACLU. *See* American Civil Liberties Union (ACLU)
admissions via lottery. *See* lottery admissions
Advanced Placement (AP) courses, 66, 141–42, 151
Advancement Project, 70, 73, 76, 139
African Americans. *See* Blacks
Aguilar, José Cristóbal, 24
Alexander, Jeffrey, 28
Alinsky, Saul, 127, 134
Alliance College-Ready Public Schools, 98
Alliance for a Better Community, 135–36
Alonzo, Richard, 77, 116
Althusius, Johannes, 157
American Civil Liberties Union (ACLU), 91, 139, 151, 154, 171–72; Crawford case, 46, 104; logics of reform, 155, 169; school finance efforts, 70, 71, 75, 76, 90, 127, 151, 172; Students Not Suspects, 83
Anderson, Roy A., 95
Ánimo Inglewood Charter High School, 107
Annandale Elementary School, 110
Annenberg, Walter, 97
Anton, William, 96
Appiah, Kwame Anthony, 160
Apple Computer, 82
Astorga, Sal, 49
Atchison, Topeka and Santa Fe Railway, 25, 26
Austin, Ben, 109, 110

automobile industry, 48–49
Ayres, J. J., 37, 38

Barlett, Dana W., 33, 42
Barr, Steve, 107–8, 114, 124
Bass, Karen, 5, 12, 131–36, 145, 162
Beaudry, Prudent, 24, 35
Belltown, Jurupa Valley, California, 134
Belmont Education Collective, 115
Belmont Zone of Choice, 76, 77, 94, 111, 116
Bernstein, Helen, 95–96, 97
Berry, Princess, 131, 137
Beutner, Austin, 87, 121, 133
Black Lives Matter, 83
Blacks, 5, 10, 38, 97, 175; charter schools, 152; churches, 44; Coco, 12; desegregation cases, 46, 103–4; housing segregation, 42, 43, 186n91; immigrants, 17, 21, 32, 36–37; janitors, 89; Latino solidarity, 143; literacy, 36; low expectations for, 69, 76; Pali High, 107; police violence against, 125, 170; reading scores, 66, *66*; school enrollment, *41*; suspensions and expulsions, 82–83; test scores, 65; unemployment, 50
Bloemraad, Irene, 129, 143
Bloomberg, Michael R., 11
Bloomfield, Bill, 108
Blume, Howard, 63
Bond, J. Max, Sr., 36, 43, 185n63, 186n94
Booz Allen, 96
Boston, 65, 100, 116
Bourdieu, Pierre, 135, 167

Boyle Heights, Los Angeles, 100, 111, 134.
See also Theodore Roosevelt High School
breakfast and lunch programs, 32, 89, 111, 141,
163
Brenes, Maria, 5, 54, 69, *73*, 76, 78, 151, 171;
on changing power relations, 67; on
charter schools, 111; Covid-19 pandemic,
170–71; on Inner City Struggle start-up,
143; New TLA relations, 85; "strange
bedfellows," 114; Villaraigosa and, 109
bricolage in policy. *See* policy bricolage
Broad, Eli, 11, 71, 73, 80, 86, 94, 108, 109, 114;
KB Homes, 61; Villaraigosa and, 109, 110
Broad Academy, 80
Brown, Edmund G., 47
Brown, Jerry, 72, 75, 76, 78, 90, 151, 157–58,
171–72
Brown, Willie, 97
Buddin, Richard, 61
Buffett, Warren, 73
Bulkley, Katrina, 113
Burbank, California, 164
Burton, Judy, 93, 98, 124
Bush, George W., 56, 62
busing, 48, 58, 72, 103, 104–5, 106

CADRE, 82
Cahuenga Elementary School, 58
California Charter Schools Association, 70,
108, 114, 134
California Immigrant Union, 29
California State Board of Education, 107–8
California Teachers Association, 107, 109
Campos, Chris, 119, 153
Caputo-Pearl, Alex, 85–87, 90, 141, 167, 172
Card, David, 60
Carver Middle School. *See* George
Washington Carver Middle School
Casillas, Maria, 115, 116
Catholicism, 28–29, 30, 134
Catholic schools, 36, 37, 100
Center for Powerful Public Schools, 70, 135
Central Pacific Railway, 36
Chan, Yvonne, 107
Chandler, Harry, 29, 44, 183n30
charter schools, 3, 55, 70, 94, 98–99, 106–14,
118, 123, 152–53; admissions, 175; Alonzo on,
116; AP rates, 66; California inception, 11;

70, 98; Caprice Young and, 93–94;
Caputo-Pearl and, 86, 87; college-prep
courses, 68; competition with traditional
schools, *102*, 122–23, 153; "conversion
charters," 112, 113, 114; elementary school
funding and, 78–79; enrollment stats, *60*;
Flores and, 149; Latinos, 111, 112, 114,
152–53; New Orleans, 6; NewSchools
Venture Fund and, 98; New TLA and, 149;
Ouchi on, 96; pilot schools compared, 78;
statistics, 100, 101, *102*, 163; as voucher
alternative, 100. *See also* California Charter
Schools Association
Chicago, 55, 56, 143, 163, 164
Chicano movement, 10, 48, 59–60, *59*, 88,
191n75
Chinese immigrants and Chinese Americans,
19, 29, 37–38; kindergartens, 43; laborers,
25, 29, 36, 185n60; massacre of 1871, 21;
mission schools, *34*; school enrollment, *41*
Chubb, John: *Politics, Markets, and America's
Schools*, 99
churches, 30, 42, 44, 136. *See also* Protestant
church kindergartens
Citizens for Justice, 75, 76
civil rights movement, 9, 46, 132, 136, 143
Civitas, 116
Clark, Detrianna, 130–31
Clarke, Susan E., 13
class size, 74, 79, 86, 112, 152, 167. *See also*
overcrowding
Clinton, Bill, 63, 95, 149
Clinton, Hillary, 138, 175
Coalition of Essential Schools, 116
Coco. *See* Community Coalition (Coco)
Coleman, James S., 103
college education. *See* higher education
college-preparatory courses, 67–69, 79, 84,
150, 151, 154; Brenes/ICS and, 69, 76, 135,
139, 151, 171; Coco and, 145; electives and,
152
common schools movement, 14, 18, 19, 23, 28,
37, 143, 157; *Crawford* case and, 103–4;
religious aspect, 32; suburbs, 38; twentieth-
century version, 63, 84
Communities for Educational Equity, 135
Communities for Los Angeles School Success
(CLASS), 54, 70

Community Coalition (Coco), 5, 12, 90, 124, 126–46, 154, 172; in broader coalitions, 67, 70, 82, 89, 171; Freedom Schools, 128, 129, 130, 138, 139; García and, 83; Harris-Dawson, 82; L.A. Unified settlement, 76, 189n48; mobilization, 154, 167; Ryan Smith on, 174; SENI and, 76

community colleges, 68, 151, 188n32

Community Magnet Charter School, 103

Compton, California, 58, 85

Connolly, William E., 15, 155, 160, 169

Coolbrith, Ina Donna, 185n67

Cordes, Sarah, 122

Cornejo, Erica, 63

corruption, municipal, 32, 33, 34–35

Cortines, Ramón, 77, 78–79, 100, 108, 110, 115, 141

Corwin, Miles, 132

Covid-19 pandemic, 7–8, 84, 145, 170–71

Crawford, Mary Ellen, 46

Crawford v. Los Angeles Board of Education, 46, 103–4

Crenshaw High School, Compton, California, 85, 140

Crocker, Charles, 36

Dahl, Robert, 13, 14, 160, 167

Dauter, Luke, 105, 112

Deasy, John, 54, 77, 78–79, 85, 89, 90, 91, 115, 120

deindustrialization, 48, 71–72

De la Torre, Julia, 137, 140

demonstrations. *See* protests and demonstrations

Didion, Joan, 27, 48

Doerr, John, 72–73

Dominguez, Miguel, 139

Dorsey High School, 130, 131, 138–39, 141–42, *142*

dropouts and dropout rates, 115, 118, 127, 128, 129, 153

dual-language schools, 70, 74, 78, 84, 87, 98–99, 123, 124; Armenian, 99, 158; popularity, 164

Duff, Joseph, 105

Duffy, A. J., 84–85, 110

Duncan, Arne, 110, 128, 138

East Los Angeles, 58, 101, 115–16; busing, 72, 106; charter schools, 111; pilot schools, 78. *See also* Belmont Zone of Choice; Zoot Suit Riots

Education Trust, 81, 91

Educators for Excellence, 70, 82, 134–35, 142

EdVoice, 108

Eire, Carlos, 184n37

English, Steve, 73, 74

English language arts, 74, 119, 141. *See also* reading and reading scores

English learners, 76, 78, 79, 152. *See also* Spanish-speaking students

Equity Is Justice Resolution, 54, 67, *117*

Esteban Torres Complex, 116

Estrada, Delia, 118

expulsions. *See* suspensions and expulsions

Families in Schools, 116

Fauci, Jeanne, 77, 78, 90, 99, 116, 124, 135

Feinberg, Walter, 7, 158–59

fertility rates, 60, 62, 76

Figlio, David, 122

Filardo, Mary, 74

Fisher, Doris, 71

Flecha, Juan, 83

Fletcher, Warren, 85–86

Fligstein, Neil, 91

Flores, Yolie, 5, 71, 119, 124; childhood, 162; school board, 110–11, 123, 146, 149; "strange bedfellows," 114, 149; Villaraigosa and, 109, 119

Fogelson, Robert, 27

Ford Foundation, 97

Franciscans, 28

Freedom Schools, 128, 129, 130, 138, 139

Fremont High School, 85, 126, 127–28, 140, 141–42, *142*

French, Dan, 116

Fritch, Brian, 115–16

Funkhouser, Peggy, 96

Gaebler, Ted, 95

Garcia, Lester, 88–89

García, Mónica, 71, 83, 88, 111, 123, 146, 190n64

Garfield High School, 115

Gates, Bill, 99

Gates Foundation, 77, 80, 81, 190n56
George Washington Carver Middle School, 72, 107
George Washington Preparatory High School, 140, 141–42, *142*
Gibson, Mary, 40
Gitlin, Todd, 52, 176
Glendale, California, 43
Goldberg, Jackie, 83, 167
Gonez, Kelly, 83
Gonzalez, Patricia, 126, 127–28
Gore, Al, 6, 95
Gould, Arthur, 42
graduation rates, 85, 141, 151, 171, 189n48; pilot schools, 118
Graham, Wade, 22, 42
"grass-top organizations," 134–35
Green Dot Public Schools, 107, 108
Griffin, John S., 14
Griffith, D. W., 33

Ham, Joshua, 82
Hancock, Henry, 22
Handler, Joel, 121
Hardy, George, 191n77
Harris, Robert, 39
Harris-Dawson, Marqueece, 82
Hart, Cassandra, 122
Hastings, Reed, 70–71, 72–73, 74, 87, 94, 109, 114; Barr and, 108; EdVoice and, 108; "few rules" prescription, 95; school board elections, 11, 86
Havel, Václav, 13, 14, 163
Hawkins High School, 140
Haycock, Kati, 81
Hearst, Phoebe, 40
Henig, Jeffrey, 12, 163, 174
higher education, 61–62, 139, 140, 145, 151, 175, 188n32; pilot schools and, 118. *See also* college-preparatory courses; University of California
Hill, Matt, 164
Hill, Paul, 110
Hirschman, Albert O.: *Exit, Voice, Loyalty*, 125
Home Gardens, California, 43, 44
Home Teacher Act, 40
Hopkins, Mark, Jr., 25

housing discrimination, 41–44, 183n30, 186n91
Huizar, Jose, 67
Huntington, Collis, 23, 25, 29
Huntington, Henry, 26, 186n92
Huntington Park, California, 39, 44, 58; Miles Avenue Elementary, 71

immigrants, 10, 18, 29, 32, 58, 143; Home Teacher Act, 40; Mexican and Central American, 56, 58, 187n9; Molokan, 33. *See also* Chinese immigrants and Chinese Americans
Inglewood, California, 107
Inner City Struggle (ICS), 67, 88, 89, 124, 135; ACLU alliance, 76; Belmont Zone of Choice and, 111; coalitions, 67, 135, 139, 171; college-prep campaign, 69, 135, 139; Deasy and, 82; García and, 83; mobilization, 87, 154, 167; new schools, 150; Ryan Smith on, 174; start-up, 143

James, Tylo, 131, 136–39, 140, 141
Janus v. AFSCME, 86
Japan, 95
Japanese Americans, *41*, 183n30
Jefferson, Thomas, 13
Johnson, Hiram, 40
Johnson, Lyndon B., 50, 58, 136

Kahne, Joe, 143
Kant, Immanuel, 166
Kearns, Caitlin, 117, 119, 153
Kerchner, Charles, 39, 96
kindergarten and kindergartners, 40, 63; busing, 58; Chinese, *43*
King, Michelle, 125
King, Rodney, 56–57
Kirschenbaum, Greta, 75
Kirst, Michael, 75
Koreatown, 58, 101
Krist, Gary, 33

Lafortune, Julien, 74
Laguna Beach, California, 72
language arts. *See* English language arts
Lankershim School, *38*
L.A. Partnership. *See* Los Angeles Education Partnership

Laslett, John, 37
Latinos, 58, 71–72, 96, 115; Alliance for a Better Community, 135–36; Black solidarity, 143; charter schools, 111, 112, 114, 152–53; Coco, 12; higher education, 62; low expectations for, 69, 76; middle class, 57–58, 60; Pali High, 107; pilot schools, 117; reading scores, 65–66. *See also* Mexicans and Chicanos
Lauen, Doug, 112
lawsuits, 46, 71, 77, 103–4, 134, 171
LEARN. *See* Los Angeles Educational Alliance for Restructuring Now (LEARN)
Lee, Joonho, 78
Lemann, Nicholas, 13, 52
Leonard, George B., 47, 186n98
Leung, Victor, 76, 171–72
light rail. *See* railways, electric
Lincoln High School, *59*
Lloyd, Henry Demarest, 33
Local Control Funding, 75, 171
Locke High School, 108
Long Beach, California, 29, 50, 58
Loomis, Charles, 29
Los Angeles Alliance for a New Economy, 87
Los Angeles Chamber of Commerce, 124, 135
Los Angeles County, 61, 62, 69, 183n24; Latinos, 50
Los Angeles Educational Alliance for Restructuring Now (LEARN), 95, 96, 97–98, 169
Los Angeles Education Partnership, 64, 96, 113, 135, 154
Los Angeles Forum for Equity (LA-FE), 76
Los Angeles High School: Temple and Broadway location, *27*
lottery admissions, 105, 119
Lukes, Steven, 6
lunch programs. *See* breakfast and lunch programs
Luther, Martin, 28, 30

magnet schools, 3, 70, 78, 83, 98, 101, 103–5, 115, 123; admissions, 163, 175; "mission-driven schools" and, 99; Romer program, 66
Mahula, Guy, 74
MALDEF. *See* Mexican American Legal Defense and Education Fund

manufacturing, 32, 36, 37, 42, 184n56; collapse, 17, 50, 56, 131–32
Marcus, David, 134, 194n5
Marsh, Julie, 56, 119–20, 121, 158
mathematics, 79, 80, 111–12, 119, 122, 151, 153
McAdam, Doug, 91, 143
McCone Commission, 48
McWilliams, Carey, 45; *Factories in the Field*, 33–34
MEChA. *See* Movimiento Estudiantil Chicano de Aztlán (MEChA)
"melting pot," 4, 7, 9, 14, 35, 60, 158, 165
Mendez v. Westminster, 46, 134
Mexican American Legal Defense and Education Fund, 171
Mexicans and Chicanos, 10, 134, 187n9; anti-Mexican legislation, 22; housing discrimination, 42; infant mortality, 34; laborers, 25, 33–34, 36, 37, 38; mutual aid associations, 44; school attendance, 36; school segregation and desegregation, 46, 134; stereotypes, 19; Zoot Suit Riots, 45. *See also* Chicano movement
Meyer, John W., 6, 30
Meza, Nancy, 67
middle-class flight, 60, 76, 105
Miles Avenue Elementary School, Huntington Park, 71
Moe, Terry: *Politics, Markets, and America's Schools*, 99
Molokans, 33
Montes-Rodriguez, Aurea, 5, 134, 140, 145, 172–73
morality, Protestant, 18, 21, 22, 28, 30, 31, 39, 159
Morrell, Ernest, 67
Movimiento Estudiantil Chicano de Aztlán (MEChA), 88, 191n75
Mulholland, William, 26
Munger, Charles, 73
Munger, Molly, 73
Muñiz-Fraticelli, Víctor, 14, 157, 161, 167

Nathan, Joe, 99
National Assessment of Educational Progress (NAEP), 64
National Association for the Advancement of Colored People (NAACP), 105

Native Americans, 19, 22, 182n17
New Media Academy, 106
New Orleans, 6
Newport Beach, California, 72
new schools, 66, 72, 73–75, 83–84, 90, 100, 123, 150–51; Brenes on, 171; charter schools, 167; East Los Angeles, 115–16; Riverside County, 134; siting, 122
NewSchools Venture Fund, 98
New TLA. See United Teachers of Los Angeles (UTLA): New TLA
New York City, 8, 11, 55, 87, 94, 116, 122
Nicholls, David, 160
Nicolaides, Becky, 42
No Child Left Behind, 56, 61, 79, 152
Nordhoff, Charles, 29
Norris, Frank, 33

Oakes, Jeannie, 30, 69, 72, 84
Oakeshott, Michael, 15
Oaks, Louis, 44
Obama, Barack, 5–6, 56, 110, 149
Open Court, 63, 79–80, 149
Orfield, Gary, 103–4
Orr, Marion, 135
Osborne, David, 95
Otis, Harrison Gray, 26
Ouchi, William, 93, 94–98, 107, 123
overcrowding, 71, 72–73, 127, 150–51, 171; busing and, 106; Dorsey High, 138; Latino/Spanish-speaking students, 63, 88, 115; school migration and, 74, 90
Oxnam, G. Bromley, 44

Pacific Palisades High School ("Pali High"), 106
Pacoima, Los Angeles, 107
parental choice. See school choice
Parker, Walter, 35
Partnership for Los Angeles Schools, 70, 77, 111, 142, 172, 174, 195n1
Pasadena, California, 30, 31–32, 43
Pastor, Manuel, Jr., 58
Pico-Union, Los Angeles, 115, 116
pilot schools, 3, 66, 70, 77–78, 80, 84, 115–16, 123, 153; Deasy on, 81; García and, 111; Inner City Struggle and, 150; principals' organization, 135, 166; statistics, 100, 101

Pius XI, Pope, 189n44
police and policing, 35, 83, 125, 126, 130, 139, 170, *173*
policy bricolage, 162, 166, 168–70
preschool and preschools, 74, 78, 87, 88, 109, 114
Price, Merle, 106
private schools, 99; competition with traditional schools, *102*, 122–23, 153; statistics, 100–101, *102*
property taxes, 41, 44, 48, 71
property values, 44, 74
Protestant church kindergartens, 40
Protestant morality. See morality, Protestant
protests and demonstrations, 53–54, *55*, 67, *68*, 107, 125, *173*
Public Advocates, 71, 90, 171
Public School Choice (PSC) initiative, 119, 120, 121
public works, 9, 16, 18, 19, 21, 25, 52, 159; Althusius view, 157; schools as, 28, 72; water supply, 22–23, 26–27
Pugh, Courtni, 88–89

Quartz, Karen Hunter, 77, 116

racialization and racial disparities, 19, 21, 22, 40, 71, 79, 97, 174; income, 61; labor, 36; profiling, 82; reading scores, 64–65; segregation and desegregation, 41–44, 46, 98, 103–4, *104*, 106–7, 134, 183n30; student performance expectations, 91, 124, 150, 171; suspensions and expulsions, 82–83. See also housing discrimination
Raftery, Judith, 21, 40
railroads, 25–26, 36, 183n21, 186n92
railways, electric, 25, 26, 183n24
Raymond, Margaret, 111, 113
reading and reading scores, 65, *65*, 72, 79, 99, 111; charter schools, 122, 153; first graders, 63; fourth graders, 64, *64*, 65; eighth graders, 64, *64*, 151
Reagan, Ronald, 99
Red for Ed movement, 86
Reed v. State of California, 77
Reiner, Rob, 109
religious schools, 40, 100–101
Resendez, Freddie, *59*

restorative justice, 82–83
Retana, Albert, 67–68, 135
Rice, Harvey, 18
Riordan, Elizabeth, 98
Riordan, Richard, 93, 95, 97, 107, 108
riots: 1871, 21; Rodney King, 56–57; Zoot
　Suit Riots, 45, 134; Watts, 1965, 47–48, *49*,
　50, *51*, 56, 71
Riverside, California, 61
Riverside County, California, 134
Roberts, Virgil, 95
Rodriguez, Richard, 22, 30
Rogers, John, 67, 69, 72, 84, 135, 142, 143
Rogosa, David, 111
Roldan, Elmer, 133, 138, 145–46, 162
Romer, Roy, 62–63, 72, 80, 81, 90–91, 149–51,
　155, 169
Roos, Mike, 96
Roos, Sara, 190n64
Roosevelt High School. *See* Theodore
　Roosevelt High School
Ross, Fred, 46, 134
Roybal, Edward, 134
rubber industry, 36
Russo, Alexander, 108
Rustin, Bayard, 48

Sampson, Robert, 61
San Bernardino, California, 61
Sanchez, David, 60
Sanchez, Luis, 88, 134
San Fernando Valley, 97, 101, 104, 105. *See
　also* Burbank, California; Pacoima, Los
　Angeles; Van Nuys, Los Angeles
Santa Fe Railway. *See* Atchison, Topeka and
　Santa Fe Railway
Santa Monica, California, 26, 31, 101
Schönholzer, David, 74
school breakfast and lunch programs. *See*
　breakfast and lunch programs
school choice, 99–101, 103, 119, 120, 121, 169
school suspensions and expulsions. *See*
　suspensions and expulsions
school vouchers, 99–100, 122
Schwarzenegger, Arnold, 108, 109
Scott, Bob, 107
SCYEA. *See* South Central Youth Empow-
　ered thru Action (SCYEA)

SEIU. *See* Service Employees International
　Union (SEIU)
SENI. *See* Student Equity Needs Index
　(SENI)
Sennett, Richard, 165
Serrano v. Priest, 71, 87
Service Employees International Union
　(SEIU), 83, 88–89
Severance, Caroline, 32
Sewell, William, Jr., 176
Shin, Hyo Jeong, 113
Shipps, Dorothy, 163, 164
Shrager, Mark, 107
Sinclair, Upton, 44
Singleton, Don, 138
Sizer, Ted, 116
Small Schools Resolution, 110
Small Schools Support Network, 64, 70, 99
Smith, Ryan, 53, 70, 76, 77, 109, 162, 173–74
social authority, 14, 120, 144, 166, 167, 169,
　170
South Central Youth Empowered thru
　Action (SCYEA), 126, 130, 131, 136, 137, 138,
　139
Southern Pacific Railroad, 25, 29, 35, 183n21
South Gate, California, 42
South Gate High School, 46
South Gate Middle School, 71
South Los Angeles (South Central), 42, 44,
　85, 98, 131–39; busing, 106; CADRE, 82;
　Rodney King riot, 57. *See also* Community
　Coalition (Coco); Watts, Los Angeles
Spanish-speaking students, 54, 63
special education, 76
spending per pupil, 44, 71, 75, 122, 151
Sporte, Susan, 143
standardized tests. *See* tests and testing
"standards-based accountability," 62
Stanford, Leland, 16, 23, 25
Starr, Kevin, 21
state funding, 70, 71, 72, 75, 76, 78–79, 97,
　122
Stebbins, Horatio, 40
Stone, Clarence, 15, 120–21, 154, 163, 164
strikes. *See* teacher strikes
Strunk, Katharine, 119–20, 121
Student Equity Needs Index (SENI), 76, 127,
　167, 171, 172, 173

Students Not Suspects, 83
subsidiarity, 75, 157, 189n44
suburbanization, 26, 41–44
Supreme Court. *See* US Supreme Court
suspensions and expulsions, 82–83, 130, 139

taxation, 48, 71, 99. *See also* property taxes
teacher evaluation, 81, 86, 190n56
teacher firing, 77, 85, 93, 115, 141; Fremont
    High, 128
teacher pay, 39, 63, 72, 86, 92, 107, 140; Duffy
    and, 84; merit pay, 56, 190n56
teacher quality, 77, 80–82, 85, 97, 115, 121, 145.
    See also teacher evaluation
teacher seniority, 77, 79, 85, 97, 106
teacher strikes, 86, 87, 96, 118, 140, 146, 167
teacher turnover, 77, 115
Teach for America, 70, 85, 108
Terriquez, Veronica, 109, 143, 144
tests and testing, 80, 123; Caputo-Pearl and,
    86; Open Court, 63–64
Theodore Roosevelt High School, 67, 88
Thornton, Patricia, 168
tire industry, 36, 42
Tocqueville, Alexis de, 157
Torres-Guillén, Sylvia, 76
Touraine, Alain, 10
Trump, Donald, 86, 175
tutors, 54, 78, 152
Tyack, David, 30, 38–39
Tynan, Roxanna, 87

United Teachers of Los Angeles (UTLA),
    77, 84–90, 110, 116, 141, 172; New TLA,
    85, 115, 149; strikes, 86, 87, 96, 118, 140,
    146; Students Not Suspects, 83; Woods,
    106
United Way, 63–54, 55, 70, 76, 82, 89, 120,
    138; Roldan, 133, 162
University of California: A-G course
    requirement, 67–69, 68, 79, 135, 151, 171,
    174
US Supreme Court, 46, 86, 99–100, 104

Van Nuys, Isaac Newton, 26
Van Nuys, Los Angeles, 26
Ventura County, California, 61

Villaraigosa, Antonio, 56, 77, 91, 108, 109–10,
    114, 119, 145–46
Villegas, Bryant, 53–54
Vincent, Jeff, 74
vouchers. *See* school vouchers

wages, 35–36, 37, 89; Chinese workers,
    185n60. *See also* teacher pay
Washington, Booker T., Jr., 43
Washington Carver Middle School.
    See George Washington Carver Middle
    School
Washington High School. *See* George
    Washington Preparatory High School
Wasserman, Casey, 110
water supply, 22–23, 24–25, 26–27, 35, 47, 182n17
Watts, Los Angeles, 26, 43; 1965 riot, 47–48,
    49, 50, 51, 56, 71
Weaver-Hightower, Marcus, 164
Weber, Max, 6
Weingarten, Marc, 21, 25
Weintraub, Roberta, 104, 105
Wesley, John, 30
white flight, 56, 57, 105, 132
"white spot of America," 29, 183n30
Wilkins, Roy, 58
Williams, Harold M., 107
Williams v. State of California, 171
Willmore, William E., 29
Wilson, Henry, 30–31
Wilson, Pete, 97
Winkes, Bill, 106
Woods, Denise Rockwell, 106
Woods, James, 19, 21
Wycoff, Robert E., 95, 98

Young, Caprice, 93–94, 107, 123
Young Women's Christian Association
    (YWCA), 186
Youth United for Community Action
    (YUCA), 173

Zacarias, Ruben, 107
zones of school choice (ZOCs), 119, 153.
    See also Belmont Zone of Choice
Zoot Suit Riots, 45, 134
Zwingli, Ulrich, 183–84n37